W9-BZJ-044

WITHDRAWN

The Sacred
and the
Feminine

THE SACRED ✿✿AND THE FEMININE

Toward a Theology of Housework

KATHRYN ALLEN RABUZZI

THE SEABURY PRESS / New York

Note to the Reader
All biblical references are to the Revised Standard Version of the Bible. Old Testament Section, copyright © 1952; New Testament Section, First Edition, copyright © 1946; Second Edition © 1971 by Division of Christian Education of the National Council of Churches of Christ in the United States of America.

Grateful acknowledgment is made for the use of excerpts from the following materials:

"The Woman at the Washington Zoo" by Randall Jarrell. Copyright © 1960 by Randall Jarrell (New York: Atheneum, 1960). Reprinted with the permission of Atheneum Publishers.

"Well Water" by Randall Jarrell. Copyright © 1965 by Randall Jarrell. From *The Lost World*. Reprinted with permission of Macmillan Publishing Co.

"Hope" by Randall Jarrell. Copyright © 1961 by Randall Jarrell. Originally appeared in "The Partisan Review." Reprinted with permission of Macmillan Publishing Co.

"The Death of the Hired Man" and "Directive" from *The Poetry of Robert Frost* edited by Edward Connery Lathem. Copyright © 1930, 1939, 1947 by Holt, Rinehart and Winston. Copyright © 1958 by Robert Frost. Copyright © 1967, 1975 by Lesley Frost Ballantine. Reprinted with permission of Holt, Rinehart and Winston, Publishers.

Lines from Dante's "Inferno" published by J. M. Dent and Sons Ltd. London, 1946.

"Anecdote of the Jar," "Notes Toward a Supreme Fiction," "A Rabbit As King of the Ghosts," "Theory," and "The Idea of Order at Key West" from *The Collected Poems of Wallace Stevens* by Wallace Stevens, Copyright © 1954 by Wallace Stevens. Reprinted by permission of Alfred A. Knopf, Inc.

"Love Calls Us to the Things of This World" by Richard Wilbur from *The Poems of Richard Wilbur*, Copyright © 1963 by Richard Wilbur. Reprinted from *Things of This World* by permission of Harcourt Brace Jovanovich, Inc.

Lines from *The Eumenides* by Aeschylus from Aeschylus The Oresteian Trilogy, trans. Philip Vellacott (Penguin Classics, Revised edition, 1959), Copyright © 1956 Philip Vellacott.

From *The Collected Poems of William Butler Yeats:* "The Second Coming" (Copyright © 1924 by Macmillan Publishing Co., Inc., renewed 1952 by Bertha Georgie Yeats) and "Among School Children" (Copyright © 1928 by Macmillan Publishing Co., Inc., renewed 1956 by Georgie Yeats). Reprinted with permission of Macmillan Publishing Co, Inc. and A. P. Watt Ltd., London, England.

1982
The Seabury Press
815 Second Avenue
New York, N.Y. 10017

Printed in the United States of America

Library of Congress Cataloging in Publication Data

Rabuzzi, Kathryn Allen.
    The sacred and the feminine.
      1. Woman (Christian theology) I. Title.
II. Title: Housework.
BT704.R3   248.8'43'5   81-18292
ISBN 0-8164-0509-3   AACR2

Acknowledgments

Many people deserve thanks for helping with this book, and I wish I could name them all. I particularly want to thank Professor William Barnett who not only read and critiqued endless drafts for me, but also initially suggested that I write the book; my colleagues who read and critiqued various portions: Professors Daniel Noel, Daniel O'Connor, Nancy Ring, Mary Wakeman, and James B. Wiggins; and above all, my family—Dan, Danny, Matthew, and Douglas—for their continued support, concern, and patience. To Douglas I owe special thanks for typing the entire manuscript.

Contents

Preface

The Land of Happily Ever After

As a child, I loved fairy tales. But I was never satisfied with their endings. What, I wondered, did the characters *do* when "they all lived happily ever after?" I always wanted details to fill in the gaps created in my mind by those familiar, but obscuring, words. Even then, I dimly sensed that most adult women spent their lives in the nondelineated Happily Ever After, rather than the exciting time-space of story.

That fairy-tale ending, perhaps more than any other, contributes to the misery most traditional women are forced to endure. Like Cadmus' teeth, those words are repeatedly implanted in impressionable minds, only to spring up and form a wall behind which traditional women are expected to live in domestic bliss. That wall, as writers from Ibsen to Tillie Olson have so often told us, more frequently demarcates a prison than a paradise.

Yet, if that is so, why does the positive pull of these words continue to haunt us? Though statistics on divorce indicate fewer and fewer adherents to the ideal of Happily Ever After, figures on remarriage suggest that *belief* in its promise still strongly persists. The intent of this book is to unlock the territory indicated by Happily Ever After.

1

Imagine, if you will, what that territory is like. It is, after all, the traditional *ending* of stories. Hence, it has not, itself, been placed *in* stories, but used to stop them. Consequently, it is almost definitionally beyond story. And because it has remained outside story, most of us have little or no consistently shared conception of it whatsoever. Instead, Happily Ever After is separated from us by a high stone wall, possible covered with flowering vines, behind which we may see absolutely nothing at all. Or a few vague structures may stand here and there, partially obscured by fog. Possibly for a few the wall encloses a region, dazzlingly bright, of flower-strewn fields leading up to a turreted castle of crumbling stone in splendid proportions. Perhaps, if you look with very great care, you can even glimpse a unicorn disappearing into the brush.

Any one of these visions forms a poor image of what the Land of Happily Ever After is all about. And yet they, or any other of the crudely formed conceptions most of us hold, are the closest we can come to envisioning that condition before we enter it. By contrast, what young adult, entering the world of work, has quite so hazy a conception of what lies ahead? It is odd, indeed, to think that so many people enter marriage (the everyday term for the Land of Happily Ever After) with little or no conception of what awaits them other than the vaguely articulated picture of their parents' mistakes or the sentimental delusions of Hollywood romances.

While this Land of Happily Ever After entraps its victims without regard to sex, traditionally it has been women, more than men, who have been forced to remain there for life without even temporary escape. For above all, despite its seemingly apocalyptical promise, Happily Ever After turns out to be the realm of domesticity, until very recently a predominantly feminine domain.

From a very young age, I had mixed feelings about entering that domain myself. On the one hand, I wanted to live happily ever after because as I understood it, that was the whole intent of every fairy tale I ever read, except those with the very different formulaic endings on the order of: "and if she's not there yet, she will be soon." Understandably, part of what Happily Ever After implied to me as a child was an absence of name-calling kids who would chase me part way home from school every day, brandishing sticks and threatening stones; and certainly it implied relief from nightmares strong enough to hurl me out of bed onto the cold, hard floor; and surely it indicated a place of peace and tranquility like that depicted in Hicks' *Peaceable Kingdom*, with the beasts so still no one would fear to walk among them. Yet that implication of stillness bothered me. Without having, at the age of five or seven, the ability to articulate it, I sensed that if this was an unstoried condition, it must not be very interesting. And without explicitly connecting domesticity, absence of story, and living happily ever after, I knew from about nine on that I did not want to spend my days in the kitchen, washing dishes and preparing meals.

Why has the story of this realm not been told? It has not been told because it could not be. Two reasons have prevented its telling. First, the story that comes after all the stories, the one about the Land of Happily Ever After, belongs to that dimension of human existence known as tacit.[1] The tacit dimension refers to assumptions so basic to a given culture that they are not made explicit, but are simply taken for granted. So implicit are they, in fact, that they are scarcely even visible to those who accept them. They function as the ground, or foundation, upon and through which everything explicitly stated appears. In that sense, the tacit dimension is very like the pages of this book which are essential for the words to appear, but which do not, themselves, contribute semantically.

Second, Happily Ever After could scarcely be told about in story because at the opposite end of the spectrum of experience it is not tacit but mystical. If you have ever had a mystical experience you know how difficult, if not impossible, it is to "return" and tell others about it. What words can you find appropriate to embody it? Admittedly, some writers, such as the author of Revelation, have done so, using dazzling imagery such as: "And a great portent appeared in heaven, a woman clothed with the sun, with the moon under her feet, and on her head a crown of twelve stars." (Rev. 12:1). But more commonly, an inability to translate such superordinary occurrences into language renders the mystic inarticulate. What we often hear then are words totally devoid of clear sensory reference. Consider the following from *The Cloud of Unknowing*:

> See that in no sense you withdraw into yourself. And, briefly, I do not want you to be outside or above, behind or beside yourself either.

> "Well," you will say, "where am I to be? Nowhere, according to you!" And you will be quite right! Nowhere, is where I want you! Why, when you are 'nowhere' physically, you are 'everywhere' spiritually . . . . When a man is experiencing in his spirit this nothing in its nowhere, he will find that his outlook undergoes the most surprising changes.[2]

According to most of our conceptions of Happily Ever After, it, too, belongs to the category of experiences barely capable of expression.

In addition to being little described in stories, the promised Land of Happily Ever After functions eschatologically. Eschatology is a term meaning doctrine of last things. In a Christian context one of its most common associations is with the concept of resurrection and the Last

Days before and during the reign of Christ. The eschatological dimension of Happily Ever After can relate both to its tacit and to its mystical poles, depending on the particular experience of an individual. For a person reared in a genuinely loving, stable family, Happily Ever After is apt to be taken for granted; it will be a tacit experience. But for someone who has experienced essential lacks within her or his home, Happily Ever After is likely to be mystical: what happens *beyond* rather than *through* the known. In the latter instance, Happily Ever After functions very much as do stories of the Last Days.

Thinking back to my own early conceptions of Apocalypse, another term often used in this connection, I recall a terrible jumble of incompatible notions. Every Good Friday, for example, I would mentally prepare myself, expecting first that the sky would cloud over. Then I assumed we would all be transformed into the Dante Gabriel Rosetti damozels and ethereal young men I encountered in strange books belonging to my artist grandfather. Out of such eclectic imaginings my notions of Apocalypse arose. But somehow, perhaps because I so greatly preferred fairy tales to Bible stories, I believed equally in eschatological peace and apocalyptical upheaval. Yet as I grew older, Happily Ever After shifted into the foreground of my awareness. While I retained my original awe of "Children, it is the last hour . . . many antichrists have come, "(I John 2:18) and ". . . I saw a beast rising out of the sea, with ten horns and seven heads, with ten diadems upon its horns and a blasphemous name upon its heads . . ." (Rev. 13:1), Apocalypse receded somewhere off in the future. By contrast, Happily Ever After seemed far less remote. From about twelve on, teenage romances replaced fairy tales as my favored reading material. Happily Ever After then became tinged with strains of "Blue Moon" listened to late at night from a radio station in New York City; and a tight black sheath dress, six-inch spike heels, elbow-length black leather gloves, a slim umbrella, and a toy poodle clasped under one arm; and softly lit restaurants, champagne glasses, and Cherries Jubilee. Above all, it became lifelong devotion to . . . . Who could possibly imagine what **He** would be like? Would he be tall? dark? handsome? intelligent? athletic? wealthy? kind?

Clearly this is a sentimental, adolescent, secularly debased vision of salvation. It is the stuff of soap opera, the vision of a Madame Bovary in-the-making.[3] It is part of what scholars generally pooh-pooh as trivia. Yet, until recently, how relatively rare were American women who came of age unscathed by just such expectations. Whether we like it or not, this is fare upon which most adolescent girls were traditionally nourished. Such a vision, fully as much as any derived from traditional religious scriptures, helped formulate the future existence and the concepts of meaning most middle class young women in the United States upheld. As such, Happily Ever After represents the scarcely articulated, tacit myth of middle-class American women's experience.

But as a child, who could not always connect my reading (which meant everything to me) with my everyday experiences, I did not know this. I was never entirely sure whether Happily Ever After applied to me or whether it was "only" confined to books. Nonetheless, I kept on wondering about Happily Ever After, trying to push back in my mind the seemingly impenetrable curtain that descended with those words. What was it like over there on the other side? Why couldn't I have just a brief vision of it? And I would lie in bed before I fell asleep, trying to imagine what it was like, extending my bedtime story beyond those final words.

It was not until I was already married that the parts began to mesh. I was sitting, one evening at dusk, on the front porch of our first house, a tiny Philadelphia row house, some four years and two and a half children into our marriage, when a chance concatenation of sights, sounds, and smells made me suddenly realize what territory I inhabited: the Land of Happily Ever After. It was a terrifying revelation. What I consciously recognized at that moment was not the childhood dream of unicorn and castle, nor even that of webbed and clouded structures: it was the mystical one of black nothingness.

In that instant of vision I realized the disparity between all my years of expectation and the reality of my situation at that precise moment in time. There I was, twenty-four years old, my husband struggling through the sixth of nine years of medical training, and me a college dropout, seemingly with only a life full of babies and household drudgery ahead. Though that moment was entirely nonverbal, I can nonetheless retrospectively translate its intensity. I knew then that I was caught, trapped in a black hole far, far away from the golden path I had always trusted would lead me from school to my intended profession of writer. How, I wondered, had I managed to lose my golden pathway and end up in a black hole?

I had plenty of time, during those years, to ponder that question. And the more I pondered, the more I realized that something was very wrong. Why should writers and artists envision so much of existence and then stop? And why, particularly, did most stories seem to tell what was possible for males and young girls without often mentioning grown women?

These are questions I have struggled with for at least half my life. It seems to me I followed a blueprint, drawn from all the stories I had ever read, up to my marriage. Then, from the moment I entered the Land of Happily Ever After, everything went blank. Almost no one had shed light on this particular territory. My only guidance, which was and still is precious to me, came from six words: Do not repeat your parents' mistakes. These I hugged to me as in younger days I had secreted magic pebbles in my hand. But why did I and others like me have to enter that realm most human beings enter at some time in their lives, so little prepared? To try and answer that and related questions, I have written this book.

Introduction

A Cultural and Theological Context for Women's Emergence

At this stage in history, fewer and fewer women are content to wait like Penelope. But awakening from the mode of waiting can be perilous. Recall what happened to Gregor Samsa in Kafka's famous "Metamorphosis." Or Rip van Winkle in the well-known legend. And then there is Sleeping Beauty, who awakened to "live happily ever after" with her princely savior, a fate possibly worse than that accorded either of the other two. But now many American women, like Gregor, Rip, and Beauty, are unquestionably waking up.

And as these women awaken, like their literary prototypes, they discover that they have been duped, and they are reminded of Plato's words in *The Republic:*

> the people. . . . are to be told that their youth was a dream, and the
> education and training which they received from us, an appearance

only; in reality during all that time they were being formed and fed in the womb of the earth, where they themselves and their arms and appurtenances were manufactured; when they were completed, the earth, their mother, sent them up. . . .We shall say to them in our tale, you are brothers, yet God has framed you differently. Some of you have the power of command, and in the composition of these he has mingled gold, wherefore also they have the greatest honour; others he has made of silver to be auxiliaries . . .[4]

While Western culture has not adopted Plato's great lie in this particular form, it has surely swallowed a closely related variant, the story of creation in Genesis 1:2. Of all the stories about women in the Bible, perhaps none has been so controversial and influential as this one. Despite the emphasis on sexual equality in the Genesis 1:1 account, it is the story of woman's creation from man's rib that historically has captured human imagination and fired numerous debates. At one extreme, inerrantists declare the account to be literally true; at the other, radical feminists argue that last is best, making the account legitimate the superiority rather than the inferiority of women over men.

Both arguments are silly: the passage *is* true, but not in the way advocates of inerrancy claim. Certainly women have been shaped in the image of men, but not as a natural, God-given process. The reversal of natural birth in this passage, in which the male births the female rather than *vice versa,* places this event in the familiar category of male initiation rites. In such rites males are characteristically born anew into a particular culture, leaving behind their natural, previous selves to become "fully human" instead. In that sense, women have been born of men, for what we call culture throughout most of the world is predominantly the product of masculine thinking. To help legitimate masculine cultures, what might be called various forms of "Plato's great lie" have been promulgated—and believed—for centuries (although there is no historical connection between the Genesis story and Plato). In much of Western culture this biblical tale of woman's creation from Adam's rib has legitimated women's political inequality, perpetuating for them a near slave-like status relative to the advantages of most men.

False Consciousness

The common name for the effect of the lies, or stories, told to and about women is false consciousness. An example, drawn from Harold Pinter's play *The Room,* goes like this:

Mrs. Sands: Now I come to think of it, I saw
               a star.
Mr. Sands: You saw what?

Mrs. Sands:	Well, I think I did.
Mr. Sands:	You think you saw what?
Mrs. Sands:	A star.
Mr. Sands:	Where?
Mrs. Sands:	In the sky.
Mr. Sands:	When?
Mrs. Sands:	As we were coming along.
Mr. Sands:	Go home.
Mrs. Sands:	What do you mean?
Mr. Sands:	You didn't see a star.
Mrs. Sands:	Why not?
Mr. Sands:	Because I'm telling you. I'm telling you you didn't see a star.[5]

At issue here is the reliability of Mrs. Sands' own experience of reality. She sees something, but her husband so strongly questions that fact that he essentially destroys the experience for her. While the example seems extreme, it merely exaggerates a situation common in the lives of many women. What female graduate student, for example, in a male-dominated classroom, has not backed down occasionally, despite her interior conviction to the contrary, when confronted by masculine reasons for a position strongly counter to her own? In my own case, I vividly recall the denial of my favorite male professor that Jung was a male chauvinist. I cited several examples, including Jung's essay, "How Women Should Dress," which enjoins Western women to emulate Indian women's plumpness and saris rather than striving for slimness and man-tailored clothes. Yet, I was told in class that these examples are insignificant in light of Jung's total *oeuvre*. That denial typifies the process by which false consciousness is imposed on women. If women from infancy on are repeatedly told by people they love and respect that what they construe as X is not X, but Y, how can they possibly learn to trust their own interior responses?

Similarly, for women to be called bitches when they stand up for their rights is to punish them for being true to their own experience of life. Yet, given cultural expectations which demand "ladylike refinement," "sweetness," acquiescence, and the like, it is difficult for women to know *how* to respond.

Consider these comments, excerpted from a paper on femininity handed me recently by an attractive young woman student: "You must never threaten a boy's ego. . . . At dinner, pick at your food. You will seem more feminine that way, and if the boy can eat half your dinner as well as his own that will make him happy. . . . When you leave the movie, prepare yourself for what is to come. Your date has spent a lot of money on you and entertained you all evening. Now it is your turn to do something for him. He will expect you to gratify him sexually." If I did not know this student, I would think the paper a put-on. But she meant every word! This is the kind of consciousness so false that it lacks even a glimmer of awareness that it *is* false. It is the same rhetoric which informs books like Marabel Morgan's *The Total Woman:*

> For an experiment I put on pink baby-doll pajamas and white boots after my bubble bath, I must admit that I looked foolish and felt even more so. When I opened the door that night to greet Charlie, I was unprepared for his reaction. My quiet, reserved, nonexcitable husband took one look, dropped his briefcase on the doorstep, and chased me around the diningroom table. We were in stitches by the time he caught me, and breathless with that old feeling of romance. Our little girls stood flat against the wall watching our escapade, giggling with delight. We all had a marvelous evening together, and Charlie forgot to mention the problems of the day.[6]

Such ideology legitimizes the status of women as objects, forced to endure "reality" as it is created and imposed upon them by masculine fantasy.

Sadly, and inevitably, the process is circular for both sexes. To the extent that men or women accept whatever the dominant culture conventionally names as "reality," they will come to doubt experiences of their own which contradict it, assuming they even recognize the discrepancy at all. Thus, if a woman grows up believing it the duty of women submissively to wait on men, she may so doubt the validity of her own anger that she represses it completely. Conversely, a man may simply assume it is his right to be so waited upon, and totally ignore any stirrings of uneasiness that might parallel comparable outrage over treatment of blacks. Or if a woman believes men excel intellectually, she may, regardless of her own levels of intelligence and motivation, actually fail.[7] In such situations "false stories" prevail, and individuals are alienated from their own actual experiences.

Fortunately, however, as more and more women allow themselves to articulate and claim their own awarenesses and feelings, such sad caricatures of human beings as Marabel Morgan's and my student's are becoming somewhat less frequent. Commonly, feminists attribute consciousness-raising among both sexes to influences of the women's movement. The connection between the two is indeed obvious, but consciousness-raising also relates to a somewhat broader context as well. Because relatively few feminists step outside a strictly feminist perspective, many tend, like any self-enclosed group, to fashion theories reflecting women's strength without necessarily showing the organic relationship between where women are now and society as a whole.

Clearly, it is essential to focus on women and their particular experience, in part to make up for previous neglect, but women must also address the entire process by which all humans come to understand more fully what it means to be human. The situation is somewhat analogous to that of the civil rights movement of the 1960s in which blacks frequently prayed for the liberation of their white oppressors in the awareness that liberation of blacks could not be conceptualized as an isolated phenomenon. To achieve transformation of the entire society—the only solution for true black liberation—black and white had necessarily to change together. Similarly, some women today argue that ordination of women in the Roman church is useless apart from a feminist transformation of the role of ordained clergy in the Christian community as a whole.[8] Only through recognizing such interconnections between women and institutions, and more fundamentally between women and men, can women's liberation ultimately succeed.

A connection less readily apparent than that of women and religious institutions concerns literature and art. Subverting status quo's has always been the province of the arts. Not until our own century, however, have we witnessed sustained artistic breakdowns of order so severe as to be truly chaotic. Consider, for example, these words from Eugene Ionesco's play *Jack or the Submission*, spoken by a character named Roberta II:

> All we need to designate things is one single word: cat. Cats are called cat, food: cat, insects, cat . . . all the prepositions: cat. It's easier to talk that way.[9]

Once artists, by such absurdities, make a certain tolerance for disorder part of many people's experience, the possibility that women and men might actually exist in a relation of equality rather than hierarchy becomes much less threatening, at least in theory. If the notion of order in general can no longer be taken for granted, then one particular kind of order based on male supremacy can no longer be accepted wholeheartedly as true. While the presence of "free" women existing equally with men in society undoubtedly threatens many men, the symbolic threat of that liberation may well be even more upsetting. Therefore, as long as the idea of something called "order" (by which "hierarchy" is intended) seems possible, it is unlikely that any actual part of that structure of thought will alter. But now that the whole conception of order has become problematic, there is no longer the same compelling need to enact, externally and literally, roles representing that concept.

Yet precisely because this is the case, many women and men who long to retain outmoded visions of reality continue bitterly to oppose liberation. That brings me to the second prong of the interrelationship between women's experience of emergence and structures of thought. Not only have new ideas allowed women's emergence to begin, but as emergence occurs, accustomed ways of thinking and familiar symbols also cease to be effective. This threat to existing symbol systems is more likely than any other obstacle to impede the process of liberation. How does this obstacle operate?

Masculine and Feminine

The key words are *men, women, male, female, masculine,* and *feminine.* They are not all interchangeable. Four belong to language used referentially and scientifically: *men, women, male,* and *female* all point to observable phenomena, flesh and blood human beings. But *masculine* and *feminine* are more slippery terms, referring to qualities of being and behavior.

Both terms may be applied to both sexes. I, who am biologically both woman and female, may and do exhibit qualities that are masculine as well as feminine. Genetically, each of us is a mixture, so that no individual is one hundred percent masculine or feminine. Jung deals with this phenomenon by labeling what he calls the masculine side of a woman her animus and the feminine side of a man his anima. The qualities typical of masculinity and femininity are not necessarily the same in everybody's thinking or experience. Generally, however, masculinity is associated with such traits as aggressiveness, violence, domination, leadership, authority, and the like. By contrast, femininity is associated with submissiveness, clinging, passivity, patience, attention to detail, nurturance, protection, sometimes even masochism.

Some feminists find this manner of labeling both stereotypic and offensive, claiming that to even use such terms as "masculine" and "feminine" is to perpetuate damaging and false stereotypes. Some go so far as to claim that no such thing as masculine or feminine exists. Instead, they argue, there is something called human nature which, though it differs from individual to individual, does not differ along sexual lines. Clearly, if one forgets that such terms are ways of naming certain qualities which exist within *both* women and men in varying degrees, such labeling is offensive. And because the terms do slip so frequently, those feminists who protest against them have strong reasons for their objections.

The difficulty arising from these labels is one that has persisted for hundreds of years. It has to do with the way human beings typically reason. Technically, the name given to this type of reasoning is ampliation—adding into the predicate something not contained in the subject. Consider the following statement: He is black. Therefore, he is stupid, shiftless, untrustworthy, uneducated, poor. Because the black man in our society is so labeled, he is far less likely to be given an opportunity than his counterpart with a white skin. Therefore, he may eventually end up being all those things just because he is barred from legitimate pursuits. But he ends up that way, if he does, not because he necessarily or even probably started off like that, but because words initially labeled him. Because of those words, he was subsequently denied the opportunities that might have allowed him to be someone totally different.

What this means in the case of the terms "women" and "feminine" is this: presumably the concept of opposition is inherent in human thinking. It is likely that awareness of opposition becomes concrete from direct observation of lightness and darkness, edibles and inedibles, and females and males. Given the ability to conceive things oppositionally, it is then natural to abstract qualities from both members of any pair. The process is obviously circular. If we initially observe that women are smaller, weaker, less aggressive than men, then once our initial concepts of women and men are formed, we naturally expect every woman and man to possess these anticipated qualities.

Throughout the long history of ideas in the Western world, a number of self-contradictory attributes of women have grown to be accepted, almost as canon law. Women are thought to be insatiably lustful, fatally alluring, dangerous to men, overwhelming, and artistically inspirational. They are also thought to be sexually anesthesized, submissive, inferior, tied to the earth, and easily dominated. But to make such assertions as these is grossly to overgeneralize. Some women may indeed possess a majority of these traits, but it is clearly impossible for any individual woman to be simultaneously both sexually demanding and sexually unresponsive, or to be too inclined towards fantasy and yet too immersed in material details. More sophisticated thinkers, therefore, prefer to distinguish between actual women and characteristics frequently attributed to them, by using the distinguishing term *feminine*. While it would be far easier to work with terms less confusingly intertwined with our conceptions of men and women, we seem to be stuck, until someone creates appropriate neologisms with the words *masculine* and *feminine*.

The careful use of these terms as distinguishing labels allows men, as well as women, to understand the pain so many women have experienced over the centuries in a way that use of *men, male, women,* and *female* may not. While it is true that more women have presumably experienced a particular kind of human pain than most men, it is untrue and self-defeating to claim that no men can know this particular kind of pain. Of course, this is a pain based primarily on the notion that women are inferior. But to assume that men, categorically, do not experience that pain, is to deny those men who have experienced feelings of inferiority their own experience, and in so doing to cut off dialogue between them and women. Yet there is a difference, which an analogy from the situation of blacks may help explain.

Obviously, there are many degrees of blackness. At least in this country, most whites are more willing to accept those blacks who seem least black. That means that blacks who are light-skinned, possess Caucasian features (particularly noses and lips), speak without traces of dialect, have straight(ened) hair, dress conservatively, are well-educated, earn a good living, and exhibit middle-class values are most likely not to be discriminated against by the dominant white caste. Such blacks can occasionally even "pass" for white.

Applying that same principle to women, what happens? Here the situation is somewhat more paradoxical and points up the confusion between the terms *man* and *masculine*. First, very few women are able to pass for *men*. A few, such as Joan of Arc, have done so for awhile, but anatomically it is difficult, if not impossible, for most women. Second, if a woman tries to "pass" in a less literal way, she opens herself up to intense ridicule. Whereas a black may be applauded (if not necessarily accepted) for adopting "our" ways, a woman trying to act like a man will be called unfeminine, bitchy, masculine, and probably dykey.

The difference between racial and sexual "passing" is this: a man may experience within himself a large number of traits generally considered feminine. He may be nurturing, gentle, intuitive, and highly verbal. But he, unlike those women who possess the same traits, can freely opt to pass for masculine if he wants to. He can cross back and forth between the worlds of feminine and masculine sensibilities at will. He can empathize and speak openly with women friends, but he can also, if he chooses, go alone into almost any bar. There, if he watches his words, he can pass for "one of the boys." For example, a friend of mine named George whose sympathies are truly feminist, admitted when I asked him that in a barroom situation he does not ordinarily defend women. In fact, he admitted he even laughs at sexist jokes.

Being a biological male, George *looks* like what we assume the word *masculine* names, even though, like any intellectual, effeminate, small, or weak man he may frequently suffer taunts from his more aggressively masculine peers. Such men, unless overtly gay, are still sufficiently more masculine-appearing than most women to avoid the frequency of painful encounters that fill most women's lives on a daily basis. What man, for example, is likely to pull up with dread to an unfamiliar gas station, wondering whether the attendant will address him familiarly as "honey" or "blondie"? Or worse, have to choose whether to skip using a restroom entirely or risk snickers and leers for asking to use the key. Whereas a professional man in a business suit generally commands at least a veneer of respect unless he ventures into the toughest of working districts, a woman (Phyllis Schlafly not withstanding)[10] no matter how well dressed, and no matter what her professional level, constantly risks sexually insinuating, demeaning remarks and behavior almost everywhere she goes among strangers.

Consider what happens to her in a situation comparable to that of George in the bar. Unlike him, she is unlikely to freely enter most bars. If she does risk it, she is asking for trouble, unless she has the courage to emulate the woman executive who squelches would-be mashers by very deliberately picking her nose.[11] But a professional woman often finds herself the only female whether she frequents bars or not. Often in such cases, as is true with tokens from other outcast groups, she will not even be told the kind of joke George heard. But sometimes she will hear one. When that happens, she is placed in a very painful dilemma. Often, if she is included, the implication seems to be that now she is "one of the boys." If she laughs, she may indeed feel accepted; she has proved that she is a good sport, that she has a sense of humor, and that she is not "bitchy." But inside, if she is sufficiently aware of the situation, she may feel a searing pain: she has just collaborated in a moment of verbal destruction. She has betrayed her own kind; she has betrayed herself.

A small, but nonetheless typical, example occurred to me just recently. A male colleague I'll call Tom gave me and another male colleague I'll call Ed a ride home. Ed was in a playful mood, having just completed a series of interviews for a prestigious foundation. Picking up a table leg oddly lodged on the floor of Tom's car, he said, "This reminds me of the last woman I interviewed." Somewhat startled, I asked why. Ed explained: the woman had come into the interviewing room and immediately planted herself on a stool, not a chair, placing it in the open doorway, more outside the room than in. Her vocation was counseling battered women. Ed thought her stance in this situation immensely funny. I admit, I laughed. But inside I kept wondering, Why? At one level, the juxtaposition of the table leg unexpectedly encountered in Tom's car with the wariness towards all potential batterers exhibited by this woman was indeed amusing. So are sick jokes . . . . Ed's banter continued; he playfully followed up his associations of battered women and dismembered tables by saying, "Now we're going to dismember you, Kathryn." I felt sick inside.

Was I "passing" in that situation? Indeed, I think not. Does a woman ever *really* pass for "one of the boys"? Whereas a man with strongly feminine sensibilities, unless he overtly swishes, can fool other men, a woman still looks like what the word *feminine* is thought to mean. While she may occasionally pass for a few moments, a sudden knowing glance, a small gesture, or a telling remark from a male colleague inevitably reminds her that her mask has slipped, if it was ever really in place at all.

Hierarchy

Whether we think of the situation of women or of blacks relative to the dominant white male caste, in both cases difference has been hierarchized. Part of what makes this treatment of difference so pernicious is the way it is built right into our patterns of thinking. In the hierarchical thinking which still dominates Western culture (although it reached its "peak" in the middle ages), there is a triangle whose apex is called God. Professional white males—kings, physicians, professors, clergy, and nowadays, corporate officers—dominate successive levels. At the next levels, lumped together variously, are women, persons of color, diverse proletarian groups, and peasants. Below them, successively, come animals, plants, and minerals.

To grow up in Western culture is to grow up with that triangular pattern predominantly shaping your thought: that is simply the way things are, even though the original roles have changed—kings, for example, are no longer what they once were. Though sociologists do recognize other types of social structure, such as the decentralized, reticulate structure of pentecostalism or even the women's movement itself, the hierarchical structures remain. This is especially true in bureaucratic societies. Even our linguistic categories are so full of inherent comparisons that some entities must automatically be construed as better than others. So strongly is this imbalance built into Western language that words which seem directional only, such as "up" and "down," connote very precise valuations. Clearly, in most situations being up is better than being down. Yet why should one direction be deemed better, rather than merely different? In *Why the Green Nigger*, feminist Elizabeth Dodson Gray concerns herself with this matter. She devotes one section to "up and downness as 'the way it really is.' " As she puts it, "Underneath it all, there is a confident assurance that what is above 'calls the tune'—and that what is below will constantly be compliant and adapt."[12] This underlying structure of what we call "reality" simultaneously creates our culture and is created by us.

What I am calling a triangle has more often been referred to as a chain of being. Either name is appropriate because both implicitly reflect hierarchy. It is puzzling the way the word *order* appears to demand hierarchy as a component. It seems almost impossible to conceive of order without implying hierarchy, although it can be done. James Ogilvy does so, for example, in *Many Dimensional Man* when he uses the term *heterarchy*.

To illustrate heterarchical order Ogilvy speaks of the game of rock, paper, and scissors in which "paper covers rock, rock crushes scissors, but scissors cut paper."[13] In the case of the "unambiguous pecking order" which constitutes hierarchy, scissors would always lose. But here recursiveness replaces the verticality intrinsic to hierarchy. Yet so engrained in Western thinking is the connection of hierarchy to order that even the *Oxford English Dictionary* defines order in terms of rank, succession, grade, or task. All four words imply gradation either according to larger or smaller or better or worse. Pursuing this line of thought, it seems that using numbers automatically necessitates valuing. This raises serious questions. *Why* must first or last automatically be assumed better than anything in between? And why has such hierarchical thinking enthralled human minds for so many thousands of years when it is possible to order heterarchically instead?

Closely related to this hierarchical conception of order is the idea, common to primitive religion in general, and traditionally attributed to Plato, of "this world" and the "other." The other world is infinitely superior to this one that we actually experience. Curiously, that other world is apprehensible only to speculative reason or faith, whereas this one we know also through our senses. Furthermore, extreme otherworldliness posits a male god so radically other that he is the image of absolute good, totally sufficient unto itself. In this particular strand of Plato's thinking "the good" is generally construed as Plato's god. This conception of God as the *ens perfectissimum* is carried forward in scholastic thought, and it has remained one conception of God throughout the ages. Examined closely, this conception of God shows a God so self-sufficient that He has no need of anything else.

The notion of a radically other, totally transcendent male god who stands in marked contrast to everything in this world bears heavily on the way women are perceived by masculine thought. This world, the realm of women, but pallidly copies the other one. By contrast with that one, this is therefore evil, lacking as it does the strength of the original.

At this point, the entanglement of ideas relative to conceptions of masculine and feminine becomes confusing and almost self-contradictory. The logic underlying this confusion is the consistency with which women are asserted to be inferior. One persistent idea derived from ancient Hellenic culture, particularly from Plato's thinking, associates women with the material world, which is usually referred to as brute matter. According to Plato's teaching in *The Republic*, the brute matter of the material world cannot measure up to the ideal, other world which it merely copies. That ideal, other world, the realm of ideas, is the divine realm which no material actuality can ever match. Although no actualized beings achieve the perfection of their ideal forms, degrees of perfection and imperfection exist. Females as a class are believed to be further removed from the ideal realm and more rooted in the material world of nature than men; hence they are inferior to males. Subsequently this Hellenic thinking through the writings of Platonic and Aristotelian philosophy, helped shape medieval scholastic theology which spoke of the self-sufficiency of God. But this view of God as not needing the natural world does not describe the biblical God. This is a point some contemporary process theologians such as John B. Cobb and Schubert Ogden have lately begun to make clear.

A second, seemingly contradictory, strand of thought derived from the Hellenistic philosophers also demeans women but for their link to nothingness rather than to materiality. This nothingness is privation of, or absence from, God or the good. In this view all being is evil save that of God which is perfect. Here, too, degrees of evil exist. In this case women are viewed, not as more material, but as less fully actualized than men.

Typical of this strand is an eighteenth-century theodicy, *De Origine Mali*, which claims that "A creature is descended from God, a most perfect father; but from Nothing as its Mother, which is imperfection."[14] Thus, two seemingly antithetical notions are consistently attached to conceptions of women. On the one hand, women are considered possessors of qualities connected with matter: heaviness, earthiness, dullness, and dirtiness. These concepts all link them to earth. Yet women are also associated with nothingness, which, as the absence of creation, is evil. (The latter view holds only when creation is considered good.) Thus, both matter and nothingness connect to chaos, and both are usually opposed to the concept of order. The difference between creation and matter is order, and order, as already stated, traditionally implies hierarchy.

Both these patterns of thought are present in Plato. But some of the specific ramifications for women do not become explicit until Aristotle. In Aristotle's writings the connection of the female with matter becomes more obvious: "The female always provides the material, the male that which fashions it, for this is the power that we say each possessed, and this is what is meant by calling them male and female. Thus, while it is necessary for the female to provide a body and the material mass, it is not necessary for the male, because it is not within the work of art or the embryo that the tools of the maker must exist. While the body is from the female, it is the soul that is from the male, for the soul is the reality of a particular body. . . .The female . . . provides matter, the male the principle of motion. . . ."[15] And it is to Aristotle that we owe the still prevalent notion, so obvious in Freud's writings, that a woman is an incomplete male.

Automatically, any child in the West is born into a world which structures reality along the lines of Platonic and Aristotelian thought. This is what feminists mean, for example, when they speak about how deeply embedded the structures of patriarchal culture are within us. That is also why a thinker like Dorothy Dinnerstein, in *The Mermaid and the Minotaur*, suggests an alternative model in which hierarchy is replaced by the notion of sibling relationships, or equality. Obviously, such thinking is not new, being present in theories of democracy and communism. What is new is Dinnerstein's suggestion that parental relationships be shifted to eliminate godlike parent figures—the father on top, followed by the mother, and the children metaphorically beneath both. Dinnerstein believes shifting that sexual arrangement would allow a new model of reality to be impressed upon the psyches of children. Presumably, then, humans could grow up acculturated to an entirely different way of being in the world. As Dinnerstein further points out, human veneration of the father figure, in contrast to human denigration of the mother, is directly proportional to the amount of time each spends with the child. Because mothers are the ones who actually have to change, feed, and connect with children for all their bodily functions, they are inevitably associated with flesh and embodiedness. By contrast, the relative absence of males from homelife automatically places them in a privileged position, detaching them from the bodily functions. Pushing her thesis further, Dinnerstein suggests that, consequently, humans automatically associate women not only with birth but with all fleshly processes including death. Thus, in part, we come to avoid women under certain conditions, whether we are female or male, because fathers seem magically removed from this world. Consequently, we connect transcendence and the ability to surmount death to male rather than female saviors. The result is that we have more male than female heroes.

Surely if we consider the way heroes and saviors typically function, Dinnerstein's thesis is convincing. For example, Superman, in the movie of that name, is able to reverse time. After the audience has already witnessed a catastrophic collapse of the Grand Canyon, Superman miraculously outraces time. Returning to the instant just before the catastrophe occurs, he manages to avert it completely. Underlying this phenomenon is the ability to reverse or even to undo the natural. Though Superman is clearly an extreme example, his behavior typifies the function of the hero.

On a more serious plane, Christ, also, reverses natural order: he rises from the dead and enables others to do likewise. Though we call it transcendence in the case of one, escapism in the case of the other, both reflect equally supernatural abilities. Following Dinnerstein's logic, both these males function in a realm totally apart from the one most women find themselves in when they are thrust into the roles of homemaker or mother. What women must cope with then are quotidian experiences in which no such miraculous intervention can occur, despite the fact that this is where they live Happily Ever After.

Of particular significance here is the fact that men, historically, have been removed from the everyday scene of domesticity unless they were farmers. To a certain extent the further removed they were, the more cultured they were considered to be. Thus kings and warriors were considered more cultivated than peasants or women. It was their deeds which were handed down through the ages in song and story, thus becoming the stuff of which culture is made; the daily concerns of their humbler counterparts were deemed unfit for recording. But it was the recorders of heroic deeds who were considered most cultured of all; they were the ones who truly shaped what we call culture, predominantly through their words.

To the extent that such recorded words have shaped the minds of successive generations, words have been more "real" than either the matter or action of which they treat. What was not encoded in words frequently seemed not to exist. In that sense words became far more important than actions for creating human experience. Obviously, some words have loomed larger in human experience than others. Such is the case with such basic terms as *black* and *white* or *feminine* and *masculine*.

Feminine Religion and Culture

Though the two oppositions of masculine/feminine and white/black have resulted in similar misconceptions about large portions of humanity, the situations of the two groups diverge also. Blacks have had distinct cultures and countries of their own. And even in this country, despite their having been brought here forceably, blacks do have a recognizable culture of their own, albeit designated as a "subculture" by the dominant culture. Furthermore, at least in principle, blacks and whites could live entirely apart. But in the case of women, this possibility has not really existed, for the continuation of the human species has clearly militated against it. Yet, despite the far greater interdependence between women and men than between blacks and whites, it is nonetheless possible to speak of feminine, as distinct from masculine, culture. Until very recently, most women, regardless of their personal predilections and qualifications, have been consigned to the former and excluded from the latter, whether willingly or not. For many of these women, feminine culture has turned out to be a sad parody of the spendid, but unstoried, existence the words Happily Ever After always seemed to promise.

To speak of feminine culture is difficult. First, the term *culture* is so broad as to be almost meaningless. Disregarding the agricultural and biological meanings of the word, culture may refer to the arts, ideas, and rituals of a particular ethnic group at a particular time in history. In this sense feminine culture is confined within the larger masculine culture of whatever sort—Italian, Jewish, WASP. Feminine culture is then an auxiliary, functioning toward the dominant culture as the Eastern Star to the Masons. From this perspective, women's modes of being reflect variations on the dominant cultural themes expressed more overtly within a larger, particular masculine culture. Thus, for example, if we consider cooking at Christmas to be constitutive of feminine culture, then the kinds of foods cooked in various women's homes would simultaneously reflect a particular ethnic culture as well. Whereas my mother always baked sugar cookies cut as stars, santas, and Christmas trees, my mother-in-law always bakes pizzelles and nut horns.

It is also possible that within any given cultural group some aspects of feminine culture are so separate and hidden that they scarcely penetrate the dominant culture even tacitly. To whatever extent this may be true, women's culture is a kind of gnosis, a special knowledge, even a heresy, with explicit rites and rituals of its own. The most notable examples in this category are various witchcraft or wicca cults, many of which trace their roots back to pre-Christian times.

But culture may also be construed in a broader sense as roughly equivalent to civilization. When culture is so understood, then without question most of what we include in that category has been overwhelmingly masculine: literature, music, drama, philosophy, theology, history. Although some women have created art, contributed ideas, or participated in recorded history, the enormously imbalanced record is disturbing. Despite increasing evidence that women have been more culturally active than official history previously acknowledged, the discrepancy in contributions is still immense. Given that situation, it is legitimate to ask why.

Women have been largely mute for several reasons. First, for centuries educational opportunities for women were either nonexistent or distinctly inferior. An illiterate is scarcely capable of writing stories. Second, in more recent times, as Tillie Olsen so poignantly reminds us in her book *Silences*, many women sufficiently educated to be capable of writing or creating in other media have been too burdened with the traditional responsibilities of child rearing to be able to do so. Finally, masculine hostility towards women artists has traditionally been so strong that few women who admitted their true identities could gain acceptance. Consider, for example, such pen names as George Sand and George Eliot.

But those answers do not adequately handle the question. While they are all legitimate, they are also too superficial. Viewed from the dominant masculine perspective, it appears as though women have little or no culture of their own. They have been, until very recently, essentially invisible, tucked away in the Land of Happily Ever After where they have experienced both imprisonment and deification.

The relationship between women's historical condition of invisibility and the similarly invisible, unspecified ideal of Happily Ever After makes studying this phenomenon primarily a theological problem, although on the surface it appears more sociological or psychological. To fully understand why this is so, a feminist theological perspective is essential. What, then, is feminist theology?

Feminist Theology

The area intended by these words is complex and far from homogeneous. But a major characteristic of most feminist theology is a high level of authorial engagement, generally in narrative form, often confessional, which sets it apart from what some feminists refer to as a contrasting remoteness and abstractness in traditional, overwhelmingly masculine, scholarship. The distinction resembles theologian Schubert Ogden's differentiation between witnessing and theologizing. Typically, even the most traditional feminist theologian witnesses, even as she or he may also blur that distinction by simultaneously and/or subsequently reflecting.

In contrast to some traditional nonfeminist theologians, who start with deity and move toward humanity, feminist theologians typically begin with humanity and ask such questions as, What does it mean to be human in female form? Or, what does the fact that I am a woman mean for me in terms of being alive at all? These are the kinds of questions which impel feminist theologians in their search toward what some still call *God*, others now call instead *the Goddess*, and some even refuse to name at all.

A case in point is Dorothee Soelle, probably one of the best-known contemporary female German theologians. Soelle brings theory and praxis together in the form of monthly "political" worship services, the *Politisches Nachtgebet* she holds in Cologne, West Germany. Despite a relatively prolific theological output (*Christ the Representative, An Essay in Theology after the "Death of God,"* and *Political Theology*), Soelle is comparatively little recognized in Germany, where she taught outside her field of major interest in the Institute of Germanic Philology at the University of Cologne, although she is somewhat better known in the United States from teaching at Union Theological Seminary. Her first book, *Christ the Representative*, which emerged out of contemporary existentialism, reflects the modern experience of God's absence, and cites Jesus as a representative for God, but not his replacement. In *Political Theology* she moves to a new stage in which she speaks of a "post-theistic 'God of the oppressed.' "[16] Neither her language (which uses the traditional sexist pronouns and the generic "man") nor her categories indicate that she is a woman, much less a feminist, although her concern for political theology necessarily posits sex one of many categories of oppression and makes her incisive thinking popular with feminist theologians. But even in her chapter on "Truth as Faith's Theory of Praxis," in which you could logically expect some discussion of her experience as a woman, she fails to use feminist categories or speak of women's oppression. Instead, her examples include references to Vietnam and Biafra.[17] A representative statement of her views occurs in these words:

> The understanding of truth in political theology, which is based on the future or eschatological unity of theory and praxis, must resist this abandonment of praxis to instrumental reason; otherwise, the feeling of having been abandoned, of being powerless, will be suggested to men.[18]

Conversely, men can engage in feminist theology as legitimately as women. One whose work seems most obviously to qualify him as a feminist theologian is Leonard Swidler. In his book *Biblical Affirmations of Woman*, for example, he emphasizes feminine imagery of the biblical God and details positive images of women. The problem is that he does not truly see through feminist eyes. Thus he makes statements such as: ". . . in fact, it can be said that in the Old Kingdom the wife was the equal of the husband in rights, although her place in society was not identical with that of her husband."[19] Or: "When we shift our focus to the world of Hellas, we also find women enjoying a relatively high status in the early period of Greek civilization. . . ."[20] In both examples women have to be *defended;* in both, women are judged against a masculine norm. The primary objective seems to be the typical masculine one of "saving the appearances," retaining the system at all costs, rather than the feminist enterprise of first penetrating and understanding *women's* experience, then relating it to a system if need be.

Within feminist theology two distinctly different approaches exist. The more traditional envisions feminist theology as theology seen through the eyes of women and men who perceive the world in nonsexist terms. Such an approach presupposes much of what is meant by traditional theology: a study of deity, often, but not necessarily, within the Judeo-

Christian tradition. This wing of feminist theologians has been labeled reformist by religionists Carol Christ and Judith Plaskow. This kind of feminist theology often construes the inherited beliefs of traditional churches or synogogues as being innately nonsexist, but subsequently contaminated because of biases of the patriarchal socities through which they have been transmitted. Hence the need for reformation.

The thrust toward this kind of feminist theology, which began approximately twenty years ago, stems from two different sources. In part, it comes from women long active within their respective places of worship. Such women wanted increasingly larger roles in their religious communities. From simply questioning why they were excluded from the most important religious functions, they grew more and more aware of what their inferior roles meant. Within Roman Catholicism, for example, some nuns wondered why they should not be admitted to the priesthood. Their Episcopal sisters, usually active lay members, wondered the same thing. Similarly, within Judaism there were women who wondered why they were excluded throughout almost all aspects of religious worship other than those centered in the home.

A second group of women involved in this kind of thinking were seminarians. Some were from Protestant denominations which did permit women clerics but espoused their beliefs in traditional, inherited masculine terminology. Others were studying because they wished to teach. Common to all these women was the realization that traditional beliefs, as they have been handed down, are clearly sexist.

A helpful point of departure for this view is provided by Catherina Halkes, who lectures on feminism and Christendom at the theological faculty of the Catholic University of Nijmegen, The Netherlands: she calls feminist theology "a reaction and a protest provoked by a theology which for many centuries took for granted that reality had its centre in the male of the species."[21] In her analysis, she characterizes feminist theology by five major traits. First, it is a theology which opposes the traditional masculine conception of two patterns of humanness fixed for all time at creation; it seeks instead, to determine what women and men are each in themselves and in relation to each other. Second, feminist theology reforms traditional theology and doctrines along nonsexist lines. Third, it is "contextual theology," theology which recognizes women's actual experiences both historically and contemporaneously and accepts the vast differences among them instead of lumping them stereotypically into one undifferentiated category known as "woman." Fourth, it is "genitive" or subjective theology in which women are, for the first time, subjects living out and reflecting upon their own faith instead of being objects manipulated by men and masculine ideologies. Finally, Halkes sees feminist theology as "a critical liberation theology."

This facet of her analysis emphasizes women's continued and historic sexual oppression much as other liberation theologies emphasize racial and economic oppressions.

In this way of understanding feminist theology, traditional structures as we have known them in Judeo-Christian thinking are respected as such. Many feminist theologians of this persuasion assume that looking at original sources and studying them carefully will reveal originally nonsexist wording, either reflecting an underlying androgynous core or incorporating feminine imagery to counterbalance the obvious masculine biases. In this view, both women and men are often thought originally to have been accorded full human dignity in equal terms. Thinkers in this branch of feminist theology typically seek to retain existing structures as fully as possible, changing only those elements reflecting masculine superiority. Representative of this approach is Roman Catholic Elisabeth Schüssler Fiorenza, who argues persuasively that it is not the original biblical texts which legitimate the subordination of women, but the subsequent misinterpretations which do so. As she points out, "All interpretations of texts depend on the presuppositions, prejudices, and questions of those who attempt to exegete them. Since most biblical scholars are men, they usually study and preach the New Testament from a male point of view."[22]

Some of the other representative Christian thinkers besides Schüssler Fiorenza whose work falls within this tradition are Phyllis Trible, Letty Russell, and Rosemary Radford Ruether. Like her Roman Catholic counterpart, Protestant Phyllis Trible uses feminist interpretation, technically known as hermeneutics, to try "to recover old treasures and discover new ones in the household of faith."[23] Her source is the traditional one of the Judeo-Christian faith, the Bible. In her biblical analyses two interpretive concerns dominate. She is first of all concerned with the connection linking the way something is written—its style, and the persuasive aspects of its language—to the way it is interpreted. Second, she tries to use nonsexist language when she translates. Her underlying thesis in *God and the Rhetoric of Sexuality* is that "a single text appears in different versions with different functions in different contexts. . . . What it says on one occasion, it denies on another. Thus scripture in itself yields multiple interpretations of itself."[24] In her critical analysis or exegesis of various familiar biblical texts, Trible persuasively argues that masculine language has obscured the biblical message of a "transcendent creator who is neither male nor female nor a combination of the two . . . . [but a] God male *and* female."[25]

The work of both Ruether and Russell, the one Roman Catholic the other Protestant, falls simultaneously within the categories of liberation and feminist theology. Liberation theology deals with the struggles of any oppressed group—black, Amerindian, Latin American, woman—to achieve freedom. Borrowing from feminist Barbara Burris' term, Russell speaks in her book *Human Liberation in a Feminist Perspective: A Theology of the oppressed world majority of women* as "the fourth world."[26] Carefully using either nonsexist language or emphasizing feminine pronouns, Russell reinterprets certain traditional biblical themes. Among them are human liberation; shalom, whose meanings include peace, wholeness, well-being, and prosperity; servanthood; service or diakonia; ministry; humanization, "the setting free of all humanity to have a future and a hope"[27]; conscientization, roughly consciousness-raising; dialogue; and community. The underlying journey toward liberation upon which Russell builds is taken from Paul in Romans 8:14–27, particularly the passage 8:22–23:

> As we all know, up to the present time, the creation in all its parts groans with pain like the pain of childbirth. But not just creation alone groans; we ourselves, although we have tasted already the *aperitif* of the spirit, we groan inwardly because we are still anticipating our adoption as children and the full liberation of our human existence.[28]

Her method, typical of both liberation and feminist theologies, is not merely limited to critical theory. Instead, it involves praxis, a "constant process of action-reflection which has led [her] in a journey with others, for others, toward God's future."[29]

Like Russell, Ruether is simultaneously a liberation and a feminist theologian. She locates the oppression of women and various Third World groups in the patterns of dualism inherent in the Western tradition, seeing the sexual dualism as the one which "sums up all [the other] alienations."[30] Her model of revolution, though couched in fairly traditional language, is truly radical, entailing

> nothing less than a transformation of all the social structures of civilization, particularly the relationship between work and play. It entails literally a global struggle to overthrow and transform the character of power structures and points forward to a new messianic epiphany that will as far transcend the world-rejecting salvation myths of apocalypticism and Platonism as these myths transcended the old nature myths of the neolithic village. Combining the values of the world-transcending Yahweh with those of the world body, the woman and the world, its salvation myth will not be one of divinization and flight from the body but of humanization and reconciliation with the earth.[31]

A male counterpart to these reformist feminist theologians is Roman Catholic Joseph Ramisch. When Ramisch reflects along these lines, typically he asks the same kinds of questions women do, but with greater emphasis on the detrimental effects of masculine assumptions to the full human development of men. Thus, where a woman feminist might attend more closely to the suffering involved in being treated as an object, Ramisch examines the harm he experiences by religious legitimation which speaks of men as "lords" and "masters."[32]

But these reformist tendencies represent only one wing within feminist theology. The other, to which this book belongs, Sheila Collins and Carol Christ have labeled revolutionary.[33] Although feminist theologians in both groups agree that religion is an essential component of meaningful human existence, the two groups differ considerably on their conceptions of where religious meaning is to be found. Whereas the reformists feel that beneath their encrustations of masculine biases, the traditional religions of our Western Judeo-Christian heritage contain a meaningful reflection of Ultimacy, the revolutionaries reject these traditional structures entirely. Viewing the so-called "major" Western religions as irredeemably sexist, they look instead to other sources of and for religious experience. Given their rejection of the biblical tradition it is not surprising that they find religious meaning predominantly in two widely separated time periods, the prebiblical and the contemporary.

And given these two major sources, it is also not surprising that what these revolutionary feminist theologians do is not always immediately identifiable as "theology." So imbued are most individuals within Western culture with the notion that "theology" means *Christian* theology, that even Judaic and Islamic theology seem somewhat alien. But theology of goddesses?

Theology in general is not easy to define because it seldom exists apart from a particular tradition. While it can be a purely disinterested, philosophical discussion about the relation of deity to the world and humanity, it more commonly reflects a particular religion. The word *theology* breaks apart into the words *discourse about God*, but what *kind* of discourse is it? It may be construed as Judaic, Islamic, or Christian, or even more commonly as more particularized versions of each such as Reformed, Sunni, or Lutheran. Cutting across all these denominational lines it may also be systematic, apologetic, historical, ecclesiastical, polemical, and the like. Ignoring these important distinctions, I may nonetheless attempt an encompassing definition of sorts.

Partially following David Tracy, I might say that theology is sustained critical reflection on my experience of God, reflection adequate to the contemporary world, but not necessarily to an inherited, traditional understanding of deity.[34] Or if I find the word "God" too problematic, I might say that theology is coherent critical reflection upon my experience of the sacred. But it is important to remember that these definitions, brief and general as they are, are not adequate for *all* theologies. If I were an Orthodox Talmudic scholar, for example, I might ignore the experiential dimension entirely, focusing instead on received texts which I would then comment on.

While theology is certainly not a vogue word, it has gained fairly common currency in the past two decades. During the 1960s, we heard variously of death of God theology, theology of hope, theology of play; now we hear of liberation theology, and, increasingly, of feminist theology. Surely lay people can ask with some justification what this proliferation of theologies means. If theology is discourse about God, what can a phrase that seems to say "discourse about God of play" or "discourse about God of feminism" possibly mean? These are ligitimate questions, made even more legitimate by the fact that some of these theologies omit God entirely. When it comes to the term *feminist theology*, which often speaks not of God but of *the Goddess*, the term theology becomes awkward indeed. Because of its awkwardness, feminist theologian Naomi Goldenberg has coined the term *thealogy* to cover an area of study comparable to what the masculine *theology* typically encompasses. While that linguistic shift helps capture the flavor of the type of feminist theology which emphasizes goddesses, it necessarily excludes androgynous visions of deity as thoroughly as its masculine counterpart does. Thus, it appropriately names only some of what feminist theology, even of the revolutionary sort, concerns.

Whatever else it may do, feminist theology does not simply look at women's issues in general. While it is relatively easy to see that feminist theology is not identical with feminism, the lines blur when it comes to the sometimes-overlapping category of women and religion. This term, adopted by the American Academy of Religion, encompasses all aspects of women and women's issues relative to the study of religion. For this larger context a book like *Women in Contemporary Muslim Societies*, edited by Jane I. Smith is appropriate because it deals heavily with women's religious roles. Furthermore, it reflects some American feminist assumptions, while still retaining its major focus on the very different Islamic context. But it is anthropology, not a book of *theology*.

A very different kind of book which challenges the concept of feminist theology, is definitely theology, but does not focus specifically on women. This is Tom Driver's *Patterns of Grace*. Here, content would appear to rule out its being feminist theology because it focuses on human experience as lived out by a male, albeit a feminist male. To the extent that feminist theology is a mode of *doing* theology rather than a content, Driver's book surely qualifies: it is confessional, it is not abstract, it seeks to locate humanity and human meaning in concrete, bodily, lived experience. A representative chapter is "Tub Water and Holy Ground." There Driver learns to ground himself, to put down roots, to say:

> . . . there are earth mothers and sky fathers. We need some earth fathers . . . . He walked on his earth father-mother toward the house. The symbols fell away. Neither father nor mother would emblem what he felt. He was full of an energy that has no name.[36]

Furthermore, the alienation which precedes this revelation is couched in terminology familiar to almost any woman. As Driver sits in his bathtub he suddenly realizes how little he knows his body. Speaking in the third person, he says:

> There was something wrong about opening your legs. This was the message he accumulated, and while he had never for an instant agreed with it in his mind, nor acquiesced with his conscious will, he knew, had long known, that the message had gotten through. To open his legs was an act of defiance.[37]

The line between what does and does not constitute feminist theology becomes even more blurred when secular components become a major focus of concern. For instance, when Judith Plaskow focuses on what she calls the "yeah, yeah, experience," of women sharing their common experiences in consciousness-raising sessions, she analyzes the religious components of seemingly pure secular experience. As she explains in her essay, "The Coming of Lilith: Toward a Feminist Theology," such an experience involves the components of grace, illumination, mission, and conversion. It is therefore appropriate to reflect on it theologically, that is to see what ultimate concerns inform it.[38] Similarly, when Mary Daly pushes beyond women's consciousness-raising groups as such, to espouse communities of women choosing to live apart from men, this move is religious as well as political. Though her militant anti-male stance and emphasis on lesbianism alienate many feminists of both sexes, there is nonetheless a compelling logic to her view that women cannot accept the existing structures of patriarchy, but instead must create entirely new, separate ones of their own. So fully does Daly espouse her own views that her theology creates new language and new imagery for and of women who eschew men. A characteristic example from her controversial book *Gyn/Ecology* concerns sparking, her term for "igniting the fire of female friendship":[39]

> . . . the Enspiriting Self is acceptable to her Self. She knows that only she can judge her Self. Because she has a strong sense of her own worth, the Amazon who has the courage to accept her Self is not self-

sacrificing. Having acknowledged the divine Spark in her Self and having accepted it as her own, she has no need to demand self-sacrifice of her sisters. This prospect is horrifying to her, for she cherishes their divine Sparks, their be-ing, as she cherishes her own, knowing that their combined combustion is the creation of Female Fire.[40]

Though the political cast of this passage is as apparent as its often controversial notion of Amazonian friendship, its religious imagery is unmistakable. This could be any gnostic group sharing its special knowledge among the initiated.

Besides women's consciousness-raising groups and lesbian communities, other seemingly secular sources for what traditionalists call revelation vary according to the predilections of individual feminist theologians. For Penelope Washbourne feminine spirituality materializes in various physiological rites of passage such as menarche, childbirth, and menopause.[41] For Carol Christ it occurs through female imagery in various women's writings. Thus she looks to the writings of authors such as Kate Chopin, Margaret Atwood, Doris Lessing, Adrienne Rich, and Ntosake Shange for revelations much as many Christians look to the Bible. For example, in words such as these from Ntosake Shange, Christ sees "a revelation of a new way of viewing the world and being a woman": "i found god in myself/and i loved her/i loved her fiercely."[42]

By contrast, Naomi Goldenberg finds a rich source of feminine spirituality in dreams and fantasies, emphasizing the tangible quality of both. Speculating on the new mysticism that will emerge in the West as the old patriarchal God is replaced, she says it "will largely be defined by women and men who will have an increasing awareness of their own physical presence within the philosophies they create."[43] She further states that "feminist theology is on its way to becoming psychology."[44] Whether or not one accepts that equation of theology and psychology, the apparent secularity of much of this revolutionary feminist theology demands close attention.

This coincidence of secularism and theology is tenuous even for theologians with a traditional masculine perspective. For feminist theologians the combination is doubly problematic, for they are departing from what the term "theology" ordinarily means in two questionable ways. To call attention to the masculine biases within traditional theology is to court the wrath of nonfeminists of either sex; then additionally to discard deity is to antagonize those who cannot accept the seemingly self-contradictory notion that there can be a knowledge of God even if there is no God and no special sphere sacred to it, her, or him. To understand this seeming paradox necessitates an imaginative leap into the world view of someone whose experience does not authentically include what the word "God" typically means.

If we stop and think how language works, it becomes easier to enter such a world view. Most people who grew up in the United States recall the power attached to certain words during their childhood. Typically these words fall into two categories: so-called "dirty" words and profanities. Thus to hear or utter words like "God," "Hell," "damn," "shit," or "fuck" is shocking to most middle-class five-year-olds even nowadays; while some of the shock merely echoes the residual middle-class proprieties of their parents, some also goes deeper, truly setting apart these words from all others. For some people these words retain the initial shock-level into adulthood; for others it diminishes or vanishes entirely.

If the entire notion of "God" loses its original specialness, then for that individual, God is effectively dead. For some people who experience God's death life goes on much as before. But for many the loss is almost unbearable: the entire meaning of their lives goes with that demise. Where the world once felt full, round, and golden, now it feels flat and gray. If God does not exist, why should I bother to, either? What difference does it make whether I try to be the best person I can be? Why bother to achieve anything?

Somewhat curiously, if I start at such a point of bleak despair, I may nonetheless end up with a stance that can only be called theological. This Alice-through-the-Looking-Glass experience can happen in one of several different ways. First, the loss of faith described above may be the temporary experience typical of adolescents whose childhood misconceptions are slowly replaced with a more mature, adult understanding of God. Such an experience usually deepens, rather than weakens, the original faith structures, returning to the word *God* all its previous intensity but at a deeper level. A person who undergoes this sort of faith loss may not view his or her structures quite the same way, but she nonetheless does not discard them. Meaning still reaches her through such familiar words as *God, Jesus, Cross,* and the like.

But someone else may experience a similar loss of faith without a comparable return. For that individual one of two things may happen. First, he may live out his life in a mood of despair, never fully recovering from his loss. Unlike his totally secular counterpart who simply goes on as if nothing has happened, he can never forget what once *was*. What he lives out is, however, a fundamentally religious story, the loss of Eden. His life's meaning springs from his loss. For him the loss of God is so great that he can't believe there once was a god who now is gone. Instead, he believes that humans were once lucky enough to hold the comforting belief that God exists. But now, for whatever reasons, humanity as a whole can no longer sustain that illusion. Thus his nostalgia is not for God, *per se*, but for the human capacity to *believe* in God. Such a negative position is dialectically dependent upon the traditional theology now stripped of positive significance.

But there is a second, less despairing, variation on that response. In this situation the individual slowly recovers from the initial shock of her loss of faith. It occurs to her one day that the grass *is* green; the earth *is* round; there is still a "goldenness" to life. It may happen to her as she watches a particularly fiery sunset, or as she catches a faint whiff of honeysuckle. But suddenly, in a kind of Joycean epiphany, she experiences what once she would have called faith. Only for her there is no going back to the old structures. The words *God, Heaven, Christ* no longer resonate for her. But yet she now and again experiences the replenishment of her world. Slowly, over a period of years, it occurs to her that she does have faith. But it is not a faith in anything she has words to name. She does not believe in heaven or hell. She does not go to church. Yet something in her life serves as a conduit to a level of experience she recognizes as sacred. What, then, is the conduit?

Secular theologians exist precisely to find the names of such conduits. For some the task involves finding within everyday life, or the secular realm, parallels to the Christian story. For others it involves discovering parallels to other stories such as those of the ancient fertility goddesses. For still others it involves finding entirely new underlying structures so that revelation may not repeat old stories but tell totally new ones or even dispense with stories completely. Revolutionary feminist theologians more commonly combine elements from the two latter categories. Whatever their particular methodologies and sources, all feminist theologians necessarily raise, sometimes in extreme form, some of the most fundamental of all human questions.

Androgyny

To try to answer these questions from within a feminist perspective, two terms are commonly used: *androgyny* and *the Goddess*. The two words name very different approaches to understanding human nature. Both raise the serious issue of whether the famous "difference" is fundamental to humanness. To even imagine that the sexual difference is not essential is startling. How could there possibly *not* be two sexes? Yet in numerous so-called "lower" organisms sexual differentiation does not exist. Instead, many one-celled and some simple many-celled animals reproduce through division, the parents breaking into two or several parts, which then become its "descendants." More complex creatures reproduce through special germ cells which produce new individuals either alone or through pairing. Those which do so alone are still asexual, or androgynous. Thus, although the sexual reproduction we take so much for granted has the great evolutionary advantage of mingling hereditary materials from two lines of ancestry, humans could conceivably have evolved as asexual creatures instead.

Sartre questions the underlying philosophical meaning of this evolutionary development towards sexual differentiation and its accompanying dimorphism by asking two crucial questions: Are humans sexual only because they have sexes? Or, conversely, do they have sexes because they are inherently sexual.[45] If humans are sexual only because they happen to possess sexes, then the differences between women and men are not essential, but accidental. In that case, cultural change might eventually reduce the famous difference. This is the view implicit in the belief that humans are potentially androgynous.

Androgyny is not a word that many people outside feminist circles take seriously. And even some within them deride it, as does Mary Daly when she speaks of androgyny as "conveying something like 'John Travolta and Farrah Fawcett-Majors scotch-taped together.' "[46] More commonly, however, androgyny is repudiated by those who don't fully understand it.

For many individuals androgyny remains roughly in the same category as the word "centaur," the mythical half man, half horse whom John Updike re-envisioned for the reading public in the 1960s.[47] Similarly, the androgyne, half man, half woman, appears almost as remote to most of us. Its most famous appearance undoubtedly occurs in Plato's *Symposium*, in which the original creation of humanity is said to have taken place like this:

> . . . the original human nature was not like the present, but different. The sexes were not two as they are now, but originally three in number; there was man, woman, and the union of the two, having a name corresponding to this double nature [androgyny], which had once a real existence, but is now lost. . . . Terrible was their might and strength, and . . . the gods could not suffer their insolence to be unrestrained. . . . Zeus said I will cut them in two and then they will be diminished in strength and increased in numbers. . . . After the division the two parts of man, each desiring his other half, came together, and throwing their arms about one another, entwined in mutual embraces, longing to grow into one. . . . Each of us when separated, having one side only, like a flat fish, is but the indenture of a man, and he is always looking for his other half. . . . This meeting and melting into one another, thus becoming one instead of two, was the very expression of his ancient need. And the reason is that human nature was originally one and we were a whole, and the desire and pursuit of the whole is called love.[48]

Out of Plato's vision of an original androgyny has emerged the romantic notion of a lost soul mate, the other half for whom one was destined romantically from before birth. Once reunited, these two halves will function as one, nearly perfect human being. With some variations, that belief has been the pattern for love in the Western world since romantic love was discovered. But this underlying belief in fundamental androgyny has so little worked that the platonic vision is precisely what it feminists are protesting against right now, for it has historically fostered and emphasized the famous difference that unites the two lost halves in the first place. Consequently, this result of Plato's myth has led to a situation just the reverse of androgynization—sexual polarization.

Jung deals with this problem of androgyny somewhat differently. Although he strongly advocates the recognition of sexual differences, he nonetheless theorizes that within every human being there exists an interior, complementary self of the opposite sex. For women this figure is the animus, for men, the anima. Thus, what Plato represented as existing in two physically separate humans, Jung posits within a single person. The problem, according to Jung, is that most people fail to develop adequately their opposite, or shadow, side. In his theory, by recognizing and developing that inner opposite, individuals can appropriately solve what is only superficially a problem of the sexes: they can integrate themselves into fully developed, rounded human beings.

But you can also justifiably ask whether androgyny is entirely a psychological issue or whether it is also physical. What, after all, do androgynes look like? The masculine/feminine dichotomy emphasizes bodiment so heavily that obvious sexual differences such as breasts and genitalia assume prodigious importance. The much-vaunted American male predilection for big breasts is a notable example. Androgyny, by contrast, neither denies the beauty of the body nor emphasizes its sexual differences. Examples of androgynous figures from the visual arts—like the women of pre-Raphaelite painters such as Rossetti and Burne-Jones—are illustrative. These women, apart from their characteristic, flowing garments, could be beautiful boys as easily as women, for they lack the accentuated breasts so often used visually to demarcate the sexes. Similarly, the strange face of da Vinci's *La Giaconda*, better known as *Mona Lisa*, is androgynous. In fact "she" has been androgynously transformed in *L.H.O.O.Q*, or *Mona Lisa's Mustache*, a photograph of the painting to which the artist Marcel Duchamps added a mustache in 1919 as part of his nihilistic Dadaist stance towards art. The 1960s emphasis on unisex dress is also androgynous.

But to suggest that androgyny is a matter of equalizing the differences and emphasizing the likenesses between women and men makes many people uncomfortable: to what extent, after all, do I want to look like my lover and have him look like me? To ask whether androgynization will make women and men literally different from what they now are is not as naive a question as it superficially seems. Behind it looms the large issue of how we conceptualize what we call "reality." Implicit in the questions are distinctions we commonly make between internal and external, appearance and reality, real and imaginery. By analogy, did Carlos Castaneda *really* turn into a crow in the book *The Teachings of Don Juan: a Yaqui Way of Knowledge?* While it is easy to avoid such questions by calling them literalistic and simplistic, or to say as the sorcerer Don Juan does, " 'You always ask me questions I cannot answer,' "[49] to do so is to miss the point that given our own linguistic framework we *can ask* these sorts of questions at all. Or more importantly, we almost cannot *not* ask them. Automatically we distinguish in precisely those ways which make such questions inevitable.

In the Don Juan situation we can, indeed, also answer on the same level as the question itself. If the question means: Did Don Juan truly lose his man shape, his limbs, and his skin to become bird-shaped, winged, and coated with shiny black feathers, then the answer is no. But if the question means: Did Castaneda subjectively experience himself as if he were a crow, then the answer is yes. He describes the experience like this:

> I had the perception of growing bird's legs, which were weak and wobbly at first. I felt a tail coming out of the back of my neck and wings out of my cheekbones. The wings were folded deeply. I felt them coming out by degrees. The process was hard but not painful. Then I winked my head down to the size of a crow. But the most astonishing effect was accomplished with my eyes. My birds' sight![50]

In the analogous case of changing images of women and men it is therefore reasonable to ask seemingly naive questions. Will androgynization make humans *look* different? Are they going to cease having sexually differentiated characteristics? Again, on one level, that is ridiculous. But that is partly because these questions are almost unbearable to ask; they reflect a fear so basic that few of either sex dare raise them. To what extent does anyone enact her or his appearance? *Do* blondes have more fun? Are fat people jollier? The questions sound absurdly literalistic, until we stop and think. A woman, after all, often exists in situations in which she is treated as a literal object of contempt. She may suddenly find the privacy of her interior space, her mind, intruded upon loudly by shouts and gestures from the driver of a passing garbage truck. Or, sitting alone, awaiting breakfast in a motel dining room, she may hear a whispered, "Psst," only to look up and see a janitor, leaning over his broom staring at her as he asks, "Was it a good night, Honey?"

Surely at the moment in which the janitor whispers his insinuation, she is as fully a sex object as Don Juan is a bird: for that one instant of shocked disbelief, she is object to his malicious subjectivity. Yet that in no way implies a visible external transformation as a literalist might assume.

To dismiss these issues as naive, literalistic, and irrelevant is to skip over the facticity of embodiment. If androgyny has nothing to do with physical appearance, but merely represents an inner mode of experience and certain ways of acting, then it ignores the actuality of embodiment. No matter how much a person seems to transcend or escape his or her body, a body is still there to be reckoned with. And given our particular culture, it is generally the body which constitutes the essence of any individual from an outside perspective. To deny that fact is to deny much of your own experience.

This issue permeates Sartre's words when he asks, what "if sex were only the instrument and, so to speak, the *image* of a fundamental sexuality? What if man [sic] possessed a sex only because he is originally and fundamentally a sexual being . . . ?[51]

Indeed, if human sexuality permeates the entire being of every individual, then the difference not only cannot be ignored, but the possibility also exists that the old Christian belief in two fundamentally different human natures is correct.

The Goddess

For feminists who do take embodiment with the great seriousness it demands, androgyny may well not provide a physically acceptable vehicle for reconceptualizing humanity. Instead, they often prefer to speak of *the Goddess*. Obviously there are multiple sources for whatever that term means. Many feminists look to ancient myths which tell of goddesses; others seek accounts of witchcraft. Naomi Goldenberg, Merlyn Stone, and Starhawk typify this group. For them the term *the Goddess* roughly correlates with *God* as the latter is broadly used by most people in Western culture. Both words signify ultimacy, to borrow Tillich's word for what *God* means.

Using the words *the Goddess*, however, causes some difficulty because so far the term remains unclear. *The Goddess*, unlike *God*, also refers to the fertility goddesses so prevalent (according to most historians of antiquity and prehistory) prior to what is ordinarily called history. This term is unclear because various cultures named their fertility goddesses with different names. Was there, as the term *goddess* seems to imply, simply one goddess, or were there many? Since certain distinguishing characteristics differentiate one fertility goddess from another, that seems a difficult issue as far as scholarship is concerned. Therefore, the monotheistic term *the Goddess* does not seem entirely appropriate.

But besides raising the issue of monotheism/henotheism versus polytheism, the term *the Goddess* is also awkward because, for many people, the word *goddess* is so foreign that it invokes something totally removed from anyone's individually lived experience. Thus, for many individuals, *the Goddess* is simply a patchwork label artificially pasted onto experience. In this sense, reviving the term is somewhat akin to modern movements in Ireland to revive Celtic, or efforts within some black communities to introduce Swahili as part of a return to African roots. But for women the link to ancient goddesses seems even more tenuous than the linguistic and cultural experiences of heterosexual outcast groups trying to connect to some known history of their own. As a kind of link to the distant past, the term *goddess* seems spurious indeed.

The fact that many people feel that the word *God* is beyond sexuality is yet another reason that the term *Goddess* is awkward. Such thinking is shared by many, both feminist and anti-feminist alike. Clearly, some evidence in the Bible and other sacred writings supports a view that sexuality is irrevelent to conceptions of deity.

God is still so heavily loaded with associations to an old man in the sky with a long white beard that entirely purifying it of such thoughts (despite the best scholarly efforts to do so) is almost impossible on a subconscious level. Yet the issue of whether *the Goddess* is appropriate or not still remains. The fact that a group trying to avoid sexually-tinged imagery cannot purposely reintroduce a term such as *Goddess* or *the Goddess* without duplicating old errors is a major problem. For them to do so simply reverses the problem raised by the masculine word *god*."

Another argument against *the Goddess* is that by using it, feminists seem to imply one goddess who is specifically a fertility figure and earth mother. In turn, that suggests that this is the image par excellence of and for women. But that particular image leads to some very real problems. First of all, few feminists nowadays support the view (more generally held by radically nonfeminist individuals) that women fulfill themselves primarily within the role of motherhood. Thus, to uphold as *the Goddess* an image whose prime reason for being has to do with reproduction seems curious indeed.

Yet, what the term intends is important, whether we like the word itself or not. *The Goddess* is a way of naming what is ultimate within the lives of women. Possibly it is the only appropriate way women have to name their ultimacy, despite the awkwardness I have alluded to. Furthermore, because the term *God* has accreted so many patriarchal associations, many women feel uncomfortable using the word. Images of the wrathful, patriarchal God so prominent within the Old Testament run counter to what seems ultimate in the lives of most contemporary women. Thus the term *goddess* can simply be a way of naming a pattern of meaning for which there seems no other especially good name.

But in using the term *goddess*, it is useful to remember that there were other goddess figures besides the various earth mothers referred to vaguely as *the Goddess*. If we consider only the Greco-Roman pantheon, for example, there are numerous goddesses. There is, of course, Hera, wife of Zeus (known as Juno in the Roman pantheon), who is the exemplar of the shrewish wife. Certainly, although she is not a figure to emulate, negative deities like Shiva or Kali have been taken very seriously as objects of worship by millions for centuries. In addition to Hera, there is Aphrodite (the Roman Venus), goddess of love. In her we see a move away from the older fertility goddess. Sexuality and lovemaking (without concomitant mothering and reproduction) characterize her, rather than procreation in the fullest sense. Another goddess of that pantheon is Artemis/Diana, the chaste goddess of the hunt who shuns male lovers in favor of a self-sufficient life of her own. There is also the curious figure of Athena, or Minerva, whose mother was not a woman, but Zeus, from whose brain she sprang fullblown. In literature Athena is depicted as anything but a stereotypic female. In fact, if you did not know you were reading about Athena, you might assume her a god, not a goddess. For example, in his Oresteian trilogy, Aeschylus shows her speaking these words of judgment in favor of Orestes and against Clytemnestra in "The Eumenides":

> No mother gave me birth. Therefore, the father's claim/And male supremacy in all things, save to give/Myself in marriage, wins my whole heart's loyalty./Therefore a woman's death who killed her husband, is, I judge, outweighed in grievousness by his. And so/Orestes, if the votes are equal, wins the case.[52]

Then there is Kore, the goddess Demeter, known also as Ceres, mother of Persephone/Proserpina, who is both mother goddess and goddess of grain, an earth mother who repines yearly at the seasonal loss of her daughter. And there is Hestia/Vesta, of all the goddesses the one with least personality. As the goddess or spirit of the hearth, she is, by extension, also the goddess of the home.

Hestia

It may seem curious for a feminist to look to a goddess like Hestia. It may also seem strange that anyone, particularly a feminist, should want to explore the world of housework for meaning. But human evolution may well be at a crossroads. The potential to rear fetuses outside their natural habitat is one of the most momentous possibilities in the entire development of human beings. The connection between this potential for human change and the current emancipation of women from traditional roles requires careful evaluation. It is puzzling to me that so many women are eager to jump "forward" into what was once labeled a man's world, without necessarily knowing what it is they are leaving behind. Granted, most of them clearly recognize that what they leave is motherhood, confinement within houses, and enforced child rearing, often with little or no support from men. Until recently, most feminists have viewed that past in just these negative terms. Yet I would argue that there are also some positive experiences in that background. Surely something has prepared women for their liberation today. While in no sense do I condone that past status quo, I am curious to learn what it was in those traditional modes of being that made women who they are today. To understand the process by which humans have and continue to become whatever it is we mean when we say we are human, we must examine any ways humanness has ever manifested itself. While viewing the haste of increasing numbers of women to leave the domestic sphere behind, I worry that they may neglect a clue vital for us all. For that reason, above all, I have chosen to visit the realm of Hestia—home, locus of the promised Land of Happily Ever After.

I

❧ Home

1

HOME AS SACRED SPACE

Where the average man in Western culture has his office, factory, or shop, and his counterpart in a preindustrial society has his tribe, a traditional middle-class woman in Western society has her home. Though it is common nowadays to speak of Western culture as being desacralized, we still call space within a church sacred, even if we do not actually experience sacrality ourselves. Curiously, however, few people notice that a comparable sacrality of space exists within a home. Like a church, home provides refuge from the "outside" world.

Familiar as it is, home is a concept most people find difficult to define. Trying to do so results in answers a bit like those provided by a roomful of second graders asked to draw God. Like their brightly crayoned images of bearded old men in the sky, home, too, can be pictured concretely. Most people would draw a house to represent it. But others might attempt an abstraction. To paraphrase art critic Rudolph Arnheim, "Of course, no two pictures of home are alike, whereas the word home persists unchanged."[1]

Although home is ordinarily a specific place, it need not be. Ultimately it is a state of mind. As Gaston Bachelard says of houses, home concentrates "all of our images of protected intimacy."[2] And although we tend to think of home as a singular concept, it may be plural, a composite of many different places or states of mind. It is often considered your place or point of origin, but that, too, is not single, for it may be the womb, the mother herself, or the home to which you were brought as an infant. But it may also be a condition to which you return, though in your absence that state or place will have changed. Or it may be the place you are now, or the place you are not and never actually will attain, being always some variant of any place but here, or any time but now. Yet home is generally considered to be where you belong, whether or not you ever actually attain it. Perhaps Robert Frost comes closest to capturing its essence when he calls it the place that "When you have to go there/They have to take you in."[3]

Despite the fact that *home* is a concept deeply embedded in our thinking, no distinct word exists for it in classical Greek or ancient Hebrew. Of Teutonic origins, it evolved through the Germanic languages, hence became part of the Hebraic and classical inheritance of Western civilization relatively late. Despite the absence of a separate word to distinguish it from the closely related *house*, the underlying idea is implicit at times in classical Greek. For instance, it sometimes attaches to the word "family" (*oikia, oikikos*), as occurs in the Septuagint, the Greek translation of the Old Testament, in I Chronicles 4:21:

> The sons of Shelah the son of Judah: Er the father of Lecah, Laadah the father of Mareshah, and the families of the house of linen workers at Beth-ashbea . . .

Or I Kings 12:19:

> So Israel has been in rebellion against the house of David to this day.

Other examples occur in I Kings 12:19; Matthew 13:57; and Mark 3:25 and 6:4. At times *patria* also suggests *home* and *family*, as when Joseph is said to be of the lineage, *patria*, of David in Luke 2:4.

Similarly, although there is no separate word in Hebrew for *home*, as distinct from *house* or *family*, the Hebrew word *het*, which comes from a root meaning "to go in" or "to spend the night" is used about 2000 times in the Old Testament, mostly in reference to a physical dwelling.[4] In its breadth of meaning the root extends from "inside" to "eternal home." In its verb form it sometimes refers to producing a family as in Ruth 4:11:

> Then all the people who were at the gate, and the elders, said, "We are witnesses. May the Lord make the woman, who is coming into

your house, like Rachel and Leah, who together *built up the house* of
Israel. . ." (italics indicate translation of *het*)

Both the Hebraic and the Hellenistic familial structures were strongly
patriarchal, but corresponding attitudes toward family life differed significantly. Although the Homeric *Iliad* and *Odyssey* reveal a comradeship
between husband and wife, women are nonetheless shown as inferior
to men. Subsequently, attitudes of male superiority came to dominate
the post-Heroic Greek attitudes toward women, and family life suffered
accordingly. Partly responsible for the shift away from early respect were
near Eastern influences and the increased refinement of the upper class
which led to educational opportunities for men, which were forbidden
to their wives. This discrepancy in educational levels is reflected in
Xenophon's *Oeconomicus* when Socrates asks his friend Critobulus:

"Is there any one with whom you talk less than you do your wife?"

The friend replies:

"There are few or none, I confess."[5]

In contrast to this strong Greek disregard for domestic life, so important was family life to the ancient Hebrews that the idea of family extends
in the Bible to cover their tribes, the nations of Israel and Judah, and to
Israel as a covenant community under God. Central to this extended
idea of family is the patriarchal concept of hierarchy which involves a
carefully gradated system of rights and obligations, with the supreme
authority vested in the male at the top. Peter stresses this notion of
hierarchical order as the root of stable social life when he says:

Servants, be submissive to your masters with all respect. . . . Likewise
you wives, be submissive to your husbands, so that some, though they
do not obey the word, may be won without a word by the behavior of
their wives. . . . (I Pet. 2:18–3:1)

He also makes clear that this hierarchical relationship entails strong
obligations from husbands as well:

Likewise you husbands, live considerately with your wives, bestowing
honor on the woman as the weaker sex, since you are joint heirs of
the grace of life, in order that your prayers may not be hindered. (I
Pet. 3:7)

Similarly within the Pauline Epistles, such as the Letter to the Ephesians, the importance of hierarchy within the home predominates (Eph.
3:15–5:22ff):

. . . I bow my knees before the Father, from whom every family in
heaven and on earth is named. . . . Wives, be subject to your husbands,
as to the Lord. For the husband is the head of the wife as Christ is the

head of the church, his body, and is himself its Saviour. As the church is subject to Christ, so let wives also be subject in everything to their husbands. Husbands, love your wives, as Christ loved the church and gave himself up for her, that he might sanctify her . . . even so husbands should love their wives as their own bodies. . . . "For this reason a man shall leave his father and mother and be joined to his wife, and the two shall become one." This is a great mystery, and I take it to mean Christ and the church. . . .

In I Timothy 3:2–5, the hierarchical conception of home is also apparent:

. . . a bishop . . . must manage his own household well, keeping his children submissive and respectful in every way; for if a man does not know how to manage his own household, how can he care for God's church?

This Pauline epistle further extends the family metaphor by urging Timothy to treat as relatives those in his pastoral charge (I Tim. 5:1–2):

Do not rebuke an older man but exhort him as you would a father; treat younger men like brothers, older women like mothers, younger women like sisters, in all purity.

Within the family it is not the rights of individuals which are so carefully detailed, but their duties. Both Ephesians and Colossians address in turn all members of a typical household—husbands, wives, children, and servants—charging each to ponder his or her duties; from these duties emerge the principles which are commonly held to make home life sacred. First is fear, or awe, of God, which includes raising obedient children as in Colossians 3:20: "Children, obey your parents in everything, for this pleases the Lord," and Ephesians 6:1–3:

Children, obey your parents in the Lord, for this is right. "Honor your father and mother" (this is the first commandment with a promise), "that it may be well with you and that you may live long on the earth."

Both extend the commandment in Exodus 20:12 to " 'Honor your father and mother, that your days may be long in the land which the Lord, your God gives you.' "

There are also laws of love and dutifulness which the home is expected to reflect. One law which is implicit in the idea of home is the law of social service, for the home is the ground of social morality. In this category falls the virtue of hospitality (Rom. 12:13): "Contribute to the needs of the saints, practice hospitality"; (I Pet. 4:9) "practice hospitality ungrudgingly to one another"; (Heb. 6:10): "For God is not so unjust as to overlook your work and love which you showed for his sake in serving the saints, as you still do"; (Heb. 13:2): "Do not neglect to show hospitality to strangers, for thereby some have entertained angels unawares," an allusion to the Sodom story in Genesis. Family life in the home is thus intended to be a training ground for love of humanity extended in the widest possible sense, although it is rooted in a strict hierarchical vision.

One need not be a feminist to recognize that this strong patriarchal emphasis on hierarchy within the home is precisely what contemporary feminists are protesting against. In the dominant Judao-Christian view women, like children and servants, are subservient to male authority, although such authority has its clearly defined limits and obligations.

Yet Jesus himself seems to have been generally free of the patriarchal biases inherent in the Jewish culture of his day, admitting women and men equally to his vision. In fact, some of his teachings radically question the strict hierarchical view as it applies to humans. For example, according to Matthew (Mat. 23: 9–10), Jesus said, ". . . call no man your father on earth, for you have one Father, who is in heaven," a message which clearly undermines the authority of earthly patriarchs although it still vests all power in one supreme *father*.

Further shifts away from the traditional Jewish conception of home and family occurred briefly with early Christianity's de-emphasis of marriage and elevation of virginity. Nonetheless, for those who did follow the traditional pattern, the old hierarchy prevailed. By the time of the Early Church Fathers, the ancient Jewish reverence for women had altered considerably. Tertullian's remark that women "are the devil's gateway," typifies the misogyny of this period.

In the Middle Ages, although the asceticism of the early Christian era had waned somewhat, marriage relationships were not highly esteemed. It was at this time that Thomas Aquinas promulgated his thesis of women's intrinsic inferiority, derived from his readings of Aristotle. Marriage now offered little in the way of love or companionship, being primarily a business or political affair among the upper classes, a physical outlet among the lower.

During the Renaissance and Reformation, however, marriage improved somewhat. Whereas parents had arranged marriages for their children during the Middle Ages, beginning with the later Middle Ages the Church insisted on free choice for the two would-be partners. Despite this greater freedom to enter marriage without coercion, the old ways did not immediately disappear.

In Europe during the so-called Age of Reason (from about 1615–1789) sexual freedom prevailed among the wealthy, and it became accepted in the upper classes for a married woman to become some other man's mistress, although middle-class mores did not readily accept such behavior. Outside of marriage there was little place for a woman except the convent.

In the wake of the Industrial Revolution, significant changes—usually for the worse—occured in lower-class family life. Often whole families now went off to work in mills or factories, leaving no supervision for children too young to work and no time left over for anything resembling family life. From about 1789–1918, a period colored by Romanticism and Victorian idealism, the interrelated concepts of family and home became strongly espoused, particularly among the middle classes. Women, for so long scorned as inferior, were now placed on their proverbial pedestals, there to be venerated as embodiments of hearth and home. This shift in emphasis was particularly difficult for American women for whom the frontier tradition had previously occasioned more economic and social freedom than was generally true for their European sisters.

As these middle-class American women became increasingly confined to their homes, they came to be identified as the sacred core of what the home stood for. In popular thought women were the ones who exerted the necessary moral force to influence the destiny of America. A number of factors contributed to this emphasis on women's roles within the sacred sphere of home. Whereas in colonial days women had frequently worked alongside their husbands on farms, in small shops, or in cottage industries, industrialization with its associated prosperity made women increasingly superfluous to the work force. At the same time, softenings of the stern orthodoxies of Puritan theology gave way to what historian Ann Douglas has called the "feminization of theology."[6] In this process, whereby the totally Other, transcendant God became immanentized, such theologians as Horace Bushnell, Henry Ward Beecher, and Dwight Lyman Moody began envisioning feminine characteristics of God. Simultaneously, the "belle ideal" of womanhood, which idealized woman's nature and influenced the accepted life style of middle-and upper-class women, permeated religious thought. The ancient belief that women are more emotional and less rational than men led to the associated view of women as gentle and nurturing. Furthermore, the romantic dichotomy of head and heart, reason and emotion, male and female undergirded the fiction which increasingly interested Americans. As theology became diluted, fiction began filling the resultant void.[7] By 1860, for example, Godey's Lady's Book had a circulation of 150,000 and women writers like Elizabeth Stuart Phelps and Harriet Beecher Stowe were widely read.

The prevailing sentimentalization of womanhood, promulgated by this fiction, is perhaps nowhere more pronounced than in the speeches and writing of Catherine Beecher (1800–1878)[8]. Building on the popular sentiments of the day, which held that the home was heaven, Beecher applied domestic pietism to American politics. She counseled her sisters that instead of practicing their Christian virtues within the confines of their own homes, they should unite and domesticate the world. Beecher's underlying metaphor saw America as an extended family, indirectly run by women educators whose capacity for self-sacrifice in the interest of the larger, public good would transform America.

In Beecher's view, as in more orthodox, patriarchal visions of the sacred, women function within the home much as Christ does within the entire realm of Christendom: both are sacrificial victims typically scapegoated and humiliated for the salvation of all *man*kind.

This situation raises the issue of whether the figure of an all-loving and forgiving Christ can be an appropriate model for women. Some of the arguments feminist theologian Valerie Saiving extends in her important essay "The Human Situation: A Feminine View" implicitly contain a negative answer, although she herself does not go so far as to say so.[9] Saiving's argument focuses specifically on the thesis that the sins of women are polar opposites to those of men. Whereas men typically have sinned through their pride, self-assertion, and will-to-power, women, Saiving suggests, have tended toward "triviality, distractibility, and diffuseness; lack of an organized center of focus; dependence on others for one's own self-definition; tolerance at the expense of standards of excellence; inability to respect the boundaries of privacy; sentimentality, gossipy sociability, and mistrust of reason—in short, underdevelopment or negation of the self.[10]

As Saiving points out, the very qualities most stressed in Christian theology are the positive faces of these feminine "sins": humility, forgiveness, selflessness, caring, and love, all of which women traditionally have been forced to develop in order to function as mothers and wives. Within the sacred sphere of home, women in general have been closer to these virtues than men. But women have also been labeled both by themselves and by men as incomplete human beings. If it is true that women are generally incomplete, then are their attempts to achieve the "positive" sides of Christian virtues to be viewed as helping or hindering their full development as persons?

But suppose that women are, in fact, complete human beings. Then it seems logical to ask whether those virtues promulgated by a masculine theological perspective are not themselves questionable. It also seems logical to ask whether the commonly accepted masculine notions of complete humanness and personhood are not also suspect.

Such questions necessarily raise the issue of whether the sacredness of home is a positive or a negative power for women. This issue was addressed and answered in the negative in one of the most important books for American women published during the 1960s, Betty Friedan's *The Feminine Mystique*.[11] As Friedan's argument implies, to the extent that home is divinized for a man by the presence of a selfless, loving woman, it may well be demonized for a woman. Conversely, to the extent that home is divinized for a woman, becoming truly her own sphere, it may well be demonized for a man. In the latter case a man often refers to his wife as a castrating bitch, and pictures his home accordingly. Thurber's famous cartoon of a threatening house looming agressively over a cowering man is typical. The extremes reflected in either of these two visions.—the one of the submissive, all-loving wife, the other of the henpecked husband—reflect two different streams of sacrality. These streams, both of which are linked to sacrifice and violence of different sorts, converge in the home.

Of the two, the gynocentric is probably the earlier according to evidence of the historical development of houses which is fairly scanty at best. According to Lord Raglan, for example, house-building in the full sense of the word, even in the late nineteenth century was still not universal.[12] He cites as illustration various tribes from around the world such as the Ona of Tierra del Fuego who made elaborate conical huts for religious ceremonies, but used windbreaks constructed of skins for their own shelter. Raglan further argues that the development of the house arose first from palaces, the houses of divine kings and queens, and then filtered down to the peasantry, rather than *vice versa.* Linguistic evidence supports Raglan's contention; the word "house" in its Latinate form "domicile" derives from the Latin *domus,* and ultimately from the Greek *doma,* meaning housetop, house, temple. The same etymology applies to the related words "domestic" and "dome."

If Raglan's thesis (which he documents with architectual details) is correct, then the original purpose of the house in its palace form was to create a sacred place for the marriage of the earth goddess and sky god. Such a marriage belongs to a very old pattern of thinking, evident in some of the earliest extant samples of human thought—our myths. There we discover that one of the most pervasive conceptions is the opposition of earth to sky. Matters pertaining to the earth are called chthonic, from the Greek word *chthon,* the earth. In Latin, the terms are *humus,* meaning *earth,* and *homo,* meaning *man.* The corresponding term for sky is *ouranian* from the Greek word *Ouranos,* heaven, or *Uranus,* as the term has been Anglicized. Ouranos was the Greek god who personified the heavens; he was variously both son and husband of Gaea, the Earth, and together they fathered the Titans, the Furies, and the Cyclopes. Eventually Chronos (Saturn), his youngest son, overthrew him. In variant forms myths of the mating of Gaea and Ouranus—the feminine earth and the masculine sky—exist around the world, although in the Egyptian Ennead of Heliopolis, a cosmogony taught by the priests at Heliopolis, the polarity reverses to make Nut (or Hathor), the sky, a goddess, and Geb, the earth, a god.[13]

According to Raglan, the building where this sacred union took place represented the cosmos, in which sky and earth are enclosed.[14] And the sacred building which housed the divine pair, the god-king and goddess-queen, came to be the prototype of the house, which was sacred because it was the dwelling of the pair who had been consecrated by the sacramental marriage. Such a connubium dated from the so-called prepatriarchal period in human history, to the time of the great mother goddesses such as Ishtar, Inanna, and Bau. The fertility rites which constituted a major part of their worship culminated in this sacred marriage. Thus, long before the Christian conception of a sacralized home developed, a much earlier, matrifocal idea had arisen. In this pre-Christian, goddess-vision of sacrality woman is the great power and source of mystery, man the son-consort who lies with and fecundates her. She is the great and terrifying mother earth from whom all life emerges, but to whom it likewise all returns. In her are centered the great mysteries of birth and death which only later become the province of a father god.

Remnants of this early goddess worship have continued to exist despite prohibitions by the "established" Western patriarchal religions—Judaism, Christianity, and Islam—against this "witchcraft." Nowadays there is a resurgence of such woman-centered religion which celebrates the Goddess in her three forms—the maiden, the mother, and the crone. Her consort is typically the horned god, whose duty is to delight the goddess sexually but not to rule her as Christianity teaches husbands must do. As contemporary witch Z. Budapest says, the horned god is the one who "makes one-night stands delightful.[15]"

This emphasis on the sexual within the sacred space of home is one which Christianity has so down-played with its emphasis on the virginity of the mother goddess, Mary, that it has come to seem the antithesis of the sacred. Thus the two strands of sacredness—the feminine and the masculine—which inform the symbolic and the actual home, frequently contradict each other.

Consecration

But not every house is sacred from either a feminine or a masculine perspective. The distinction between houses that are sacred and those that remain profane relates to the familiar house/home distinction which is particularly clear in these words of an American woman who married an Arab sheik just prior to World War II:

> For a long time it was hard for me to think of the house in which we
> all lived as my home; and Hayat [her sister-in-law and fellow-member
> of the Harem] and I had great discussions on the subject, as well as we
> were able. It was easy for her to conjugate the house into "mine, yours,

hers, ours," but I was not accustomed to communal living and insisted that although I lived there it was not *my* home. "How nice it would be," said I, "if I had my own home."[16]

The means by which an ordinary house is transformed into a home is consecration, the ritual by which any space is formally sacralized. A poignant example of the intangible quality which comprises consecration occurs in *The Grapes of Wrath* when Ma manages to sacralize the Joads' end of an open box car, not by any particular act, but more importantly, by her attitude. Steinbeck describes the situation this way:

> The Joads had one end of an end car. Some previous occupant had fitted up an oil can with a stove pipe, had made a hole in the wall for the stove pipe. Even with the wide door open, it was dark in the ends of the car. Ma hung the tarpaulin across the middle of the car. "It's nice," she said. "It's almost nicer than anything we had 'cept the government camp."[17]

Formal rituals of consecration are universal; often they begin with appropriate site selection, for it is essential that a site be favorable to deity or in some cases, the fairies. In Sweden, for example, a housebuilder first queries the fairies and carefully avoids their domiciles.[18] Around the world various prognostications are made, from the Yugoslavian custom of rolling a cake down a hillside to see if it will fall on its face to indicate a favorable spirit, to setting flour beneath a tree as the Maravi of Nyasaland do to test whether the ancestral spirits choose to eat and hence confer their blessings on the spot. Consecration as such sometimes follows, the rites again ranging widely from the old German custom of sprinkling holy water on the site to the marking of magical symbols with offerings of flowers and boiled rice as in South Camara, India. Far more widespread is the foundation sacrifice. This universal practice once involved protective measures ranging from the burial of a simple charm to sacrifice of an animal, but now generally revolves around the formal laying of the foundation stone, no longer commonly performed for private dwellings. Finally, when the house is completed there is typically a housewarming ceremony of some sort to safely install the human occupants.

Aside from the formal housewarming which is usually shared by both husband and wife, most consecration rituals are typically the province of the men who build. But the underlying meaning of such, rites of consecration is more often gradually and informally accomplished at the tacit level, where it is traditionally the woman who officiates. This meaning is as central to the home-centered feminine religion as the ritual transformation of wafer and wine into flesh and blood within Holy Communion. Apart from its sacramental significance the communion wafer has nothing to recommend it: it is tasteless and gummy. No one would select it for either nutritional or gourmet purposes. A house unsanctified as a home may be equally dreary, as Walker Percy indicates in these lines from his book *The Moviegoer:*

> It is good to see the Smiths at their fishing camp. But not at their home in Biloxi. Five minutes in that narrow old house and dreariness sets into the marrow of my bones. The gas logs strike against the eyeballs, the smell of two thousand Sunday dinners clings to the curtains, voices echo round and round the bare stairwell, a dismal heart forever points to itself above the chipped enamel mantelpiece.[19]

Even if a house is not dreary, but fine, it may also remain simply a house because it has not been consecrated in any way. Such a structure tends to be depersonalized, often containing a motel-modern or decorator interior. Nathanael West brilliantly satirizes the extreme of this type in *Day of the Locust,* when he describes a Hollywood bungalow, an "Irish cottage" made purposely crooked with an enormous roof "thatched" with fireproof ribbed paper. Inside, its decor varies from heavily Spanish to fake New England. Two identically decorated bedrooms match so precisely they even contain the same picture of a "snowbound Connecticut farmhouse, complete with wolf."[20]

Demonic Houses

Some houses which are sacred do not reveal the divine, positive face of sacrality, but instead reflect its demonic, dark, negative pole. This demonic—as opposed to divine—side of home's sacredness is readily apparent in some forms of its external symbol, the house. In Leviticus 14: 43–44, disease is the form such demonization assumes:

> If the disease breaks out again in the house, after he has taken out the stones and scraped the house and plastered it, then the priest shall go and look; and if the disease has spread in the house, it is a malignant leprosy in the house; it is unclean.

The pollution of Oedipus which contaminates not just his own dwelling but his entire kingdom is comparable. A similar connection between a "sick" inhabitant and a "sick" house exists in Edgar Allan Poe's short story "The Fall of the House of Usher," in which the eventual collapse of Roderick Usher occurs simultaneously with the collapse of the house.

The poltergeist phenomenon likewise involves a close link between occupant and house. Repeatedly, experts called in to solve such baffling phenomena as teleported objects and crashing china discover within the household a highly emotional teenager whose psychic energy somehow manages these otherwise puzzling feats. Folk wisdom makes a similar, totally physical, connection between house and occupant with its belief in "cancer houses," whose inhabitants supposedly are highly prone to the disease.

More commonly, instead of disease, demonic possession of houses is attributed to haunting, frequently caused by ghosts, the ancestors of those who once lived there. Shirley Jackson's *The Haunting of Hill House* incorporates most of the elements of this belief in addition to the motif of "sickness." In this story a number of carefully selected strangers are brought together by a doctor who wishes to study the house in question. Unlike some haunted houses, this one is personified:

> No human eye can isolate the unhappy coincidence of line and place which suggests evil in the face of a house, and yet somehow a maniac juxtaposition, a badly turned angle, some chance meeting of roof and sky, turned Hill House into a place of despair, more frightening because the face of Hill House seemed awake, with a watchfulness from the blank windows and a touch of glee in the eyebrow of a cornice. Almost any house, caught unexpectedly or at an odd angle, can turn a deeply humorous look on a watching person; even a mischievous little chimney, or a dormer like a dimple, can catch up a beholder with a sense of fellowship; but a house arrogant and hating, never off guard, can only be evil. This house, which seemed somehow to have formed itself, flying together into its own powerful pattern under the hands of its builders, fitting itself into its own construction of lines and angles, reared its great head back against the sky without concession to humanity. It was a house without kindness, never meant to be lived in, not a fit place for people or for love or for hope. Exorcism cannot alter the countenance of a house; Hill House would stay as it was until it was destroyed.[21]

Occasionally, as in a well-known Monty Python skit of the 1970s, an evil house eats its inhabitants—a variant of the folkloristic motif of the devouring mother. The story of "Hansel and Gretel," in which the witch and her house are closely identified, is illustrative. On the fringes between divine and demonic possession of a house lie the house spirits so common to folklore: the elf who repeatedly makes shoes for the shoemaker until the shoemaker inadvertently breaks the spell by making him a coat; the brownie who sweeps and tidies up around the house in exchange for milk; or the more sinister kobold who tricks the householder by undoing work already done.

Space Becomes Place

Part of what distinguishes the sacred—whether in its divine or its demonic form—from the profane is the quality of its being set apart. To be sacred, space must be set off in some way from the surrounding profane world. Another way of speaking of this spatial separation of the sacred is to distinguish between space and place as philosopher Suzanne Langer does.[22] In the most general sense, the word *space* is used to designate anything undifferentiated. Thus, if a city dweller is plunked down in a rural setting, she may find it impossible to distinguish one aspect of her new environment from another. Everything looks alike. For her there are no places, only undifferentiated sameness, or what she loosely refers to as open space. Each tree resembles every other; every meadow seems to roll in just the same way. There are no golden arches or fancy grillwork facades by which she can "place" herself. Such displacement is highly apparent in these words of an American woman reflecting on her first glimpse of Saudi Arabia:

> When we landed I peered out to nothing but desert, but taxiing I saw
> the great crowd of men—a striking sameness in their robes, their head-
> dresses, and their bearded faces. The scene was completely foreign to
> me as if I had landed in a separate world. There was nothing with
> which I could identify—men, plane, or desert.[23]

This woman confronts only sameness: sameness of men, sameness of desert: it is one vast, apparently featureless landscape.

By contrast with the absence which space implies, place is positive. It, like the solidity of a statue, focuses attention and pronounces itself to *be there*. We cannot help but know it exists, whereas we scarcely notice space. The poet Wallace Stevens presents this same phenomenon in his poem "Anecdote of the Jar":

> I placed a jar in Tennessee,
> And round it was, upon a hill.
> It made the slovenly wilderness
> Surround that hill.[24]

The placing of the jar, which domesticates the surrounding wilderness, is like the building of a house: it creates out of the surrounding, undifferentiated space a place. Where all was previously vague and general, now there is particularity.

What is involved in this space-into-place process is not necessarily the erection of a human construction. It is not a culture/nature distinction, for there are places in nature: Mt. Saint Helens, Niagara Falls, the Grand Canyon. In these cases differentiation from the surrounding environment is so physically great that we automatically "placify" them. But often the process involves far more subtle gradations not picked up by just any eye because they are less physical than emotional.

When "place" is created for emotional reasons, it is personal, reflecting the interaction of a group or individual with the surrounding environment. For a very small child a particular backyard tree may acquire the status of a very special place. Perhaps she crawls in under heavy spruce boughs, there to play house with her dolls on the ready-made bedding of soft needles underneath, the air above pungently scented. Or a particular bush in an otherwise impenetrable hedgerow may serve as unofficial gateway between her house and that of her best friend. Whether a spot is humanly or naturally constructed is not important; its status as a place depends primarily on personal investment.

But the mere existence of space set apart as place is not sufficient to account for sacredness. If it were, any building, bridge, or roadside cairn would be sacred. In addition to being physically set apart, a sacred place is distinguished by an almost wholly intangible quality in which certain objects, people, places, and events are more highly charged than others. Traditionally that charge, as in electricity, can be both positive and negative. In its positive form it is called divine or holy, in its negative, demonic or damned. Therefore, the set-apartness so crucial to the sacred is not only physically tangible, it is also highly charged in contrast to the neutral. We typically give the names *secular* or *profane* to this particular kind of neutrality.

The need to separate one sphere from the other is analogous to a situation in which I have one punch bowl containing a quantity of very strong alcoholic punch and next to it three of pineapple juice mixed with ginger ale. To maintain the "charge" of the one I must keep it physically separated: any mixing of the contents of these bowls will contaminate both and lead eventually to almost equalized punch bowls. A comparable rationale exists in setting apart whatever is sacred: to intrude upon it with weakened or different elements which might draw away some of the power from the sacred spot is to profane it. Conversely, the opposite possibility must also be guarded against: because the profane is "weaker," it must be protected from power it may not be capable of withstanding. Obviously the dividing lines between the sacred and the profane will vary significantly from one culture to another. To the Oglala Sioux Indians, for instance, Harney Peak in the Black Hills is sacred, whereas to most other Americans it is but one of many profane, though lovely, places in the West.[25]

Sacred Space

The sacred is difficult to define. I derive my concept partly from my own experience, partly from writers like Rudolph Otto, Mircea Eliade, and Paul Tillich, who speak of numinosity, the contrast with the profane, order in contrast to chaos, mystery, otherness, centeredness, ultimate concern, and Being to describe sacrality.

Applying the concept of sacrality to space, two issues are central: The intended purpose of the space and the experience of those entering it. Certainly the purpose intended by many Unitarian churches differs considerably from that of most traditional Roman Catholic ones. Externally that difference is indicated by the typical bareness of the Unitarian church interior: its lack of symbols—stained glass, crosses, candles, and altar—and its related lack of rituals—prayer, kneeling, Holy Communion, and absolution. By contrast, the traditional Roman Catholic church is characterized by all these things. Consequently, although a Unitarian church is often called a church—hence designating its difference from houses, schools, and government buildings—it differs considerably in terms of its interior spatial quality from many other buildings also called churches.

A further necessary distinction depends not on the intended purpose of the church space, but on the response of the person within it. A Buddhist might conceivably experience no quality of sacredness upon entering a Roman Catholic church. Even a regular parishioner might never experience it. Conversely, an agnostic or atheist might unexpectedly experience it whether within a church or in some totally nontraditional locale such as a bar, a house, or the natural environment. It is important to recognize that the sacrality you may assume is present may never or seldom be felt; conversely, it may be experienced in unlikely places.

One view of the power (in Greek *doxa*) inherent in sacrality is that mere proximity to a sacred space or object is enough to bring the observer within its orbit. Such is the case, for example, regarding the relics in the altar stone of a Roman Catholic church. A contrasting view does not consider sacrality or high charge to be a quality which exists entirely without reference to a participant. Unlike an electrically charged fence which will shock me whether I know or believe it is charged or not, in this view sacrality does not come into existence apart from my experience of it. It exists only for those who participate in it since it is activated, so to speak, by the interaction that takes place between them. Thus, if I go to Harney Peak and wait suspiciously for "something to happen," my presence will be passive and non-participatory. By contrast, if Black Elk goes there and dances an elaborately patterned sequence of steps or prays for a vision he participates in the spot. Hence he allows for the possibility of a sacred experience, whereas by doing nothing I almost preclude any happening at all. Yet most religions stress that the experience of sacrality cannot be imposed, willed, or created (although I may will to be where the sacred is, and thus to a degree will the experience of the sacred in that sacred place). Although some religions such as Canaanitic Cult, for example, have been based on the idea that humanity can manipulate deity and thus the experience of sacrality, more often this is not believed to be possible. Like grace and revelation, the experience of sacrality is generally thought to happen to one who approaches correctly, but it cannot be forced into being.

With these distinctions in mind, it is easier to understand why and how home, which is generally construed as part of the profane world in contrast to the sacred spheres of heaven and hell, can nonetheless be experienced as sacred. As with any place, it holds the potential for divinity to break through its boundaries and potentiate what we usually consider neutral or profane territory.

Because home is so familiar we tend to think of it as ordinary. In one sense it is; we so take it for granted that it exists for us only tacitly. Yet ordinariness is not necessarily the same as neutrality. In fact, the qualities that make home sacred are the same ones that most people find so commonplace. When we distinguish between the ordinary and the extraordinary, the profane and the sacred, home and heaven, we are not making exactly the same discrimination in each case. Each set of polarities is different, yet one word of each set does possess some affinities with its counterpart in the other two sets.

Home, ordinary, and *profane* all reflect generally familiar categories whereas the corresponding terms speak of the strange and distant. But as Wordsworth so ably demonstrates in his poetry, what appears familiar also possesses strangeness and vice versa. Thus, within the seemingly profane or ordinary, the sacred may often be found. This view sees deity as immanent, or inherent, within the universe. The contrasting view separates deity from the familiar, seeing it as transcendent, existing totally outside the world of sense experience. In this conception a church is profane to the extent that it is physically in this world, but sacred for what it symbolizes. As with all such polarizations, this one breaks down if carried too far: generally immanence and transcendence overlap somewhat in all conceptions of sacrality.

Two poems help clarify this distinction. One is Randall Jarrell's "Well Water," which likens the "dailiness of life" to "water/Pumped from an old well at the bottom of the world." The well image immediately connects the familiarity of "dailiness" to the unfamiliarity of fairy tales from which Jarrell borrows the motif of the well at the bottom of the world. In closing this poem Jarrell turns this dailiness into an image of Holy Communion by saying

> . . . sometimes
> The wheel turns of its own weight, the rusty
> Pump pumps over your sweating face the clear
> Water, cold, so cold! You cup your hands

And gulp from them the dailiness of life.[26]

By contrast, in a poem with a similar Holy Communion image entitled "Directive," Robert Frost emphasizes the retreat from dailiness by opening this way:

> Back out of all this now too much for us,
> Back in a time made simple by the loss
> Of detail . . .

Frost ends with words very similar to Jarrell's:

> Here are your waters and your watering place.
> Drink and be whole again beyond confusion.[27]

Elements reflective of both these approaches—the familiar and the strange—belong within the sacrality of home. But in contrast to the belief system of the Church, the familiar and the immanent outweigh greatly the strange and the transcendent within the home.

These contrasts between the sacred and the profane, transcendence and immanence, power and comparative weakness all reflect an underlying world view which assumes deity without question. Whether or not deity is multiple or single, anthropomorphic, theriomorphic (in animal form), or amorphous and nonspecified, it is usually more powerful than any mortal. Yet some cultures have, indeed, envisioned gods who die (as in the case of the generations of gods in ancient Greece). Other characteristics vary according to the particular religious tradition which conceives the particular deity. But a term common to this power or deity in all forms is numinosity, a word derived from the Latin *numen*, meaning an indwelling spirit.

One form of numinosity that most people instantly recognize is sublimity. The "height" implicit in this word, whether literal (as in the case of mountains,) or figurative (as in Beethoven's Ninth Symphony,) helps to vivify the concept. When we stand outdoors on a very clear evening gazing up at a starry sky, we may experience the meaning of the word. Something exists out there so much greater than we are that we marvel at the idea of our own existence.

Church architecture frequently plays on certain bodily sensations, particularly those of weight and weightlessness, or gravity and grace, to emphasize the qualities of sublimity associated with sacredness. The Gothic style is particularly successful in this regard for it combines the solidity of stone with a skyward thrust in such a way that stone defies the limitations of gravity and achieves transcendence. Thus the incredible height and airiness of truly great Gothic cathedrals such as Chartres, Reims, and Notre Dame seem to lead the human straight up to heaven. Further sublime effects achieved by glass and stone, perhaps most ably demonstrated in Ste. Chapelle in Paris, make stone all but disappear, lifting the viewer skyward on glass-filtered light alone.

The feelings occasioned by such truly awesome spectacles as these great Gothic cathedrals, the fjords of Norway, or art works like Picasso's *Guernica,* are our response to numinosity in its large scale form. This kind of numinosity clearly falls at the transcendent end of the spectrum, because although the heavens are part of the physical universe, their distance and immensity so remove them from us that they function as symbols of total Otherness. Rarely, if ever, is this sublime quality of the numinous found within a home; home exists almost entirely at the opposite end of the scale.

At this opposite end of the numinous are places or objects of a small intimate scale. Almost any one of the many tiny Byzantine churches in Athens—some as miniscule as an apartment kitchen—possesses a "pull" that can only be considered numinous. This pull consists of a characteristically dark blue ceiling leafed with gold stars, a heady smell of burning incense, interior gloom, and a general hush. This pull is not skyward, but earthward, stressing both rootedness and containment. Both these qualities are typical of home, for home is the place you stand, the foundation of your being and the entire surrounding environment. Hence, home both supports and envelops at the same time. To stray from home or to become lost consequently involves both loss of footing and loss of air. Plant imagery appropriately captures this sense of home as that in which one is rooted. Our clichés and everyday metaphors tell us that: we speak, for example, of transplanted New Yorkers living in California.

Furthermore, since the airing of the 1970s television series of that name, many Americans have spent time searching for their "Roots." Home in this sense is the medium in which we are grown, the earth which holds us fast. Though we all "know" this, in a way, we tend to forget that what this says about us as human beings is a very old concept indeed, one "deeply rooted" in human thought—the desire to place ourselves firmly in a context and trace back our origins.

This chthonic, origin-connected side of home is generally taken for granted. Though for most people it exists very much at a tacit level it is nonetheless clearly known. This aspect of home constitutes the "reality" we accept without question.

But there is another side to home, one linked more to the ouranian, transcendant dimension of religion than to the chthonic.[28] In contrast to the norms set by the chthonic, the ouranian tries to idealize home and lift it out of its earthbound setting into some airy beyond. This

"beyond" is named variously according to the predilections of the individual contemplating it. Within a religious framework it is either
heaven or hell, the divine or the demonic. Within a profane perspective
it is simply death. No matter which of the terms we use—home, heaven,
hell, or death—all four function the same way: all name a place or
condition where we are thought to belong, a place proper to "house"
us at a given stage. But of these terms only "home" remains clearly
"rooted," or chthonic; the other three all reflect states presently beyond
us. Thus the earthbound quality of feminine religion and culture is
typically transformed into something "airier" by its masculine counterpart: to "lift it up" it is put on a pedestal just as the goddess is assumed
into heaven in the guise of the virginal Mary.

Very closely related to numinosity in either its divine or demonic form,
but not identical with it, is the concept of mystery. This is not mystery
in the popularly understood sense of the word as suggested by mystery
stories. Rather it is reflected in the technical term *mysterium tremendum*,
something beyond human knowledge, a divine secret. In this sense,
mystery refers to those most basic human questions: Why am I here?
How did I come to be here? Why me and not some other combination
of gene cells? Why is there something instead of nothing? What happens
when we die?

The general dimness of most church and cathedral interiors—whether
Romanesque, Gothic, Norman, Renaissance, or Baroque—reflects this
quality of mystery, strongly countering the airiness and transcendence
with which light filtering through stained glass pierces this gloom. In
addition to these qualities of space, height, light, and dark, which exert
primarily visual and gravitational effects, most such sacred spaces also
play upon auditory and olfactory sensations. Organ notes echo resound-
ingly within large stone spaces as do the words of deep-voiced priests.
And the pungency of incense mixed with the odor of melting wax combines with all the other sensory effects to create a matrix of associations
that contribute to what most Christians consider the essence of sacred
mystery.

In the home comparable sensations may also be aroused through
various combinations of stimuli. Though the particulars will vary from
individual to individual, the underlying principle is unforgettably expressed by Proust when a bite of cookie dipped in tea suddenly evokes
for his persona the home of his childhood:

> . . . immediately the old grey house upon the street . . . rose up. . . .
> And just as the Japanese amuse themselves by filling a porcelain bowl
> with water and steeping in it little crumbs of paper which until then

are without character or form, but, the moment they become wet, stretch themselves and bend, take on colour and distinctive shape, become flowers or houses or people, permanent and recognisable, so in that moment all the flowers, in our garden and in M. Swanns's park . . . sprang into being . . . from my cup of tea.[29]

Here a particular taste evokes the entire setting of time past; it can as easily be an odor, sight, sound, even the touch of a particular object: all work, singly or collectively, to create for the percipient a sense of mystery comparable to that of any churchly organ tune or scent of incense.

Home evokes its mystery because of its links to family and origins. Despite the fact that few contemporary homes actually function as family seats, metaphorically, every home an individual lives in with her or his family of origin blends together to become a composite family seat. Since it is within the home that many of our earliest memories arise, in a sense, any child experiences herself as having sprung full-blown into existence within her earliest home of recollection. It is therefore difficult for most people to contemplate home without also associating their origins with it.

In this regard many people particularly connect home with their mothers. Aside from the fact that in traditional households it was mothers who most often stayed home tending the children, other associations, too, strongly link mothers with homes. Ever since Freud, houses have functioned as womb-symbols, with heavy sexual implications. But long before Freud, before common knowledge of birth control had made sex and fertility separable, homes, caves, and mountains were associated with the female attributes of womb and omphalos (navel), the latter in its maternal aspect. Such places have traditionally been places of safety for those who belonged, but locations of great danger for trespassers. Both qualities pertain to home, and both suggest the protective function of mothers. To the extent that home provides sanctuary and protection it serves as a kind of surrogate mother. A dramatic literary instance occurs in Ray Bradbury's short story "There Will Come Soft Rains," in which the protagonist is a house so automated it fulfills all conceivable needs, making it a twentieth-century rendition of the age-old motif of the all-providing mother.[30]

The counter side of the deep appeal of the all-providing mother is the fear such obvious creative power elicits. Yet relatively few people speak fearfully of having come into existence in the first place the way those who are honest do about dying. An exception is Vladimir Nabokov, who does so in his autobiography, *Speak, Memory*, as he tells of a chronophobiac's panic at first seeing movies predating his birth:

He saw a world that was practically unchanged—the same house, the same people—and then realized that he did not exist there at all and that nobody mourned his absence. . . . But what particularly frightened him was the sight of a brand-new baby carriage standing there on the porch, with the smug, encroaching air of a coffin; even that was empty, as if, in the reverse course of events, his very bones had disintegrated.[31]

From the perspective of Nabokov's chronophobiac, the nothingness from which we emerge is truly awesome. To feel, even for just a moment, the power that can allow existence at all is indeed to know the terror or wonder of sacred mystery. Those homes which focus heavily on memorabilia, family photographs, and heirlooms heighten this mystery by emphasizing the presence of ancestors among the living.

Still another important quality of the sacredness of home is centeredness. The notion that a sacred place or object lies at the center of the universe appears in many religions. This center is the spot from which life flows into the world. As mythologist Joseph Campbell puts it, "the torrent pours from an invisible source, the point of entry being the center of the symbolic circle of the universe, the Immovable Spot of the Buddha legend, around which the world may be said to revolve."[32] Underneath this spot, by whatever name, lies a symbolic figure representing the world-generative quality of deity. Usually this figure is a uroboros, a snake devouring its own tail, which symbolizes the infinitely creative, regenerative qualities of the divine life force. Such is the case with the King of the Serpents who guarded Gautama, the Buddha, during his seven days of Enlightenment. From this central point variously grows the *axis mundi*, the tree of life, which is the universe itself, or the cosmic mountain, cosmic man, or cosmic woman. Sometimes, too, the world navel is the hero, through whom sacred energies flow from eternity into time. No matter how it is manifested, this world navel, or center of the universe, symbolizes continuous creation.

For any individual, whether hero or antihero, to be at this center is to partake of the sacred power inherent in such a spot. Samuel Beckett exploits this notion in his play *Endgame* when the invalid Hamm in his wheelchair, seeks to be pushed "right 'round the world," continuously asking if he is right in the center. Of his caretaker, Clov, he demands repeated small adjustments:

> I feel a little too far to the left.
> (Clov moves chair slightly.)
> Now I feel a little too far to the right.
> (Clov moves chair slightly.)
> I feel a little too far forward.

(Clov moves chair slightly.)
Now I feel a little too far back.
(Clov moves chair slightly.)[33]

This desire to be at the center of the world signifies the wish to be centered within your whole self. Jung says of this process that "The self is not only the center, but also the whole circumference which embraces both conscious and unconscious; it is the center of this totality; just as the ego is the center of consciousness."[34]

Applied to home, such centeredness involves the ability of the symbol *home* to help hold an individual together. Often home functions as a Jungian mandala, a symbol of integrated selfhood or wholeness.[35] Whatever this "center" is, whether it manifests itself as a spiral, a navel, or home, it is ultimately unknowable. It is the opposite of what Yeats expresses in the lines, "Things fall apart/The Center cannot hold."[36] Home holds things together by providing a familiar foundation within which you can orient yourself to the universe as a whole. Sometimes, as with the Cross, just the presence of the symbol is sufficient to help a troubled individual center herself. But often some ritual—as is also true within most organized religions—is necessary. Consider the otherwise puzzling phenomenon of people who react to the shocking news of a family member's death by plunging into a frenzy of cleaning and straightening. While such behavior may strike observers as callous or bizarre, actually it serves to center the performer. By immersing herself in a series of familiar activities, she is able to "touch base"—to discover where she is before confronting in all its terror the full impact of what has just occurred.

Such home-centered ritual is a way of reassuring herself that, yes, the world does still go on. Though one of the most awful things she can imagine has just occurred, she is still able to do some of the same things she has always done: many of her familiar routines are still available to her. Though her husband may never again sit just so, pipe in hand, right leg swung casually over left, a contented smile on his face, she still has dishes to wash, counters to scrub, and a kitchen floor to sweep up. And those grease spatters on the wall—how they upset her. She attacks them with vigor. It is a way of testing the limits of her world, of reestablishing whatever remains of it.

To be centered is to be in the middle of whatever exists. It is to be a self within a world. But as existential analytic theory suggests, the worlds in which we all stand are not single, but multiple.[37] There is *Umwelt*, the environment generally thought of as the natural world, *Mitwelt*, the world of fellow humans, generally called community, and *Eigenwelt*, the world of relationship to oneself, which presupposes self-awareness. The latter two worlds are unique to humans, but *Umwelt* is present to all sentient beings. To center yourself in the sense that Home allows is specifically to center yourself within the *Eigenwelt:* to be at home with yourself. This ability to be at home with yourself relates directly to the fact that home, as opposed to a merely profane house, functions as a symbol of both salvation and damnation, making it above all a symbol of ultimate concern.

2

HOME
AS SYMBOL

Home, as a symbol of tacit feminine religion and culture, must not only be distinguished from *house*, it must also be discriminated from *home* with a small *h*. The difference between the two is akin to that of cross and Cross.

In contrast to symbols like the Cross and the Star, or Shield, of David, however, which have ostensibly guided and informed most Western (and some Eastern) women's lives, Home has actually and more immediately done so. Home also contrasts sharply with Church, which refers to Christendom in general and symbolizes a particular body of predominantly otherworldly beliefs.[1] Standing within this world for what is essentially this-worldly, Home is far more a symbol of immanence than of transcendence.

As with most religious symbols, Home is primarily a symbol of salvation. For most people it automatically implies salvation in the sense of safety—safety from the elements, from animals, from dangerous people, and from fearful encounters of any kind. But that kind of physical salvation is quite different from what the term ordinarily means within a theological context. There it typically refers to the salvation of what was traditionally called your soul.

As soon as the term "soul" is introduced, an ancient world view of predominantly Greek and Hellenistic Christian origins enters along with it. This world view is built on the old conception of a three-storied universe consisting of Heaven, Earth, and Hell. Whereas Earth is here and now, Heaven and Hell are correspondingly removed in space and time, being "then" and "there." As long as humans were entirely earth bound this metaphor of a three-storied universe worked, for indeed, the heavens then seemed so remote that they could function appropriately as seat for the ultimately unknown and unknowable—deity by whatever name.

Within this context, if I adhere to the traditional Christian doctrine of General Resurrection, I will believe in the salvation of my body and soul after death. But if my belief is less traditional and more influenced by inherited Hellenized conceptions, only the immortal part of me, my soul, can be saved. From the evidence of my senses I know my body will eventually die and decay, so it obviously will not be "saved." Because the body and whatever pertains to it belong to another context entirely—the purely secular, profane realm which eventually must fade away—my body has no ultimate concern for me. Only the soul, that invisible part of me abstracted out on faith as a continuation of "me" after death, so concerns me from this inherited Hellenized Christian perspective.

In contrast with these beliefs, traditional or Hellenized, there are numerous newer theologies which take account of a more contemporary world view in which the old three-storied universe no longer figures. Once science opened up the way for spatial exploration the heavens lost their previous strong association with the unknown. When that happened their mystery drained out, revealing them to be not so radically different in kind from the air directly above us, and they became desacralized. Following the metaphor of the preceding chapter, the bowls of nonalcoholic punch became mixed with their alcoholic counterpart, so weakening the entire mixture that it all appeared to be uncharged.

Yet the fact that the older theological edifice no longer works for some people does not mean that either the underlying need it once filled or the deep meaning it symbolized has ceased to exist. It simply means that, as frequently occurs in science, the need for a new paradigm has been acknowledged by scholars. To replace the outmoded imagery of these stories, many mid-twentieth-century theologians thus began speaking of inner and outer realms, frequently using the term *depth dimension* to speak of the sacred instead of the terms *heaven* and *hell*. Others retained the traditional terms but envisioned them differently, with the sacred spheres referred to as *inside*, and the profane, earthly ones as *outside*.

With this shift some theologians have retained otherwise traditional imagery of ultimacy. They still speak of God and Christ. However, others (particularly, but by no means exclusively, women) have found the traditional words too heavily freighted with connotations they find increasingly difficult to connect with their own lives. For them new God-language has become necessary. Still other thinkers and scholars, such as Thomas Altizer, William Hamilton, Gabriel Vahanian, Richard Rubenstein, Paul van Buren, and others prominent in the 1960s came to speak of God "dying." In so speaking they did not all mean precisely the same thing. Some meant by it the ancient pattern of gods dying only to eventually rise again. Others meant that cultural changes have now precluded the possibility for belief in deity. But all were speaking of the experience, peculiar to modern humanity, in which not only the experience of the sacred but even its possibility have come to seem increasingly remote, whether because of a change in deity or in humanity.

Despite these various "deaths," however, faith, surprisingly, did not entirely vanish. Though understanding of the long-held myth of Jesus Christ shifted, its underlying meaning was repeatedly reaffirmed in different ways. Sources of revelation, rather than drying up, as might be expected, actually multiplied. As the old, rigid split between sacred and profane gave way to a scientific perspective which seemed to desacralize everything, a corresponding shift occurred within the once so-called "profane" world, revealing in it numerous instances of sacrality. Thus, the Bible once was considered by Christians to be the only authentically sacred text; subsequently, for many people literature in general has become an additional source for many of the same kinds of spiritual revelations detailed there. While works with obvious "Christ figures" such as Faulkner's *Light in August* with its Joe Christmas, or Steinbeck's *The Grapes of Wrath* with its sacrificial Tom Joad, were obvious candidates, less overtly "religious" writings were often the most fertile sources. Beckett's works, with all their despair, are illustrative. As critic Michael Robinson asserts,

> Godot's existence is the result of man's profound need for meaning. When man is shown, as here, to be incapable of accepting his own significance in a slowly dying world, and of realizing that his suffering is meaningless, Godot is the necessary unknown at the end of the series who is introduced to justify existence by the rational leap into the dark. He is the missing quantity in the universe which the tramps can define in no other way, the answer to the unanswerable question who would, if he appeared, integrate the world that is always disintegrating and restore man, out of meaninglessness, into meaning.[2]

A story more simple than any of Beckett's which vividly illustrates this twentieth-century shift away from traditional to secular theology is Hemingway's "A Clean, Well-Lighted Place." It also shows how secular theology replaces the concept of life after death with concepts of salvation and damnation tied to the here and now conditions of living human beings. In this short story the modern shift in sensibility is most dramatically apparent in the altered words of the Lord's Prayer:

> Our nada who are in nada, nada be thy name thy kingdom nada thy will be nada in nada as it is in nada. Give us this nada our daily nada and nada us our nada as we nada our nadas and nada us not into nada but deliver us from nada; pues nada.[3]

Yet despite this nihilism in which God is replaced by nothing, the possibility of salvation has not entirely disappeared. The story focuses on the experience of one of two nameless waiters working late in a café. The older, more reflective waiter restrains his impatient, younger colleague who cannot understand why the lone old man they are serving must stay up so late. Understanding the old drinker's pain, the older waiter protests against his co-worker's statement that the old man can drink at home: "It's not the same." As they finally lock up, he also says, "I am of those who like to stay late at the café . . . With all those who do not want to go to bed. With all those who need a light for the night."[4] Here the "clean, well-lighted café," like Home in its fullest sense, functions as a place of salvation. By contrast, the bodega to which the waiter, in turn, goes to forget his own pain does not quite sustain him. Though "the light is very bright and pleasant . . . the bar is unpolished."[5] Yet the potential for salvation offered by "a clean, well-lighted place," whether café or Home is clearly of a very different sort from that understood by a theology which separates out something called "soul" from body. Nonetheless, what the café and Home in their divine aspects offer those who "believe" in them is alternatively salvation or damnation every bit as encompassing as that of any other theological symbol.

First of all, much as churches once supplied sanctuary to criminals, Home in its house form still does. The right of sanctuary is very old. In Egyptian, Greek, and Roman temples it applied to the area in front of the statue of the god long before Christianity existed. And in Judaism it existed, also, as attested to, for example, by the recently discovered horned altar of Beersheba, to which any offender might cling in safety.[6] The theory behind this right of sanctuary is intertwined with the concept of sacredness, which primitive thought believes to be contagious. Once someone enters a sacred space, he or she becomes sacred too. Consequently, to try to remove the individual is to violate the holiness of the place.

Nowadays sanctuary still legally attaches to homes in the sense that no house in this country or in England may be entered without a legally signed search warrant. An extension of this kind of legal safety exists also in laws designed to forbid wiretapping of telephones or bugging of rooms. In these prohibitions we also see the kind of safety that the word *home* implies when it is used in games. In baseball, for example, a player is not ultimately safe until he reaches home plate. In games this legal sanctuary changes imperceptibly to become safety of a more psychological cast in which home is a refuge from diverse incursions from the external world. Coming "home" in hide 'n' seek to be finally safe from capture involves both these components. And such psychological sanctuary is also apparent when I am hospitalized for serious illness and typically think, "If only I can get home, I will be all right." Novelist Anne Tyler well captures this particular kind of home-generated safety in describing how the grandmother in *Waiting for Caleb* enables her newly married granddaughter to reexperience in adulthood the safety of her childhood home:

> . . . she led Justine back to her room, and covered her with the quilt handstitched by great-grandma, and sat with her a while. The quilt gave off a deep, solid warmth. There was a smell of coffee and cinnamon toast floating up from the kitchen, and a soft hymn of Sulie's with a wandering tune. Justine's jaw muscles loosened and she felt herself easing and thawing.[7]

Not surprisingly, the demonic side of such Home-generated salvation is often insidiously close to its divine manifestation. As is also true within a Christian framework, the problem is how to distinguish the Devil from God, the demonic from the divine. A case in point occurs within Charlotte Perkins Gilman's short story "The Yellow Wall Paper," which focuses on the postpartum depression of its nameless protagonist. To help her overcome her condition, her physician-husband arranges a retreat to a family home in the country, where she is confined to a one-time nursery with barred windows and a bed nailed to the floor. Its fetid yellow walls so pervade the atmosphere, in contrast to the green of nature's growth outside, that the room even "smells" yellow. Daily the woman traces the busy patterns of the wallpaper. In this demonic parody of women's work she discerns body parts which reveal to her a hidden woman. Observing this hidden woman's crazy, babylike behavior soon demands all her attention; the hidden woman crawls incessantly. As the story climaxes, the protagonist frantically claws off all the wallpaper, finally releasing the other woman. The story closes with her telling her husband, "I've got out at last . . . and I've pulled off most of the paper so you can't put me back!"[8]

For this woman, the presumed home is clearly not a place of salvation but of damnation, a hell instead of a heaven. For her, and others of either sex like her, the orthodox belief that it must be a house which symbolizes Home simply does not work. Like multiple divisions within Christianity, diverse interpretations of Home also exist. While Gilman's protagonist would obviously select a heterodox view, others do not necessarily choose to do so. For them it is circumstance, not choice, which dictates that Home will function in unorthodox fashion.

Such is the case for Harold Stahl, a Syracuse, New York, man who was saved from life on the street because two nontraditional places functioned as Home for him. In the Top Hat Tavern "he often sat in the back booth nursing a beer for hours. . . . he made like he was playing piano at the bar. . . . he danced. . . . he kept his plants in the front window." And in Unity Kitchen, "where he usually had a free supper at five in the afternoon. . . . they called him "Happy Harold." . . . [And] almost all of the good old boys loved him."[9]

On a slightly different scale, nontraditional Home-centered rituals exist among more affluent men who may, if they are unhappily married or psychologically driven to overachieve, feel more at home in the office than the house. Sometimes deliberate choice may even dictate a move from house to "essential hangout" or "third place," as sociologists Ramon Oldenburg and Dennis Brissett call spots which differ from both home and office in being places without purpose beyond "unorganized enjoyment of the company of diverse others."[10] Predominantly male, such spots more commonly prevail at either end of the social scale, existing as clubs for upper-class men and street corners or bars for their lower-class counterparts. In both cases these places also typically provide refuge from the opposite sex.

Perhaps nowhere is this tradition quite so strong as in the British Isles where the neighborhood pub—which appeals there to the middle as well as the lower classes—with its typically dim interior, cozy low ceiling, comfortable chairs, and fireplace offers an obviously womb-like surrogate home. James Joyce's writing abounds in instances of this masculine home-away-from home. This scene from the short story "Counterparts" in *Dubliners* is representative:

> From the street door he walked on furtively on the inner side of the path towards the corner and all at once dived into a doorway. He was now safe in the dark snug of O'Neill's shop, and, filling up the little window that looked into the bar with his inflamed face, the colour of dark wine or dark meat, he called out:
> —Here, Pat, give us a g.p., like a good fellow.
> The curate brought him a glass of plain porter.[11]

And later:

He felt his great body again aching for the comfort of the public-house.[12]

By contrast, "He loathed returning to his home."[13] But in this instance the allure of the bar is demonic, not divine, ultimately destroying the man rather than saving him.

Often the distinction between the divine and demonic faces of a surrogate home is more problematic than is the case with Joyce's bar. A dramatic example occurs in Peter Shaffer's play *Equus*, in which the young protagonist, Alan Strang, feels so alienated from his working-class family that his place of refuge and comfort becomes a stableful of horses instead of a houseful of humans. There he eventually enacts the savage mutilation of all six horses, the incarnation of his primitive god whom he invokes with the call, "Equus." For him, as for many housewives, Home in its traditional form has become an imprisoning structure from which he must escape. The place where he comes to life in the fullest sense of the word, his place of salvation, demonically inverts Home-centered beliefs. Yet he does gain salvation there, until the time he violates his own conception of the sanctuary through nearly succumbing to a stable girl's sexual advances.

But damnation does not always occur from variations within the system itself. As with more traditionally recognized religious systems, it can occur in two broad ways—from outside or from within. Automatically those without membership are considered damned. Thus within the feminine Home-centered religion the generally outmoded dichotomy between heathens and Christians becomes that of the homeless in contrast to those with homes.

Homelessness

The damnation represented by homelessness may be homelessness of the most literal sort—that of having absolutely no place of your own to go day or night, a situation still not readily imaginable for the majority of middle- and upper-class Americans who take homes for granted. That some people actually exist as street people or bag ladies almost defies comprehension for those who take private shelter for granted. Yet the existence of such homeless people points up by contrast the still pervasive centrality of Home in the lives of almost everyone else. In fact, so far beyond the pale of acceptability is homelessness to most people that those who lack homes are perceived as severely threatening to those who have them. During the fall and winter of 1980–81 in Syracuse, New York, for example, a controversy among business people, city councillors, and members of various social welfare agencies raged in the local papers regarding the large downtown population of street people. Whereas in milder climates street people might conceivably fend for themselves, in Syracuse they would freeze to death in winter without benevolent intervention. The issue was not whether something should be done or not, but the manner in which it should be handled; should the rights of street people take precedence over the accepted, middle-class order of things?

Such people threaten this order in several ways. Most frighteningly they prove that such anomalous individuals do exist. If some people can live this way, their presence implies, then what about me? To acknowledge that thought is to be threatened indeed, because the barest reflection shows that street people had to come from somewhere: to drop through the bottom necessitates having fallen *from* some other place. Babies aren't born and raised on the street in the United States, so at one time these people, too, lived in something resembling a house or apartment. Their existence is thus a prominent and visible reminder that classless though this country pretends to be, we, too, have our outcasts/es who are essentially untouchable.

To see these people many of whom do "look funny"—hair flaring out in wild, stiffly uncontrolled strands, plastic bomber jackets too short at waists and cuffs matching trouser legs too short and wide above salt-faded, cracked leather boots—is to be reminded of the uncanny distortions of funhouse mirrors. To be homeless the way they are is not only to have no place to go, it is scarcely to exist within the category of humanity as most people construe the term.

In some ways street people threaten Home-centered values more acutely than did the hippies of the 1960s. Though the hippies flouted conventional values in ways calculated to irritate middle-class America, nonetheless they did not stray far from the system they sought to discredit. By mirroring it, they inverted it—hence neither destroyed nor escaped it despite their rhetoric; eventually most even found their way back to middle-class life styles. True street people, by contrast, are largely those who have no place at all, having simply fallen through the grids of both culture and counterculture alike. Whereas hippies were frequently communards, hence very much ensconced within surrogate families, street people typically have no one. Their presence thus visually reminds passers by of such unthinkable questions as: "What would I do in this situation?" "Who would take care of me?" "How could I possibly manage?" "What if I became ill or even began to die?" Answers like "nothing" and "no one" are not reassuring.

Although street persons or hippies are not entirely responsible for their situations, in a way both groups can be said to have brought on

their conditions through their own behaviors. In that sense their damnation is akin to that of atheists. By contrast, a group of people for whom
Home may be still more irretrievably lost are those who experience
nervous or spiritual breakdowns. For them, the loss is more akin to
unexpected loss of faith. For someone who has previously known only
what is loosely called "normalcy" or psychic health, this form of homelessness may feel even more extreme than the situation of being without
a physical place to call Home. In such cases what happens is much like
what Epictetus describes in the following passage quoted by Matthew
Arnold:

> 'A man rushes abroad,' he says, 'because he is sick of being at home;
> and suddenly comes home again because he finds himself no whit
> easier abroad. He posts as fast as his horses can take him to his country-
> seat: when he has got there he hesitates what to do; or he throws
> himself down moodily to sleep, and seeks forgetfulness in that; or he
> makes the best of his way back to town again with the same speed as
> he fled from it. Thus every one flies from himself.'[14]

Such an experience is the psychological counterpart of the experience
of a street person. While the specifics vary from one individual to another, the inner feeling is well expressed in these words from the general
confession for Morning Prayer in the 1928 Episcopal Prayer Book: "And
there is no health in us."[15]

The inability to work and carry on a normal routine that is associated
with a breakdown represents a sharp disruption of the tacit level of
existence. What is thrown out of balance is the taken-for-granted level
which Home ultimately represents. By analogy, it is comparable to the
feeling that occasionally overtakes one who has driven a car for many
years and long ceased thinking about the actual process. Preoccupied
with an inner train of thought, she may suddenly feel herself jerked
abruptly back to the task at hand. For a moment, she may wonder where
she is and which pedal to step on next. She may well shift from fourth,
where she has been all along, thinking to attain a higher gear. Instead
she goes back into third, only then recollecting that she has no gear
higher than fourth in this car.

The person who experiences such psychological homelessness experiences an amorphous, almost cloudy feeling, well captured in the cliché
phrase "to be up in the air." Not only is he out of his element, there is
no place to put his feet, no place to stand. The entire earth, sometimes
even the universe, seems closed against him.

At this level homelessness approximates two conditions frequently
used to characterize the negative aspects of our era: anomie and alienation. To be anomic is literally to be without law. Because laws inhere

within every culture, to be without law is to be outside any cultural system whatsoever: it is to be outside humanity. To feel you do not belong at this level is to be fully alienated from your own kind. An extreme of such homelessness is autism, in which an individual, from childhood, so little identifies with humans that she or he entirely fails to communicate. In some cases machinelike behavior results. Bruno Bettelheim details such a situation in his book *The Empty Fortesss: Infantile Autism and the Birth of the Self* when he describes Joey, who decides to be "a mechanical contrivance instead of a person."[16] In that situation qualities generally categorized as human are missing. From the perspective of outside observers, Joey is homeless in the most complete way imaginable. Whether he himself so experiences it, however, can only be conjectured.

Joey's situation more closely approximates the consignment to Limbo of unbaptized babies than it does damnation per se. By contrast, the Homelessness of most refugees, while less extreme, is at the same time more consciously and fully experienced for what it is: exile from salvation.

Frequently the nostalgic praise refugees indulge in sounds entirely disproportionate to the actual merits of their last homelands. Occasionally their nostalgia is so pronounced that they devote entire works of art to it, as the long tradition of writers in exile attests—novelists such as Katherine Mansfield, expatriated from New Zealand; Henry James, from the United States; and James Joyce, from Ireland. Possibly, however, Vladimir Nabokov outdoes them all in his autobiography, *Speak, Memory*, where he tells of recreating artifacts of his lost home in order to place them within his books. Thus he establishes for himself a home comprised of words:

> Somewhere, in the apartment house of a chapter, in the hired room of a paragraph, I have also placed that tilted mirror, and the lamp, and the chandelier drops. Few things are left, many have been squandered. Have I given away Box I . . . that old brown dachshund fast asleep on the sofa? No, I think he is still mine.[17]

In Nabokov's case nostalgia is artful, but more often it turns sickly, giving way to sentimentality and falsehood. Such is the case with many emigrés to California, as historian William Irwin Thompson indicates:

> Southern Californians imagine ivy-covered, leaf-strewn squares, and villages clustered around white frame New England churches, and lacking them in reality, create them in the plastic towns to which they go to find themselves.[18]

Such sentimental versions of lost homelands keep gift shoppes in business. They also suggest the correctness of William Carlos Williams' contention that " . . . no whiteness (lost) is so white as the memory of whiteness."[19] As with Dante's Carnal Sinners,

> When they arrive before the ruin, . . . the shrieks, the moanings, and the lamentation . . . there they blaspheme the divine power.[20]

With their backward-looking yearning refugees engage in recreating one of the most famous of all Home-centered myths: the loss of Eden.

While homelessness is often associated with the condition of being a refugee, at times it is more severe, as when the home itself disintegrates. Such erosion of Home may occur naturally from disasters of the magnitude of earthquake, flood, or volcanic eruption which suddenly destroy the earth itself. Many of Woody Guthrie's songs written during the time of the Dust Bowl attest to homelessness of this sort, as the words of his first well-known song indicate: "So long, it's been good to know you, this dusty old dust is a-gettin' my home . . . . "[21]

Any such physical dissociation destroys the physical foundation of your entire existence and renders the concept of Home meaningless. Suddenly there is no stability anywhere. What had always been solidly indestructible now possesses the volatility of gas. Instead of standing on firm land, you are suddenly bucked by violent seas or plummeted through alien sky: no supports exist. The whole taken-for-granted nature of things collapses along with the earth. All the terror associated with a medium other than your own is suddenly activated: you fear falling, hurtling through a substance not strong enough to support you. It is a nightmare familiar to all who dream. Nausea and dizziness engulf you along with the earth itself. Gone now is the comforting belief that there is somewhere a safe place on which to stand.

This process may be even more devastating, however, when erosion of Home is not physical, but political. These words of the Czech novelist Milan Kundera reveal the insidious horror of political machinations:

> If someone had told me as a boy: one day you will see your nation vanish from the world, I would have considered it nonsense, something I couldn't possibly imagine. A man knows he is mortal, but he takes it for granted that his nation possesses a kind of eternal life. But after the Russian invasion of 1968, every Czech was confronted with the thought that his nation could be quietly erased from Europe, just as over the past five decades 40 million Ukrainians have been quietly vanishing from the world without the world paying any heed. Or Lithuanians. Do you know that in the 17th century Lithuania was a powerful European nation? Today the Russians keep Lithuanians on their reservation like a half-extinct tribe; they are sealed off from visitors to prevent knowledge about their existence from reaching the outside.[22]

In cases such as those Kundera mentions, the symbol, rather than the physical Home is jeopardized. Its occupants are left in the anomalous position of occupying the same space geographically, but experiencing the slow and systematic obliteration of habitual associations and meaning. In these cases the fixity you typically assume is central to Home erodes even as you still live there.

The connection between such disruptions of Home and the metaphoric system of symbols surrounding it is readily apparent in the following passage from Jean Rhys's novel *Quartet*:

> Still, there were moments when she realized that her existence, though delightful, was haphazard. It lacked, as it were, solidity; it lacked the necessary fixed background. A bedroom, balcony and *cabinet de toilette* in a cheap Montmartre hotel cannot possibly be called a solid background.[23]

The words *solidity, fixed background,* and *solid background* all highlight qualities we assume about the earth, the foundation upon which we plant our homes. When that foundation betrays us, whether physically, psychologically, or politically, we lose our capacity to speak meaningfully within the symbol system to which we are habituated. When that situation occurs it is the equivalent, within the Home-centered belief system, of the so-called Death of God within the Judeo-Christian tradition.

In these instances of such extreme homelessness, when the foundation that Home symbolizes disintegrates, we are left in a precarious situation. Contemporary philosopher Michel Foucault speaks of it as heterotopia, "the disorder in which fragments of a large number of possible orders glitter separately . . . without law or geometry."[24] He likens this foundationless place to the inability of aphasiacs to coherently sort varicolored skeins of wool into meaningful categories:

> Within this simple space in which things are normally arranged and given names, the aphasiac will create a multiplicity of tiny, fragmented regions in which nameless resemblances agglutinate things into unconnected islets; in one corner, they will place the lightest-coloured skeins, in another the red ones, somewhere else those that are softest in texture, in yet another place the longest, or those that have a tinge of purple or those that have been wound up into a ball. But no sooner have they been adumbrated than all these groupings dissolve again. . . .[25]

Such homelessness distinctly threatens those who believe in what the concept *home* implies, for *home* seems to promise that somehow everything will be all right, that you will survive. This is part of what makes Home, like the Cross, a symbol of salvation. Therefore, to encounter obviously homeless people is to experience cognitive dissonance. Believing that you could not possibly survive homelessness yourself, it is shocking to discover that some people actually do. Does that mean they are somehow stronger? Or does it mean they are less than human, that they lack the sensibilities to care? Or could it possibly mean that Home is not as essential as you had always assumed? The situation reverses the one detailed in Hawthorne's story "Young Goodman Brown," in which Brown discovers, with horror, that all the supposedly good people of his community are hurrying to a witch's sabbath. The jolt thus occasioned Brown's faith is rivalled within the Home-centered belief system by the sight of homeless people who yet manage to survive. Such a sight may either occasion a crisis of faith sufficient to shatter your Home-centered belief system or else inordinately fortify it so that Home becomes a fortress.

3

HAPPILY EVER AFTER

The strain placed on followers of a Home-centered belief system by the external threat of diverse homeless people is matched by a serious internal flaw—a strongly American, overwhelmingly feminine, belief that marriage automatically leads to the salvation implicit in the words *happily ever after*.

Much as the Cross promises Heaven, Home seems to imply Happily Ever After. Fairy tales tell us so; Hollywood romances reinforce the notion. But these three words are slippery and ambiguous. As one of many variants of Plato's great lie, these words more often turn and damn their adherants than save them.

Happily Ever After: these three words have both a romantic and a sentimental overlay. The romantic stems from the familiar belief that a prince will "save" every languishing Cinderella, whisking her from her cinders to a life consisting of storybook elegance, romance, and sexuality. Yet the fairy tales from which these three words come are notable for what they seem to omit: Eros, one of the gods our age devotedly worships is scarcely present in recognizable form. How odd that these tales, which antedate much of Western literature and are thought to embody the wisdom of "the folk," exclude one of the qualities of life we most value. The fact that we now consider fairy tales to be primarily for children is no explanation, for that is our misconception. Originally they were intended for everyone, regardless of age. Granted, these tales are full of boy-meets-girl situations. But how very different these situations are from what we have come to expect through the subsequent literary tradition of realism and its frequent odd couplings with romance. Although the misconceptions engendered by this odd coupling are held to some extent by both sexes, it is overwhelmingly women who have the time and inclination to read romances, hence women who typically suffer far more delusions about Happily Ever After than men.

A major part of the difference between the fairy tale and romantic/realistic visions of Happily Ever After is the locus of fairy tales. Though most individuals, even when very young, realize fairy tales are not "real," they also know at another level that such tales are very real indeed. As adults we call their reality psychic, not bodily, even knowing that to make that distinction is to perpetuate a misleading mind/spirit versus body dualism. Being wary of the distinction that our Cartesian heritage makes it difficult to avoid, we may nonetheless say that fairy tales point us in the direction of an inner reality that we typically contrast with the world of external affairs. Both the vagueness and the artificiality of these structural terms are bothersome, but they suggest the way our received thought places fairy tales. Even as we distinguish between psyche and soma, inside and outside, we also realize that very young children do not always make those distinctions. Nor do we ourselves always do so.

The old question, "Am I actually a human, asleep, dreaming that I am a butterfly, or am I a butterfly dreaming that I am a human," also relates to this dichotomy. Though that question may seem like amusing double-talk, certain experiences dislocate my assurance of existence in such a way as to make it personally meaningful. Often it is a dream so vivid that it rivals the reality into which I awaken. When that happens my awakening self struggles momentarily to decide which of two "selves" it "really" is: Didn't I *really* just see my mother standing before a wood-burning stove, a green and white small-flowered apron over her brown wool dress? Didn't she really turn to me and say, quite calmly, "Tomorrow I am going to die"? But isn't she already dead? Such may be the sequence until slowly a pattern of memories recalls her actual death several years back. The present moment's frightening intensity fades and finally, in an hour or two, the dream dissolves.

Such generally rare moments when inside and outside, dream and waking, psychic and somatic distinctions fade are often instants of great waking, psychic and somatic distinctions fade are often instants of great insight and power, as the writings of mystics attest. They are also times of great danger to most of us. Artificial or not, the boundaries our Western tradition of thought has taught us to make protect as well as mislead us. They give us our sense of what it means to be a separate "self" and they enable us to act in the arena of "not-self," the world.

Given such conventions as the belief that self is definitely separate from world and dream from waking—conventions which inform and undergird our Western culture—what happens when any two such realms are confused and conflated? Aside from children's misunderstandings and occasional adult confusion over dreams, such conflations may occur experientially in certain drug-induced states, in what we label as madness, and in some mystical experiences. But these experiential confusions aside, there may also be cases of cognitive conflation. These situations, which involve confusion in thinking about the two realms of inner and outer, Faerie and "real" world lead to one of the most common perversions of Happily Ever After.

Hollywood dramatizations of Happily Ever After with their emphases on sex and romance depart significantly from their fairy tale prototypes. Yet for most people, even those seldom exposed to fairy tales, the two realms are confusingly intermixed. The result does not work very well.

To understand the distinction between these two visions—the Hollywood and the fairy tale—we must consider fairy tales as Jung does. For him the typical figures of fairy tale—the helpful animals, the helpful old woman or man, the witch, the Princess, the Prince, the dragon, and the like—are all images contained within the psyche. These *dramatis personae* are not highly characterized, but remain indeterminate. Typically, they are not even given names, but appear simply as the Princess or the Witch. Such indetermination reflects their universality. That means that these images are archetypal, belonging to all humans, much as blood, bones, skin, and hair do. They are as essential to being human as is a body.

By this thinking fairy tales do not tell the kind of girl-meets-boy stories they superficially appear to; instead, they tell self-meets-self stories. The archetypal princess who meets the prince is one inner psychic component of ourselves interacting with its opposite. If I, as a woman, dream about a young man killing snakes for me, that dream reflects the very common fairy tale motif of the dragon-slayer. The young man, according to Jungian thought, represents my male side, my animus, battling evil. If the young man and I subsequently marry and live "happily ever after," that marriage symbolizes a conjunction of opposites—formerly nonintegrated parts of myself are now united. Thus these archetypal fairy tale images exist much like individual puzzle pieces which the psyche constantly arranges and rearranges into different patterns of order, or different "stories."

But few readers of fairy tales are likely to arrive intuitively at Jung's position, even if they construe fairy tales differently from novels written in the realistic tradition. Possibly they recognize that Faerie is more like dream than waking reality; nonetheless, when they also encounter Hollywood boy-meets-girl romances—whether cinematic, televised, or novelistic—the dividing line between internal psyche and external soma blurs. To further diffuse the distinction, advertisements for products ranging from mouthwash to automobiles also play with and upon these archetypes, making clarity and appropriate discrimination highly problematic.

It is therefore not surprising that fairy tales, which actually disclose psychic ordering principles, are often confused with stories that have evolved out of them, but have lost touch with their original focus. An appropriate way to picture this evolution in story is to see it as a movement from deep within the human interior out to its surface, the skin of the body, and on into what we conventionally call "the world." However we name that interior—soul, psyche, spirit, the realm of the gods—it is a far different "place" from the external one called world. While there are obviously strong and deep connections between these two realms, to confuse them with each other is to collapse a distinction that otherwise helps us to function appropriately in the world as we now understand it. Such confusion is the true meaning of the phrase *to profane.*

Another way to explain the difference is to say that fairy tales tell us stories about the interior realm or depth dimension of human existence. By contrast, realistic stories—in the broadest sense—take the same archetypes but apply them to and on the surface dimension of existence. On the surface level, of course, boy meeting girl implies a meeting of two separate individuals with two separate bodies and opposite sexes. That is a very different situation from the meeting of two psychic components within the dream or story of a single individual. To try and celebrate the inner reality by looking to a person of the opposite sex rather than to my own capabilities to complete myself is to misappropriate the dream.

The point where this difference is most crucial for understanding the divergent meanings of Happily Ever After is, of course, the marriage (once enacted on behalf of feminine earth and masculine sky) which typically leads into that seemingly blessed realm of Happily Ever After. Marriage as a conjunction of opposites within a single individual is not at all the same thing as the marriage of two separate people resulting from romantic attraction. But the common, faulty identification of the two repeatedly leads people to expect a literalization of what the words Happily Ever After seem to imply. Looking at this source of confusion from the perspective of the 1980s, those of us living in the Western world almost automatically equate marriage with love. The idea of arranged marriages strikes us as quaint or offensive; to think of romantic love not figuring in marriage puzzles us. How can marriage be initiated without love? Yet love as we conceive it is a relatively new human phenomenon.

Before romantic love, with its emphasis on the desires of two individuals, came to be the *sine qua non* for most Western marriages, order—specifically social order—was the dominant marriage consideration.[1] When maintaining the cosmic order of earth and sky no longer occupied humanity, the paramount concern became the positions of the two families involved relative to kinship, status, wealth, and politics as in *Romeo and Juliet*. The wishes of the bride and groom seldom entered into the alliance-making process. Whereas nowadays marriage primarily culminates the shared erotic desires of two individuals, in the older conception it externally symbolized a relationship between two families. Marriage then represented a social, rather than an individual, alliance. Often, as in the case of royalty, its repercussions extended far beyond the two families involved as occurred with Mary of England and Philip II of Spain. Marriage was thus a method of *placing* people within a larger social context, rather than a way of pleasing them individually. While reproduction was the major focus, its purpose was primarily to increase a specific social grouping rather than to satisfy the parental urges of these individuals. Marriage, in this view, enabled society to follow a strict order to which individuals submitted themselves without regard for their personal desires. In the mother-goddess phase of religion, the social order necessitated sacrifice equally from both women and men, for sometimes the sacred wedding ended in the ritual murder of both bride and groom. By contrast, in the patriarchal phase, particularly in Christianity, order had assumed a rigidly hierarchical form with woman typically sacrificed to the interests of masculine supremacy.

Only slowly did arranged marriages go out of fashion in the Western world. The still extant tradition of the young man's asking the father for a young woman's hand is a relic of that pattern. The conviction of most young people that their families should welcome their romantic choices also continues this old tradition, although it is also natural to want your beloved to be liked by family members. But the general emphasis in our era almost totally reverses the older tradition. We unquestioningly believe that something called *love*—a strong sexual attraction combined with affection, mutual respect, and liking—is the basis for marriage. Considerations of order, in terms of interrelationships between families and place in the community, have now lost prominence, sometimes not mattering at all. Likewise, concerns for similar background, ethnicity, and religion also figure less frequently. Furthermore, procreation (with children the visible emblems of the newly adjusted social order) now remains optional for many couples. Even as recently as thirty years ago you typically assumed something was "wrong" with a childless couple; nowadays few people are surprised by those who choose not to reproduce.

Given such changes within the general conception of marriage and the continuing use of the same word to describe a relationship whose avowed end is no longer the same, it is no wonder that the even more nebulous belief in Happily Ever After should be so confusing. Out of such confusion it is logical that some obviously imbalanced, overly literalistic visions of Happily Ever After should occur.

The difference between such imbalanced, overly literalistic visions and their more authentic counterparts hinges as much on a sentimental as a romantic misunderstanding. Often it is the children of the homeless or the products of distorted homes who create sentimental images of Happily Ever After. To compensate for the physical and emotional poverty of their actual lives, such deprived children may create prettified images mistakenly believing them to be authentic. The distinction between authentic and prettily sentimental images is often a fine one. Gideon, a black South African artist in Nadine Gordimer's novel *Occasion for Loving*, helps clarify the distinction when he speaks of his wife's conception of art:

> She looked at his paintings, when he really was beginning to paint, as the wife of a gangster might look at the guns and knives present in the house. She cared only for prettiness, for the little sweetnesses and frills that clerks acquire to soften the rough chunk of the labourer's life. She was only concerned with covering ugliness and did not know the possibility of beauty.[2]

Individuals who sentimentalize Home into an unrealistic vision of Happily Ever After similarly cover ugliness, without understanding the difference Gideon intends when he distinguishes the pretty from the beautiful. The illustrations of Norman Rockwell may at times approach prettiness but they lack the depth for true beauty. Such "prettifying" is also apparent in the following description of a believer:

> He has a clear sense of being totally a part of, filled up with, and wrapped in a state of faith. That is to say, his faith is such an inseparable part of him that it shows in everything he does, says, and is. . . . Wow! That sounds like there should be a surge of fantastic music and at least

a ship sailing off into the sunset, or something! I mean, it is so wonderful, and it really is the way things ought to be![3]

This selection too easily glosses over the deep level of meaning it seems to be telling about. An idolatrous, sentimental interpretation of Home similarly involves "worshipping" the image divorced from its roots of good and evil, beauty and ugliness. But false worship creates a deceptive, mirage-like image which floats rather than remaining anchored to its source. As such it is as nonsustaining an idol as this one promulgated by Dorothy, a gentle woman reared in a strongly middle-class home which emphasized fidelity to parents, weekly church attendance, and like virtues. Her husband, reared similarly, has rebelled against his upbringing by becoming an alcoholic. Although he can be exceedingly charming, and frequently is, when he is drunk he taunts his wife, telling her she's nothing but a strumpet, a word he never uses when sober. This couple's only child is a daughter aged eight, who frequently wakens in the night, shrieking, because of recurrent nightmares. To reassure her frightened child, Dorothy always rushes in, asserting in the face of all evidence to the contrary that "everything is all right." Though her intentions may be good, they are based on a sentimental, rather than an honest, conception that Home is Happily Ever After. Presumably her thinking goes somewhat like this: Home is supposed to be the place where you are always safe, and mothers are supposed to ensure that safety. Therefore, when my daughter cries out in fright, it is my duty to reassure her that things are as they should be, as I hope they soon will be.

Whether it is through false words, false behaviors, or false interiors, however, sentimental beliefs in Happily Ever After distort, trivialize, and artificially sweeten Home so that it loses its full meaning. A sentimentalized concept of home has all the solidity of an airplane cruising at 35,000 feet above a bed of fluffy white clouds which obscure the sky and ground beneath. Looking at those clouds makes you feel safe, for surely they look like they will hold you up. While this illusion may make you feel better temporarily, if it were put to the test those clouds would let you drop to the ground just as quickly as if the sky were cleanly devoid of them. Similarly, Dorothy's falsely soothing words, instead of providing her daughter with a secure place on which to stand, give her only fluff instead. In this case, the mother tries by her words to create a boundary that does not actually exist. The "badness" her words seek to banish is present *within* the home. No matter how much she tries to manipulate the situation of her husband's drinking and consequent abusiveness, his behavior continues to belie her words. Consequently, she creates a dissonance between her child's experience of the tacit reality of the situation and its sentimentally expressed veneer.

Carried to such extremes, sentimental distortions are far removed from the amusing lapses of taste of gemutlich cuckoo clocks and Ye Olde Gift Shoppe frilly gewgaws; instead, they are downright demonic. In Pirandello's play *Henry IV*, for example, the era of Henry IV so captivates the central character that he chooses to remain locked into that period of history as Henry IV for the remainder of his life. In his refusal to leave the refuge of this role which he originated for a pageant, he enacts a totally falsified version of existence. Is he the madman everyone takes him for? Or is he, on the contrary, so sane that he prefers this existence to the greater madness of his chronological era? On a lesser scale those same questions apply to sentimentalized versions of home. Are the inhabitants of ruffly, Priscilla-curtained Cape Cod houses full of quaint little multicolored glass bottles hiding from their time, or are they providing appropriate refuge from an external environment over which they can exert no control?

A sentimental misappropriation of Home by Happily Ever After, whether in art, literature, or actual experience, involves a misunderstanding—a standing under a false sign. In fairy tales this kind of falseness appears in the motif of the valuable fairy object which metamorphoses into junk when transported out of the realm of Faerie. Most often the object is gold given to the mortal by one of the fairies. Upon returning to human territory, however, the beneficiary discovers to his or her chagrin that it is only a lump of coal. Its golden aura was only fairy glamour, the magically deceptive substance fairies love to spread around for the amazement of their mortal rivals.

To misname coal as gold is to lose experience—is to shut out, ignore, or abstract qualities you do not wish to see in order to experience only those you desire. But that behavior not only distorts, it causes you to miss certain aspects of life entirely. Thus sentimental words which seek to comfort and cover over provide false comfort because they are empty. Not actually being connected to the situation they pretend to describe, they simply float. Those who use them anticipate that their hearers will listen to the words and be soothed, rather than listen *through* the words to the disturbing images beneath them. Consequently, although people like Dorothy do not necessarily utter their false words conscious of their falsity, the difference between such sentimental glossing over of the truth of a situation and an authentically transcending story is enormous. The transcending story does not blink at the real situation. It appropriates its important elements, no matter how horrifying, and then proceeds to envision an alternative future which incorporates the present situation without denying it. By contrast, the deceptive speaking and hearing of sentimentality block the possibility of the emergence of authentic meaning. While sentimental words may protect you momentarily from harsh truths they eventually choke you with their false sweetness.

But such sweetness is not the fare of deprived individuals alone. It is a diet common to all strata of our culture. Frequently, as children, both girls and boys experience Home much the same way, although some families do make very early, rigid sex-role distinctions. In such cases little girls may be expected to help out while boys escape housework entirely. Certainly the little girl asked to tote her younger brother everywhere she goes—or worse, to stay home because of him—is not likely to develop positive associations with Home. But for those children, particularly of middle- and upper-class origin, who are asked to do almost nothing, Home is likely to be a place of relaxation and freedom from responsibility, a middle-American version of the age-old Land of Cockayne. And so these children develop a falsely sweet belief in a Happily Ever After to which individuals are born and from which they need never depart.

For many men this infantile experience of dependency remains relatively unchanged throughout adulthood. While these men assume full adult responsibilities at work, when they come home they expect to be cosseted by wives who adore them as much as their mothers did when they were little boys. For them Home ideally functions as a refuge catering specifically to masculine needs, as the words of this letter, dating from 1845, indicate:

> Man is strange, but his heart is not adamant. He delights in enterprise and action but to sustain him he needs a tranquil mind and a whole heart. He spends his whole moral force in the conflicts of the world. His feelings are daily lacerated to the utmost point of endurance by perpetual collision, irritation and disappointment. To recover his equanimity and composure HOME must be to him a place of repose, of peace, of cheerfulness, of comfort, and his soul renews its strength and again goes forth with fresh vigor to encounter the labors and troubles of the world.[4]

These masculine words counter the stereotypical feminine vision of Happily Ever After as the realm in which a savior prince will forever save a woman from all worldly dangers. In either distorted vision the dreamer remains infantilized, while a rescuer of appropriate sex functions as an all-protective savior figure.

For a girl, this supposedly ideal situation of perpetual *salvation* changes unless she marries into great wealth. Suddenly, instead of existing as a Princess, she discovers it is she who must enact the role her own mother once performed for her. If she is not emotionally prepared to assume it, she may suddenly experience a sharp dissonance between her old image of Home and her new experience of it. That means that she may come to oppose the term *Home* in ways very different from her husband. While both are likely to construe homelessness as Home's most fundamental opposite, she may also exclude qualities he incorporates into it. For example, unlike her husband, she may associate relaxation, fun, and sexuality only with motels and vacation spots, and home increasingly with drudgery. Thus she may slowly evolve from the fun-loving, carefree Princess into the Witch who rigidly forbids anything but duty in her conception of Home. The "right-eousness" of her new, witch-like behavior is then likely to exclude her husband from Home, so that he, too, comes to associate pleasure with persons and places outside it.

When this happens, a woman's actual home begins to push out too much of what the traditional Home-centered belief system attributes to Home in its idealized form. Then the boundaries of her living space may become strained to the point of explosiveness, as occurs in Euripides' play *The Bacchae*. In this play Dionysus dramatizes deity in its ecstatic form. Angry because no one worships him in his hometown of Thebes, Dionysus reveals to the Theban women not the divine, but the demonic, face of his ecstatic religion. In states of uncontrolled madness these women feel compelled to leave their homes, fleeing to the mountains "where they wander, crazed of mind,"[5] and whirl to strange dances. Eventually they dismember Pentheus, the son of one of them.

Dionysus is a way of naming a certain pattern of human behavior. The intoxication he incurs—whether alcohol-induced or unaccounted for—if not controlled, quickly turns destructive. Disavowed, the force he names destroys the one who ignores it, as the fate of Pentheus so clearly attests. Such a "return of the repressed," as Freud called such situations of psychic denial, will similarly attack the most conservative guardian of Home if she (or he) too rigidly excludes elements which must eventually find entry. Like the deceptive premarriage expectation of Happily Ever After, this postmarriage danger of rigid exclusion raises a crucial question for women: can Home, as a symbol of salvation within the tacit feminine religion, continue to function for women any better than various officially accepted symbols such as the Cross, Star (or Shield) of David, or Sword of Islam?

To appropriately answer this question demands careful reflection on the sacred presence which infuses Home: Hestia, Goddess of the Hearth. In her countless housewifely incarnations, what does this unstoried goddess do? Understanding enactments of her role can help illuminate the meaning Home continues to exert both in contemporary American culture as a whole, and in its tacit counterpart, feminine culture.

II

❦ Housework

HOUSEWORK AS RITUAL ENACTMENT

Danny: What is there to be done about the house—will you tell us
        that?
Lizzie: There's the pig 'n the heifer 'n the hens to be fed 'n tended.
        There's ironing, cooking, washing, 'n sewing to be done.
Sean O'Casey, The End of the Beginning[1]

In a memorable scene from contemporary playwright Olwyn Wymark's play *Loved,* two women crawl across a slightly skewed Oriental rug, beating on it with their hands to the strains of Strauss' "Also Sprach Zarathustra," Subsequently better known as the theme song of *2001.* The viewer need not be a deliberate symbol hunter to realize that something ritually significant is occurring here in this highly unusual scene of spring furniture moving and rug beating. But how often do the arts consider such homely material? Generally more "lofty" procedures (such as Hemingway's endless details about how to bait a fishhook) have been deemed artistic, while women's work has been considered too trivial for art. The fact that such a scene even appears in Wymark's play suggests that finally the strong taboo against artistically rendering women's traditional work may be breaking down.

I would like to go a step further. Not only is the artistic acceptance of women's work a major step forward, but such work also makes sense in a whole new way when it is so viewed. And yet most contemporary feminists still refer to housework as "shitwork." Such denigration makes women who claim to enjoy housework appear to be dupes of false consciousness, retrogressive upholders of the male-dominated status quo. Yet these traditional women are actually in touch with a level beneath our visible, still largely Platonic, masculine vision of "reality." At this level, whether we speak psychologically or archaeologically, there exists a woman-centered foundation so deep that few of us consciously realize it is there. Psychologically, this level relates to the early symbiosis between mother and child; archaeologically, it relates to evidence, drawn from around the world, of prepatriarchal goddess worship. This woman-centered foundation is so deeply embedded within human beings that it belongs to that dimension of human existence which Michael Polanyi refers to as tacit.[2]

In the case of women's traditional work, the business of housewifery, only the purposeful aspects—those concerned with producing and maintaining order and cleanliness and preparing food—are visible: everything else is tacit. But apart from these ends, when woman's housework is viewed as having intrinsic merit for its own sake, then we begin to glimpse beneath the articulated visible masculine edifice of culture a tenacious belief system for which there is cultic ritual but essentially no mythos. And at the heart of this cultic ritual lies the shadowy presence of deity—the goddess Hestia.

When I say Hestia, I do not mean Hestia literally. One of the most curious things about this goddess is the virtual absence of myths about her, for unlike such sister goddesses as Hera, Artemis, and Aphrodite, Hestia is unstoried. In fact, she is not even personified—her name actually means "hearth."

Consequently, to follow some sort of pattern of development through artistic sources is not possible. What I am speaking about is a pattern of being for which Hestia provides a name. After all, when we look at the Greco-Roman pantheon, what we are really looking at are names for certain modes of being—those Jung calls archetypes. When I look at Hestia, therefore, I am examining some ritual patterns of behavior that women in traditional societies have enacted within their lives—those essential for the role of housewife.

The importance of Hestia is indicated by her position as oldest of the twelve great Olympians. Similarly, her centrality to the household and its cult is apparent from rituals related to her—every meal beginning and ending with a libation to her, newborn children being officially ensconced in the family by being carried around the hearth, and all public as well as private liturgical acts beginning with special recognition of her. One reason for the paucity of stories about her is the fact that she is not, as you might expect, a married goddess like Hera, but a virgin. To gossip about her, the representative of pure homelife, would not have been appropriate.

But the fact that Hestia is so little noticed despite her importance probably extends beyond the issue of propriety. How aptly her role reflects that of traditional women, who, like her, represent the comfort of home for others, without seeming to achieve full personhood in their own right. Furthermore, Hestia, unlike other members of the Greek pantheon, remains chained to the hearth: she is never seen in other locations. For the traditional woman that situation has frequently obtained. Unless she remains a half-child, as in fact, many traditional women seem to do, she will typically make a home for others, but will often have no home that is recognizably her own. For her, the place her husband and children call home will actually be a workplace, the domestic sphere. Thus, for her, the important difference separating "the world" and home will not exist as it does for them. And without that distinction she will have difficulty experiencing for herself the joy of homecoming, in which home assumes its fullest meaning. Although she is often like a prelapsarian Eve, inhabiting Paradise, she does so without awareness, having no basis for comparison. Functioning as a priestess who performs for others, she typically has no one but herself to perform those rites for her.

Metaphorically, all the domestic rites a housewife performs are designed to maintain Hestia's fire property. If she allows the fire to go out, her house is no longer a home; when heat, warmth, comfort, relaxation, and security go, only the outward, physical structure remains. Conversely, if a homemaker allows the fire to rage out of control, her home will vanish along with its physical embodiment. A housewife's task, therefore, involves a careful balancing of these two extremes.

Despite the fact that Hestia is, by definition, a virgin goddess, it is nonetheless she, of all the ancient goddesses, whose unvoiced story most closely approximates the experience of traditional women locked into the twin roles of housewife and mother. Often the major emphases of traditional marriages are both motherhood and domesticity, neither of which reflect the promised sexual fulfillment implicit in the happy endings of our fairytale dreams. Even in a "happily ever after" kind of marriage, more time is spent by most wives in domestic rituals than in sexual communion. Turning that relationship around, most women, except the very wealthy, have had to function to some extent as house-keepers, whereas not all women have chosen, or been capable of, motherhood. We need to explore this aspect of traditional women's experience as well as the more frequently studied dimensions of motherhood, reproduction, and sexuality to more clearly understand the underlying significance of what it has meant, until now, to grow up female as opposed to male, to live predominantly in the domestic realm of Hestia.

In this domestic realm, centered on hearth and home, cultic rituals surface primarily through housework, a general term denoting all the chores associated with cleaning and ordering a house. To call such chores ritual almost seems laughable, until you consider what housework can mean to its performer and those who live with her. It is not *what* is done but *how* it is done that makes housekeeping chores rituals, although you can argue that the how transforms the what. A helpful illustration is provided by the following Zen *koan:*

> Seeker: How do I achieve enlightenment?
> Zen Master: What do you do when your begging bowl is dirty?
> Seeker: I wash it out.
> Zen Master: Then go and wash your begging bowl.[3]

Whether enlightenment occurs depends more on the understanding of the seeker than on the particular task she undertakes. Many times, probably most, the performance of housework is totally profane. But sometimes a qualitatively different experience occurs, transforming the ordinarily profane chore of housekeeping into a sacred process because it is seen from a cosmic viewpoint.

This transformation can assume either a demonic or a sacred form, but in either case the performer is caught up in something much larger than herself. In its demonic form housekeeping is extremely distasteful, sometimes even frightening, as the myth of Sisyphus, with its endless, meaningless repetitions, appropriately suggests. But in its sacred manifestation—or cosmic perspective—housekeeping creates an entirely different experience, one analogous to what psychologists call *flow* in sports. Then performer and performance are virtually indistinguishable, as Yeats indicates with his question, "How can we know the dancer from the dance?"[4] Such moments manifest a hierophany; instead of the performer performing her tasks, something is performed through her. The poet, Rainer Maria Rilke, in *Lettres à une musicienne,* beautifully describes what happens when such a transformation of the ordinary, profane world occurs. Because his cleaning woman was absent, he had polished his piano:

> Under my zealous dustcloth, it suddenly started to purr mechanically
> . . . and its fine, deep black surface became more and more beautiful.
> When you've been through this there's little you don't know! . . . Po-
> liteness tinged with mischief was my reaction to the friendliness of
> these objects, which seemed happy to be so well treated, so meticu-
> lously renovated. And even today, I must confess that while everything
> about me grew brighter and the immense black surface of my work
> table, which dominated its surroundings . . . became newly aware,
> somehow, of the size of the room, reflecting it more and more clearly:
> pale gray and almost square . . . well, yes, I felt moved, as though
> something were happening, something, to tell the truth, which was
> not purely superficial but immense, and which touched my very soul:
> I was an emperor washing the feet of the poor, or Saint Bonaventure,
> washing dishes in his convent.[5]

What happened to Rilke serendipitously may happen more regularly for a housewife. Such an experience makes the individual a player in a scene far older and larger than her individual self. No longer does she participate in profane historical time; instead, she is participating in mythic time, ritually returning as a priestess to the time of origins, the primordial time in which the gods and goddesses originally created order out of chaos.[6]

Yet by no means can all housework be considered cultic ritual. Much of it, in fact, is contrastingly profane. In its ordinary, profane manifes- tation, it is common for the housewife, like any alienated worker, to experience disjunction between herself and her work. Robert Coles viv- idly portrays such disjunction in "Mountain Dreams," one chapter in his book *Women of Crisis*. Quoting the words of Hannah Morgan, a displaced Appalachian woman living unhappily with her family in Day- ton, Ohio, Coles presents the experience of disjunction like this:

> Suddenly, I started to cry. I didn't even know why I was crying. I was
> afraid Tim would notice, but he was lost to himself—the way I am, a
> lot of the time, when I come home from work. I'm not really in touch
> with what I'm doing. I'm in a daze. I end up getting my work finished,
> but I'll be going to bed, and I'll think back, and I'll wonder if I did one
> thing or another. I'm ashamed to say that sometimes a whole day will
> go like that for me.[7]

These words express just the opposite of engagement. For this woman, daydreams are essential to lift her out of the Dayton supermarket in which she must clerk to earn a living. Only by returning imaginatively to the Appalachian hollows of her origins can she get through the day. While these daydreams are necessary escapism for her, they preclude any possibility of truly enacting her work.

Hestian ritual enactment of housework not only must be distinguished from its profane counterpart, it must also be separated from other kinds of ritual enactment. Superficially, some performances of housework which appear to follow a Hestian pattern are actually patriarchal instead. The situation of the young Catherine of Siena comes to mind. Forced as a child to perform servant's work in her own home, she would imagine herself waiting upon Christ. In her case, the business of housewifery serves some purpose other than itself. It is a patriarchal rather than a Hestian enactment for what she does leads her away from the task at hand into a "reality" unrelated to the work itself in which she figures in the stereotypic relationship of submissive woman to savior man. This differs considerably from the situation to which I refer.

Enactment relates both to a way of performing tasks and, in the case of housework, to a mode of relationship the housewife establishes between herself and her home. As the term implies, it is first of all an acting out. That means it is active and physical as opposed to quiet and contemplative. It is therefore more akin to the performance of actor or singer than the product or writer or composer.

But although enactment has strong affinities with the theatre, it is not primarily a verbal mode dealing with "word-presentations," but a physical one having to do with "thing presentations."[8] Some of Antonin Artaud's ideas in his Theatre of Cruelty point to the kind of "language" a housewife typically employs. For example, he says that "instead of harking back to texts regarded as sacred and definitive, we must first break theatre's subjugation to the text and rediscover the idea of a kind of unique language somewhere in between gesture and thought. We can only define this language as expressive, spoken dialogue potential."[9] It is particularly Artaud's emphasis on the *spatial* dimension of the language he is calling for that relates to a housewife's enactment. In this sense her "language" more closely reflects that of a dancer than an actor, for it is above all her body in action that bespeaks the meanings of what she does. As dancer/choreographer Marlene Pennison says of her work, "I start with the movement, because that's the deepest root for me. . . ."[10]

But for most people, the "movement" involved in housework has been scarcely noticed. Because "ends" issue from housework, typically they have been emphasized almost to the exclusion of performance. Characteristically these ends—cleanliness and orderliness—have dominated the general conception of housework to the extent that its actual performance has remained almost entirely tacit. Yet three aspects of housework as action need to be distinguished to clarify its potentially sacred component. Explicitly housework includes all the tasks necessary to make a house function properly. But implicitly two other factors converge. First, these tasks may have additional purposes other than their tangible "products" of cleanliness and order. And second, the actual performance as such, regardless of any end whatsoever, may also hold meaning in and of itself.

Yet just as many women as men seem to have been oblivious to these distinctions. For example, the December/January 1980–81 issue of the *National NOW Times* printed the following quote from and about feminist author Diana Silcox:

> "It's not that women don't want to relinquish these roles," Silcox says. "A lot of us just don't know how." A prime recommendation in her portfolio is the acquisition of hired help in the home; even for women who can't afford it yet, Silcox says, "it's important to want that kind of help, to get rid of the attitude that a woman must do everything herself."[11]

But a woman may *want* to do these things. If she truly experiences her home as sacred space, then to have someone else, a total stranger, come in and "do" for her may be to transform that space from "special" to "ordinary." That in turn makes it into a workplace for someone else. A woman who truly sees her home as a bodily extension of herself may not want anyone to intrude on it. For such a woman to have someone else performing tasks in her house would be akin to having a surgeon probing the organs inside her body or poking a breathing device up her nose to draw air into her lungs for her. To live in a house entirely taken care of by someone else, while agreeable to her in one sense, would be exceedingly uncomfortable in another. And what if the worker performed her tasks wrong or inappropriately? What if she were to break some heirloom china? Worse, what if she were to steal?

Such incursions by an essential stranger into a housewife's own space would leave a certain kind of woman feeling that she no longer lives inside her own house. Instead, it would appear to belong to someone else. In her relationship to the house she might come to feel herself a stranger, albeit a petted one, much as you do when staying in an elegant, well-appointed hotel.

On the surface, the difference between living in a household maintained by a servant or cleaning woman and one managed exclusively by a housewife and her family appears to focus on time and labor. But at the tacit level the difference between these two modes of living is very great indeed. The woman whose interior living spaces and prized objects are all touched and cared for by someone else does not live in close physical intimacy with them. Nor does she possess them in the same way as the woman who physically interacts with them.

Living on the surface of her environment is not at all the same for a housewife as digging into it and immersing herself therein. Such a surface existence may foster boredom with her environment because there is so little of herself invested in it. In that case she may experience restlessness like that of a young child forced to visit elderly relatives in a non-childproofed house. The reverse phenomenon also occurs when relatives, in-laws, or other guests descend for lengthy visits. The resulting disturbance of her routine disrupts her not just at the obvious surface level, but more deeply within the tacit dimension where her habitual actions are attached to their sacred sources.

Some women feel so strongly about the way they relate to home and possessions that they distinguish sharply between owning their own home or merely renting it. Those women who most strongly identify themselves with their homes are least likely to feel satisfied with rented space. For them the dream of ownership may have significance far deeper than the obvious goals of financial security and status. The dream may well reflect a desire for ownership in a slightly different sense— desire for totally private space into which no janitor or superintendent can unexpectedly intrude. For this kind of woman enactment is most free within space she and/or her husband own, without the interference of any outsiders, not even an occasional cleaning woman.

Ritual enactment of the Hestian sort deepens the actual experiences of housework rather than avoiding or altering them, although it, too, in its own way, transfigures and transcends. The following passage from Solzhenitsyn's *One Day in the Life of Ivan Denisovich* helps illustrate this difference:

> More than once during his life in the Camps, Shukov had recalled the way they used to eat in his village: whole pots full of potatoes, pans of oatmeal, and in the early days, big chunks of meat. And milk enough to bust their guts. That wasn't the way to eat, he learned in camp. You had to eat with all your mind on the food—like now, nibbling the bread bit by bit, working the crumbs up into a paste with your tongue and sucking it into your cheeks. And how good it tasted—that soggy black bread![12]

The difference between these two ways of eating is immense. In the prison way, three factors dominate: duration, quantity, and quality. Where once there was plenty, now there is nearly nothing. Yet, somewhat paradoxically, the scanty ration becomes a ritual feast reminiscent of the loaves and fishes. Both quantity and quality, from a nonimprisoned perspective, appear lacking. But viewing the occasion relative to its setting, this soggy black bread becomes entirely sufficient. How greatly it differs from the heedless consumption Shukov recalls from before. And it is just because so much heed goes into the task at hand for the starving prisoner that the occasion of eating becomes so meaningful. Eating, for this man, becomes an all-consuming task. There is not part of him left over, so to speak, to engage in some other competing activity. Every part of his being is concentrated totally. Consequently, what he is doing really matters. Similarly, for the woman who enacts her role, no part of herself is disengaged at the time she is performing her tasks. She and her work fully occupy her whole being. She thereby transcends the half-heartedness and partial involvement typical of dissatisfied workers whose performance is profane. Equally, she avoids the fragmentation and divided attention common to time-pressured executives.

As with the prisoner in Solzhenitsyn's book, a traditional housewife frequently experiences fewer stimuli than do many workers outside the home. Yet the prisoner analogy, while helpful, is not extreme enough. Unlike him, the traditional housewife is not simply a victim; she is also, typically, an idol or priestess. Consequently, her plight is infinitely more complex than his, making her more closely resemble the priest-king at Nemi, so extensively, if inaccurately, detailed in Frazer's *Golden Bough*. A contemporary feminine variant of the sacrificial priest-king is Nepal's "Raj Kumari," the Royal Virgin Goddess. In the fall of 1980 the most recent incarnation of the Goddess, Sunina Sakya in ordinary life, was dethroned. But

> . . . for 10 years, Sunina was . . . worshipped. She lived according to a strict code in a special temple in the capital. Every morning her servants bathed and dressed her . . . . The few times each year she briefly left the temple—normally she was not allowed out even into the courtyard—she was carried so her feet would not touch the ground.[13]

In exaggerated form this account reflects the simultaneously glorified and sacrificial status of the middle-class Western housewife.

Though most feminists readily acknowledge both these facets of a woman's traditional role, few admit that anything positive can emerge from either. Following Virginia Woolf, they typically scream that a woman needs "a room of her own."

But it is this "room of her own" that is, precisely, an essential result of enactment. Enactment creates what Susanne Langer calls "virtual space" by allowing a housewife to create and participate in a symbolic space of her own as well as to create and order an environment for her family. Whereas, on the surface, a woman picking up last night's paper, several dirty coffee cups, some tramped-in leaves, and a bouquet of wilted roses may simply appear to be straightening her living room, she may actually be enacting her own psychic environment. As she sorts, cleans, and rearranges, she is able to externalize her inner needs for order. Much as literary critic I. A. Richards claimed that reading a poem patterns a reader,[14] so can physically shifting the contents of a room pattern the person doing it. To the extent that such a fit between inner and outer worlds occurs, a housewife is able to focus the meaning of her task in such a way that there is neither need nor reason to escape or make it something other. For enactment does not fundamentally alter the nature of the task as daydreaming, for example, does. On the contrary, it deepens and intensifies it.

In addition to its strong aesthetic component, the ritual enactment of housekeeping typically links its performer back in time to the company of female ancestors. Such linking back to origins is a frequent and important element of most religious ritual. Just as family stories or memorabilia may be handed down within families, so may traditional ways of doing certain tasks. As Mircea Eliade says, "To do the rite again is to join with the ancestors and regenerate the ideality of their lives . . . ."[15] Thus, one benefit ritual behavior confers is to convey special knowledge in nonverbal fashion from one time period to the next.

To do a task precisely as you observed or were taught by your mother or grandmother is to experience a portion of what they each once did. Two kinds of knowledge are thus imparted: knowledge of what it is to be a housewife and knowledge of what it was to have been Grandma X in her homemaking aspect. For example, at times, catching myself in what was presumably a characteristic gesture or attitude of my mother, I have the eerie feeling that I AM my mother. The ritual enactment of housework thus helps provide continuity from one generation of women to another. Consequently, although housework as it is generally practiced is a solitary occupation, some sense of community is provided by the *method* of doing, when that method reflects the performance of earlier women. Obviously, for women who hire their work done or those who have rejected the methods and attitudes of their mothers this connection will have been severed. But homemakers in general are the largest group in the post-industrial world still to connect back in this particular fashion to their forebears. In the days when sons more frequently followed the occupations of their fathers, most men also engaged in handed-down ritual enactment. Now, however, except for those who are farmers or those who apprentice in skilled trades, even individuals who do pursue a parental career are apt to be trained outside the family in professional or trade schools. Furthermore, relatively few children nowadays grow up fully aware of the day-to-day activities which fill their working parents' lives. Not many share even a few hours a week with a parent at her/his place of work outside the home. Therefore, the experience of learning to enact a task precisely as your mother or father did it, even if you follow the same trade or profession, is increasingly rare except for avocational pursuits such as woodworking or sports. In that regard, homemakers and peasants, like tribespeople, appear to be beneficiaries of a mode of knowledge now essentially lost to most people in our post-industrial age.

The linking back in time provided by this kind of knowledge is one of the major benefits ritual enactment bestows on its participants. It is one of the major ways that women (whose lives have typically been isolated from the public sphere dominated by men) have been able to share in the entire community of women. In such enactment women celebrate the unstoried pattern of Hestia, goddess of the hearth.

5

COSMIZATION

Few would deny that historically most women in Western culture have been both secluded and excluded from what many individuals construe as "the world," meaning by that term the world of masculine affairs. But in a far larger sense even the most traditional women have been in contact with "the world," have, in fact, been free to create it.

Ritualized housework not only sets a housewife in the context of female ancestors, placing her in the larger family of women, it also determines her place in the largest context of all: the world. The process by which such placement occurs is cosmization, the creation of world out of chaos. Whereas community with ancestors connects human to human across time, cosmization relates human to environment in both time and space. These two inherently religious connections—the one to community, the other to cosmos—usually complement, but occasionally clash with, each other.

As a major aspect of ritual housework, cosmization attempts to create or renew wholeness. Typically, ritual patterns of enactment, if they are religious, are intended to bring together two worlds—the ordinary, profane world and the ideal, sacred world which alone has "reality." To the extent that home can be considered a sacred space, what lies beyond it—the world of masculine affairs—is contrastingly profane. But home, like church, is not automatically sacred. Various rituals must be performed in both to maintain their sacred character. In ritual housekeeping the profane world is apt to intrude in the form of freshly tracked mud, baseball mitts on the dining-room table, lint on the rug, and ants marching towards the sugar bowl. Beyond that chaotic face, however, in many people's minds, lies a world of perfect order, one envisioned perhaps, from fragmentary memories of a grandmother's lovingly ordered home.

The process of cosmization often involves a preliminary tearing up, as when a housewife periodically determines to sort through her family's accumulated possessions. To initiate this task she may first occasion more chaos by pulling accumulated possessions out of closets, upending drawers, and emptying shelves. As she takes up each displaced object in turn, she is apt to run her hand over it and hold it up to the light for careful inspection. Constantly she is torn between the desire to retain in tangible form some link to past memories and the urge to weed out and create more space. As her pile of potential throwaways grows she feels satisfaction. To be able to throw out is to enlarge her living space and banish clutter from it. And yet she continually feels a tug in just the opposite direction: to put back all those things she has managed to discard, thus retaining her connection to the past they represent.

The complement of this surface struggle between retention and elimination of accumulated objects, which is the process whereby she creates a world, is the creation of herself. What she chooses to keep and what she decides to discard reflect inner qualities she either wishes to expand or delete from herself. In her ritual ordering she is creating *place* for herself and her family as she is also simultaneously mimicking the process by which she herself continuously comes into being. That is why she cannot simply go through and systematically throw things out as she could so easily in somebody else's house where no sacred history exists for her. For Jane, Rosemary's icons are nothing but objects, heavy in their materiality, but with no glowing, sacred core of meaning.

How often Jane has heard friends make the statement, "I would make the best housekeeper for somebody else. I love to throw things out, only I can never bear to part with any of my own possessions." For every object she throws away, a small part of herself seems to vanish, too. Yet with some objects she has no difficulty at all: the black plastic salad bowl with silver-speckled red lucite servers, the hand-carved walnut cuckoo clock, and the milliafiori glass paperweight from Murano, Italy, give her no difficulty at all. Though given to her as gifts, they never "belonged" to her at all, for she never cared enough for them to incorporate them into herself. But the multiflowered silk print cocktail dress, long out of style and far too youthful for her now—that is a different matter. She sewed that dress herself; it was one of the first she ever made, years ago when she and her husband had no money at all. And the gold filigree cigarette lighter in the shoebox usually stuffed under her sweaters: even though she hasn't smoked since she was in college she can't give that away. Aunt Emma gave it to her as her graduation present. These are her icons: to lose one is to lose touch with the past that helps sacralize her existence by telling her who she is.

But the world she creates is not only rooted in the sacred past. It simultaneously looks forward, too, being a continuous creation rather than an entity fixed once and for all. Thus, as she sorts, decisions must be made; often she finds them impossible to arrive at. After a morning of plunging her hands into boxes and closets she may leave the whole mess still uncategorized in the middle of the floor. As evening approaches she may frantically stuff it all back, or if she is a different kind of woman she may shift the accumulation of one room to another, so that what had cluttered her own closet may wind up in an attic trunk, there to be brought back bit by bit at some later time. Sometimes the retrieval process may not occur until just as she is about to slip a bag of discards into the Goodwill box.

In these sporadic, often indecisive attempts at ordering, a housewife tries to come to terms with elements within her own life. What appears unnecessary because it is worn, outdated, or too small nonetheless may matter essentially at the level of inner meaning. Similarly, within her own personality, traits she thought she did not need she may actually wish to retain.

This personally meaningful aspect of ritual housekeeping relates to anthropologist Geza Roheim's distinction between autoplastic and alloplastic cultures.[1] In his view, in earlier, less-civilized cultures humans performed rituals and acted upon their own bodies in order to effect changes in the external world. The underlying belief system thought to govern such behavior is magical. Specifically, it is magic of the homeopathic sort in which, as Sir James Frazer says, "like produces like. . . . The magician infers that he can produce any effect he desires merely by imitating it in advance."[2] Thus if the female initiates of a tribe are forced to endure ritual clitoridectomies, the underlying reason may be to ensure the submissiveness of women.

By contrast, according to Norman O. Brown, who develops Roheim's ideas, Western civilization is alloplastic, meaning that humans have learned to act directly upon the environment through various technologies, rather than indirectly on their bodies, to shape the world to their ends. Whether Brown's global application of alloplasticity to Western civilization is appropriate or not, it is nonetheless useful to distinguish along the lines of the two terms to understand what sometimes occurs during housework.

On the surface, housework appears to be entirely alloplastic: a housewife takes one of her implements, a vacuum cleaner, perhaps, pushes a button, and whoosh! a few minutes later her living room is clean. She has applied technology to the problem of a dirty room. That is certainly the visible aspect of what she has done. But at the tacit level what she does actually reverses the concept of alloplasticity without, however, becoming autoplasticity: instead of working on or with her body to effect a clean room, she works on the room to effect a "clean" self.

Furthermore, in her acts of cosmization, a housewife not only creates world, she also places herself in certain very special ways into the world she is creating. The interior space of her home represents an opening or hole whose space a housewife metaphorically fills. Sartre suggests an analogue when he speaks of the symbolic nature of holes:

> The hole is originally presented as a nothingness to be filled with my own flesh. . . . It presents itself to me as the empty image of myself. I have only to crawl into it in order to make myself exist in the world which awaits me. The ideal of the hole is then an excavation which can be carefully moulded about my flesh in such a manner that by squeezing myself into it and fitting myself tightly inside it, I shall contribute to making fullness of being exist in the world.[3]

What Sartre is describing is a body-sized hole which can be filled completely. Applied to a larger space, the feeling Sartre describes may become elongation of my body as if it possessed the elasticity of taffy: I might feel myself extend in much the way Stephen Dedalus imagines for himself in *Ulysses:* "His shadow lay over the rocks as he bent, ending. Why not endless. . . . Endless, would it be mine, form of my form?".[4] What Stephen ponders about his shadow elongating endlessly relates to what a housewife may experience relative to the space around her. But instead of merely elongating, she may metaphorically stretch out her body so as to be large enough to fit *all* the space.

In that case, what happens is a little like the experience of Alice in Wonderland:

> . . . before she had drunk half the bottle she found her head pressing against the ceiling, and had to stoop to save her neck from being broken. She went on growing and growing, and very soon had to kneel down on the floor; in another minute there was not even room for this, and she tried the effect of lying down, with one elbow against the door, and the other arm curled round head. Still she went on growing, and, as a last resource, she put one arm out of the window, and one foot up the chimney, and said to herself, "Now I can do no more, whatever happens. What *will* become of me?[5]

A housewife, however, may experience something more than what Carroll, Sartre, or Joyce describes. Their images are heavily masculine, a fact which is clear in Sartre's case when he continues with a highly phallic discussion of filling holes. While the feeling these writers detail can be experienced by women as well as men, it only partially describes what can happen for a woman in her relationship to interior spaces. Whereas a masculine response to a large space may very well be what Norman O. Brown refers to as being "a little man in a large room," a feminine one is quite different. In fitting the space around her a woman does not necessarily *fill* it the way a solid plugs up a hole. Instead, what happens for her is apt to be a circular stretching such that she touches all the edges without filling up the center, thus still allowing to the interior its essential emptiness.

All of Henry Moore's open-centered sculptures appropriately capture such central emptiness without indicating the dynamic quality of this shape-shifting process. Also relevant, but equally static, is a work by contemporary artist Saint-Phalla entitled *Hon*, a "gigantic reclining woman whose interior is a total environment reminiscent of a circus fun house."[6] The actual experience whereby a housewife expands her interior emptiness is far more similar to the movement of a gas dispersing than to a solid being fitted or fitting itself into a space. This process is reflected in the following lines of Rainer Maria Rilke's poem, "Evening," translated by Randall Jarrell:

> Your life: the fearful and ripening and enormous
> Being that—bounded by everything, or boundless—
> For a moment becomes . . . stars.[7]

The sense of simultaneous dispersal and space present in these lines is what differentiates this feminine experience from its otherwise close, masculine counterparts.

During this extended process of metaphoric stretching which mimics the uterine stretching of childbirth, a housewife eventually comes in contact with most or all of the surfaces within her house in various ways. In so doing, she and the surface she is working on exist briefly in extended relation to each other. For example, when she bends down on hands and knees and carefully scrubs every inch of her kitchen linoleum, she and that surface are interrelating in such a way that she is impressing her bodily weight upon that floor to alter its surface appearance. At the same time that she impresses herself on the floor, she also feels its impress against her knees. As she moves from one section of floor to the next the nature of what is occurring is twofold: ostensibly and obviously she is creating a dirt-free surface to replace the previously scuffed and sticky one. To note her visible accomplishment is to mark what she is doing to the floor. But that is only half of the relationship. In turn, the floor enables her symbolically to stretch herself along its surface so that she fills its entire space, extending out from the center of herself to become, in poet Wallace Stevens's terms, "a self that touches all edges,"[8] or "a giant of herself."[9] This process, by which she enacts herself in space, allows her metaphorically to undergo body transformation. Much as the water in her pail alters its "shape" from pail-sized cylinder to floor-sized square, a housewife typically experiences a similar topological distortion. Yet, unlike the water, she retains her original shape. In this way she is able to extend herself into a realm of being totally alien to herself without actually metamorphosing. A housewife when cleaning is consequently able to relate her body to her surrounding space in ways potentially as varied as those of a dancer, depending, of course, on her agility. The difference is that the dancer is consciously aware of the symbolic impress her body makes upon the space and that the space makes against her body.

To become aware of this body-dimension of cleaning is to gain some understanding of why some women undertake the particular tasks they do. To reach up with a rag-covered broom to clean scarcely visible or even nonexistent cobwebs from a ceiling, for example, may appear needless, yet in so doing a housewife touches the upper surfaces of her house as she more frequently does the floors she scrubs. Both kinds of contact connect her with the vertical dimension of her house. Phenomenologist Gaston Bachelard associates this dimension variously with rationality and irrationality:

> We become aware of this dual vertical polarity of a house if we are sufficiently aware of the function of inhabiting to consider it as an imaginary response to the function of constructing. The dreamer constructs and reconstructs the upper stories and the attic until they are well constructed. And . . . when we dream of the heights we are in the rational zone of intellectualized projects. But for the cellar, the impassioned inhabitant digs and re-digs, making its depth active.[10]

In this age of frequently attic less and sometimes basement less houses, the house-related experience of verticality that Bachelard analyzes is more apt to be experienced through cleaning the heights and depths of a single room rather than a three-storied house. In so doing, the body and mind experiences of the performer so converge that the conventional Cartesian split between them disappears.

Thoroughly cleaning an entire room also allows a housewife to fill its space completely. Such relating to space has very ancient origins in practices such as walking deasil or widdershins—to the right or sunwise—in ritual circumambulation. This is an ancient Celtic practice thought to be lucky. Carried to extremes, of course, such behavior inverts into its demonic counterpart. Such is the case for many of Samuel Beckett's male characters whose preoccupation with their bodies in relation to space is notable in many of his works. A representative example occurs in *Watt*:

> Watt's way of advancing due east, for example, was to turn his bust as far as possible towards the north and at the same time to fling out his right leg as far as possible towards the south and then to turn his bust as far as possible towards the south and at the same time to fling out his left leg as far as possible towards the north . . . and so on, over and over again, many, many times, until he reached his destination, and could sit down.[11]

By contrast with her larger tasks of cleaning—bending down to scrub floors or stretching to remove dust and cobwebs from ceilings—ordinary dusting of objects typically places a housewife in a different relationship to her environment. Here, instead of her body stretching or elongating to shape itself to fill or fit the contours of a room, she herself now becomes a container, but within her own human scale. When she picks up a small ivory Buddha brought back to her from Japan by a friend, and holds it gently and carefully in her hand to remove its coating of dust, she experiences possession in its most tangible form. Because it is small enough to lie almost fully enclosed within her palm, the figurine is able to "be" part of her while yet retaining its own integrity of form as a completely separate object. To feel against her palm its smooth, hard shape, punctured here and there by a groove or sharp point, is to incorporate it into herself without its actually becoming identical with her or she with it.

In addition to enabling her to extend herself and to physically possess objects, cleaning can satisfy a housewife in still another way. The change in appearance from furry (in the case of heavy dust) or dull (in the case of light) to shiny satisfies an inner need for transforming the physical world. While shape and size are not ordinarily affected by removal of dirt unless long-accumulated debris is being removed, surface sheen and texture are. To thus return a previously dull, lustreless surface to a softly glowing patina is but a difference in degree, not kind, from what the sculptor does if her avowed technique is to "uncover" the form latent within her raw marble. Difference in kind does exist, of course, when the sculptor's ideology tells her to impose her own preconceived forms on the stone.

Transformation of one quality into another also predominates in ironing. In this task turning the wrinkled into the smooth and starching the flaccid into the stiff allows the housewife to enjoy the act of doing for its own sake. Here, to a lesser degree than in scrubbing the floor or dusting the ceiling, she extends herself in the act of bearing down with the iron on the soft white cotton of the shirt before her. In this situation she feels herself become an appendage to her arm which in turn is an extension of the hot iron connecting her to the shirt.

Comparable variations on her relationship to her home and the objects in it exist for all the maintenance tasks she performs. To the extent that a homemaker relates to her home as an external image of herself she is simultaneously both making a space, or a world for herself, and, by enactment, enlarging the interior of her body so that she herself becomes a world for herself and for others.

But an ever-present threat to this creation of cosmos is the incursion of chaos. The things that inevitably go wrong around a house tend to assume overwhelmingly disproportionate significance for a woman attuned to the underlying meaning of her role. An invasion of cockroaches, for example, while annoying from a profane perspective, is devastating when perceived as an intrusion of chaos into order. Besides the obvious association roaches have with filth and the implication that they are present because the priestess of the home performs her task inadequately, there is an even more disturbing element present in such an invasion. First, it is likely to be a shocking surprise—something that might happen to someone else, but never to me. Where could such horrible creatures come from? It is as if a plague of locusts had suddenly been visited upon me. Still more threatening is the need to dismantle the kitchen so that the exterminator may spray his smelly poisons. Then to discover that one, two, and even three applications at weekly intervals may not suffice, is to be forced to acknowledge the overwhelming strength of antagonistic chaos. In this small domestic drama occurs a minor reenactment of the ancient fight of Marduk and Tiamat.

I could multiply examples: leaky roofs, erupting sewer systems, broken furnaces—all remind the priestess of her limited powers, her frailty in the face of the enemy. Symbolically, such devastation is far more potent than the actual physical harm it causes.

Far more overtly terrifying are intrusions by strangers. To return home and discover her house vandalized is apt to demoralize a typical housewife far differently from the way it does her husband. To see piles of undergarments and nightwear mixed in with carelessly strewn magazines and dried flowers makes her start. Her nearly empty jewelry box and the gaping hole where the television set used to be occasion heart palpitations. This is *her* house, *her* space. At one level what she feels, along with her husband, is loss of ownership, the indignation so well expressed by E. M. Forster in his essay, "My Wood," when he asks:

Pray, does my wood belong to me or doesn't it? And, if it does, should I not own it best by allowing no one else to walk there? There is a wood near Lyme Regis, also cursed by a public footpath, where the owner has hesitated on this point. He has built high stone walls each side of the path, and has spanned it by bridges, so that the public circulate like termites while he gorges on the blackberries unseen.[12]

But for a housewife the mixture of pain and outrage is likely to go far deeper. Her own inner space has been violated, making her feel almost physically ill. It is as if she had been raped.

The inevitable cleaning up which follows any such major sign of chaos helps relieve her anxiety as much as it returns her home to order. This is also true of less threatening episodes of chaos, for even if she is merely washing dirty stains from her children's clothes, scrubbing greasy frying pans, or disinfecting bathrooms, she is ridding her home and its objects of actual or imagined contamination. Ostensibly such cleansing is done only to restore the unsightly. But many women extend these activities so far beyond that goal that the tacit significance of what they are doing is readily apparent.

In the first place, Western culture in general, and that of the United States in particular, places an unusually high premium on cleanliness. While rites of purification are known in most cultures, such insistent emphasis is not universal. Thus, to assume that what Western or American housewives typically do to the interiors of their houses is a human "norm" is not accurate. You can very well ask those women whose efforts go beyond making a house "look nice" what they are doing. Why, for example, need any floor ever exemplify the well-known saying, "It's clean enough to eat from?" Who really wants to eat from the floor? And what difference can it possibly make if the inside of a collar, which is not visible when worn, has a ring around it?

Often what these women are doing serves exactly the same function as the ritual action of a priest absolving a parishioner from guilt, except that they must function as priestesses for themselves. To absolve or free someone from guilt has obvious affinities with the word "solvent." Both words derive from the Latin *solvere*, meaning to free, release, or loosen. These two words clearly reveal the analogy between dissolving or washing physical stains and washing away the sins of the world. What they fail to reveal is that dissolving a physical stain may function not only to rid a garment or wall of an unsightly blemish, but also to exorcise, for the woman washing it, her own spiritual deformities. Thus while her washing serves the surface purpose of cleaning the garment, the meaning of washing may well be larger. The case of Lady Macbeth with her pitiable cry, "Out, damned spot! Out I say!" accompanying her ritual hand washing, is suggestive.

When a housewife purifies she ensures that the cosmos she creates and maintains is safe. Often the underlying meaning of her housewifely performance resembles that of several American Indians—the Californian Hupa, Karok, and Yurok tribes—whose priests reestablish the cosmos every year through various rituals of cleaning accompanied by appropriate words such as these: "Ixkareya yakam [one of the Immortals] is sweeping this time, sweeping all the sickness out of this world."[13] Other representative rituals besides sweeping include straightening the tipped earth and filling its cracks. What the traditional housewife does may equally destroy "sickness," not just in the obvious physical sense, but in a more abstract, moral fashion as well. If she is a very traditional, strongly family-oriented woman she may not distinguish much between herself and her family. In that case the family unit will be primary, the separate individuals, including herself, secondary. But if she reverses self and family unit she may realize that her needs frequently do not coincide with those of other individuals in the family as a whole. Hence what she enacts may be for herself fully as much as, or even instead of, for them.

A woman who engages in ritual purification for her family needs may quite overtly maintain that she won't allow "filth" in her house, possibly meaning by the term anything from *Playboy* to *Catcher in the Rye*. If she is extreme, she may extend her vigilance from the family-shared rooms to include surveillance of her children's bedrooms, looking there for signs of what she calls dirt: condoms, birth-control pills, and "dirty books," all the way to playing cards and movie ticket stubs if she belongs to a very strict fundamentalist church. In this kind of "purification" she acts primarily as family guardian.

Less apparent variations on this theme are apt to surface if a housewife enacts her purification rites primarily for her own benefit. These variations have to do with her inner conception of what home is all about and, conversely, what it excludes. Although her awareness of this matter is not likely to be fully conscious, she may oppose "home" in her mind to some morally "unclean" place. This may be a topless bar, a brothel, or any such public place, but it is more likely to be a private spot with primarily personal associations. Perhaps she may inwardly recall a spot from her childhood which she has ever since associated with shame and impurity. If as a small girl she was caught and chastised for playing "doctor" with a neighborhood boy in his "hideout," a sloping dirt surface underneath a cellarless house, she may unconsciously envision home and hideout as opposites in her mind. Whether or not the hideout was actually as physically dirty and repugnant as her memory reconstructs it, it is likely to be so in her mind. It is consequently the physical embodiment of whatever the word "shame" means to her.

No matter what the particulars of her inner concept, however, they are likely to incorporate a sense of dirt. Even if shame was no more than her mother saying, "shame, shame," to the dog when it had an accident on the rug, dirt—here in the particularly unacceptable form of excrement—would attach itself firmly in her mind. Ever after the "dirtiness" of the dog's deed would immediately transfer itself to any situation in which she was shamed. Since the dog experience would teach her absolutely that dirt does not belong in the house, she has learned by extension to separate shame from home as well. Consequently, to feel at home with herself is to feel absence of shame. As a result, at a deep level, part of what a housewife purifies when she cleans are her own inner feelings of shame or guilt. Like Lady Macbeth she may well wash for reasons other than the desire for clean hands.

But these sacred processes of ordering and purifying which both alloplastically and autoplastically repeatedly transform chaos into cosmos, are frequently carried to extremes. When that happens, the results, instead of being holy and self-affirming, are demonic, for the ritual enactment of housework can manifest itself in either way. When it is demonic, cosmization is not only highly disagreeable, it is also menacing. The myth of Sisyphus, with its relentlessly repetitive rock-pushing appropriately captures this face of the process. The poet Wallace Stevens puts it well when he says:

> A violent order is disorder: and . . .
> A great disorder is an order. . . . [14]

Instead of being alive, the overly ordered environment is lifeless: a tomb instead of a cosmos. The deadness of such a milieu is readily apparent in Wright Morris' short story "The Ram in the Thicket," whose male protagonist, Mr. Ormsby, feels constrained to tiptoe through his own house. So cowed is this man by his wife (referred to as "Mother" throughout), that he accedes to her dictum that they should actually *live* in only one room: "It was the only room in the house—except for the screened-in porch in the summer—where he could take off his shoes and open his shirt on his underwear."[15] Otherwise, it is the kind of house that is totally protected from life, in which he "couldn't find a place in the house to sit down. . . . Mother had spread newspapers over everything. There hadn't been a chair in the place—except the straight-backed ones at the table—that hadn't been, that wasn't covered with a piece of newspaper."[16]

But while everything that *shows* reflects such "violent order," the inner deadness of this order is obvious in hidden places. For example, when the protagonist

> . . . put his head in the icebox door—in order to see he had to—[he] stopped breathing and closed his eyes. What had been dying for some time was now dead. He leaned back, inhaled, leaned in again. The floor of the icebox was covered with a fine assortment of jars full of leftovers Mother simply could not throw away. Some of the jars were covered with little oilskin hoods, some with saucers, and some with paper snapped on with a rubber band. . . . A jar which might have been carrots—it was hard to tell without probing—was now a furry marvel of green mold.[17]

Here, ordinary household artifacts have clearly been transformed into death's heads.

In some houses, such overt signs of death and decay are never present. In them, deadness may be less insistent: no books, magazines, or newspapers ever accumulate. Dishes are cleaned the moment they are dirtied. Shoes are removed at the door. The dog *never* has an accident. No one ever smokes in such a house. Nothing is ever left half done: everything is always put neatly back in place before a new task is begun.

Such ordering takes immense effort. For its performer, no time is left over. If every cookie baked must be exactly round, then baking takes double the average time. If every item must be ironed, then permanent press might just as well not have been invented. If every object in the house must be dust-free and sparkling, then. . . . There is never enough time. And this is one of the most salient facts of the demonic tug of housewifery: every moment of every single day is precisely accounted for. For some women who succumb to housework's demonic pull, time is so filled that there is no room for surprises. Housework is certainly not done by these women because it needs doing—it is done because they feel compelled to do it. Such women's scrupulosity seems pointless and absurd. And their lives actually appear contentless: what do they *do* all day?

Though external appearances suggest these women don't do anything, if we were to follow some of them around through several typical days, we would discover that they work very hard indeed at tasks less demanding women would not even think of doing: vacuuming already immaculate houses, hand washing every dish before placing it in the dishwasher, ironing sheets, and the like. It only seems like they don't do anything because nothing ever visibly changes in their houses. Such apparently meaningless actions reflect the ever-present threat that the demonic rather than the divine face of ritual enactment will emerge. When this facet of the demonic does take over, the performer is so submerged by her ritual tasks that she hardly continues to exist apart from her work. Instead of the balance between worker and task which exists when enactment is divine, in this case the task swallows up the performer instead. That relationship to housework is just as far removed from divinity as is the ordinary profane performance of the woman who hastens through her tasks heedlessly only longing to get them over and done with.

The objects or props with which a woman surrounds herself are of great significance to the meaning of cosmization and its component, purification. As Wallace Stevens says in his poem "Theory," "One is not duchess/A hundred yards from a carriage."[18] Likewise, many people may not fully experience themselves without certain objects around them. Thus, to be surrounded by familiar objects is part of what is involved in the whole notion of home. Anyone who has been away from home for extended periods of time knows that homesickness means longing for familiar things as well as for family and friends. Much of any individual is reflected in the objects with which he surrounds himself.

Clearly, you can surround yourself in vastly different ways. In our highly suburban, upwardly mobile culture keeping up with the Joneses frequently determines the objects a person selects. Although that syndrome is not sex specific, women more frequently than men are accused of a materialistic preoccupation with objects. Norman Mailer stereotypically makes this point in his essay, "The Case Against McCarthy: a Review of *The Group*," in which he claims that in McCarthy's novel "Everything in the profound materiality of women is given its full stop until the Eggs Benedict and the dress with the white fichu, the pessary and the whatnot sit on the line of the narrative like commas and periods, semicolons, italics and accents. The interplay of the novel exists between the characters and the objects which surround them until the faces are swimming in a cold lava of anality, which becomes the truest part of her group, her glop, her impacted mass."[19]

But critic Patricia Meyers Spacks thoughtfully counters Mailer's patriarchal construction of women's preoccupation with objects. She says that:

> Through things, much fiction implies, women convey their natures. Concretions serve the psyche. Destined by society to assume responsibility for the artifacts of domestic life, women invest with meaning the objects they protect. To perceive clothing as an expression of the self requires no great effort of imagination; to extend human significance to remoter objects, a more demanding exercise, seems equally characteristic of many female novelistic characters. The phenomenon may be taken to illustrate that women are less, not more "crass" than their male counterparts, since their interest focuses not in objects but in the objects' signification.[20]

At a very deep level, objects do appear to possess a power of their own. Some function overtly as amulets: carefully preserved four leaf clovers, rabbit's-foot key chains, found pennies. And some are believed holy: crosses, Bibles, rosaries. But most are not readily categorizable, deriving their "power" less from generally accepted sources than from the personal involvement and associations of their owners, from the investments we individually put into them. In the home, it is not one single article which dominates to become the paramount attribute of the homemaker, but the entire environment, composed of numerous objects. Not all concern for objects is necessarily frivolous and superficial. Clearly, many people strive to keep up with the hypothetical Joneses, and some are Silas Marners driven to hoard for no reason beyond the act of hoarding. But for other people, acquiring, possessing, and giving goods definitely assumes a ritual significance.

This process of acquiring goods can often lead the homemaker out of ordinary space-time into wish space-time. When a homemaker enters wish space-time, she is typically transported into it by one of the ubiquitous women's magazines like *Woman's Day* or *Good Housekeeping* or a mail-order catalog like those from Sears and Penney's. As she pours over her source, gleaning ideas, she vicariously enters the imagined dimension of some other, usually totally anonymous, woman. If, as she enters this wish space-time, she is deepening her commitment to her role, finding in this excursion a heightened pleasure about who she is and what she does, then she may well experience transcendence.

On the other hand, this power of things to transform ordinary space-time cannot be predicted. As with grace, sometimes transformation occurs, sometimes not; neither can be taken for granted. The poet Richard Wilbur in his poem "Love Calls Us to the Things of This World" well illustrates the difference between objects charged with sacred meaning and those which lie heavily within a deadened, totally profane context:

> The eyes open to a cry of pulleys,
> And spirited from sleep, the astounded
>   soul
> Hangs for a moment bodiless and simple
> As false dawn.
> Outside the open window
> The morning air is all awash with angels.[21]

The "angels" with which the morning air is "awash" are laundry: "bedsheets," "blouses," and "smocks." But inevitably

> The soul descends once more in bitter love
> To accept the waking body. . . .[22]

And when that happens the language of transcendence ceases. Wilbur uses the words *gallows, thieves, heaviest* and *dark* to indicate the drop into the profane. Such an occurrence seems to flatten objects so that you can almost *see* their meaning pour out, as if a handleless tap had been turned on. All you can do is stand by, helpless against its loss.

In marked contrast to the absence of meaning objects exhibit in their profane aspect, when their demonic face predominates they are highly powerful. Only this time the power is dangerous rather than potentially redemptive as in their divine manifestations. The broom in the *Sorcerer's Apprentice*, which refuses to cease its labors regardless what command the desperate apprentice shouts is illustrative. It brings in more and more pails of water, flooding the floor instead of merely cleaning it. And when the panic-stricken apprentice seeks to stop it forever by breaking it, each splinter becomes a new broom capable of bringing in its own pails of water. Here is chaos indeed! This motif of the inexhaustible object—whether it is the frenzied broom, the salt-mill which refuses to cease grinding salt, or its less tangible variant, the Midas touch—symbolizes the negative side of the powers inherent in sacrality. Any housewife who has had to stand by as her dishwasher, washing machine, or water heater disgorged water onto her floor knows this demonic power of objects.

For individuals who regularly experience only the profane or demonic aspects of objects it is understandable that consumerism should appear banal or even evil. Indeed, when consuming objects becomes a replacement for self-worth, substituting external props for internal strengths, consumption is as negative as any other form of escapism. In this regard a major argument often levelled against ritual buying, or consumerism, is that it is anticreative. Certainly buying something is not the same as making it yourself. But just because the two processes differ does not mean that only one can be creative. The relationship of buyer to object cannot be so peremptorily dismissed. The buyer who has previously entered wish space-time may well have invested significant time and energy in considering the object she is now about to buy. Though she is not its actual fabricator, the object may well feel like "hers" in a way that renders it extremely significant to her. Surely all of us have experienced such a highly personal sense of possession with at least some of the objects surrounding us. Consider blue jeans, for example. Who is willing to settle for just any old pair? Who would send away for them sight unseen? Why do we feel that way about jeans?

While some people appear not to care about any objects whatsoever, most fall along the middle of a scale between the extremes of excessive indifference or intense concern. What many people feel towards their jeans or other favored clothes, a creative homemaker feels towards the possessions in her house. Each one says something about her. The cumulative effect of one more added to the rest matters considerably. And this cumulative effect can transform consumerism into ritual buying, making the act far more creative than it is ordinarily considered to be. Assembling a pleasing array of objects demands creativity. It is, after all, the same principle as that involved in creating a collage, an assemblage, or an environment. But because a home is thought to be primarily functional, its creation is seldom considered comparable to that of an art work except when executed by "professionals"—architects and decorators.

Yet often the line separating a homemaker's enactment (by which she creates her interior space) from similar creations by artists is extremely tenuous. Consider the artistic phenomenon of the "found object" as opposed to the intentionally created one. Such an object is precisely what its name implies; it may originally have been natural, machine-made, or crafted, and it may be as simple as a pebble or as complex as a machine. A found object exists at one level of artistic complexity below a collage or assemblage, which also consist of ready-made items. In the case of both collages and assemblages, however, the components are physically reformed into some other entity. By contrast, a "found object" retains its own original identity, receiving no further physical or external transformation aside from the possible application of a title and a frame. What it definitely receives is a change of setting. It would seem, basically, that it is primarily this change, combined with the intent of the artist, which elevates the found object to its status as art. Now what happens when this same impulse to find an object strikes a housewife and she feels impelled to bring into her house an assortment of seashells and water-polished pebbles? Why are they not art?

While it is relatively easy to dismiss the marine assortment as trite because it has been "done" so many times before, it is important to recognize that similar urges often motivate the officially recognized artist and the housewife: both may be trying to make statements; both may revel in aesthetic components such as color, shape, and texture; both may desire to express themselves. Both, therefore, may actually be engaged in doing the same thing, although one may succeed better than the other.

The difference between the two of them begins to shrink when we consider the homemaker who disdains obvious found objects but delights in scavenging dumps and junk shops. If the Dadaists were able to shock by placing a toilet in a museum, why can't a housewife be credible if she displays rocks, glass, and scrap metal? Why must the altered setting be a *museum?* As a matter of fact, nowadays much officially acknowledged art is not museum art. The trend toward earthworks such as Robert Smithson's spiral road built into the great Salt Lake in Utah (*The Spiral Road, 1970*), for example, is about as far removed from traditional museum art as anything could be. Yet the home, generally, is not accorded the same dignity as the museum or "acceptable" alternative settings. What has been created there has typically been denigrated as something "lower," as mere craft in contrast to high art.

Yet there are some exceedingly interesting cases of recognized artists who have extended their art into their homes in ways far beyond hanging paintings or displaying sculptures. One is Kurt Schwitters, the Berlin artist who turned the interiors of three of his own habitats into strangely angled environments incorporating openings and objects commemorating his constructivist and Dadaist friends. Throughout the 1920s his first *Merzbau,* as he called these "sculptures," so filled his Hanover house that he had to extend it to the second story. These strange plaster constructions somewhat resemble three-dimensional Cubist paintings of the analytic type.

Then there is the curious case of Simon Rodia, the uneducated, self-taught Italian immigrant whose early jobs included quarry, railroad, construction, and tile work. At age forty he suddenly began building his towers, strange glass, shell, tile, pipe, and bed-frame constructions that he felt impelled to erect. Though these were not interior environments, they massively patterned the lot in the Watts area of Los Angeles where he erected them because he "had in mind to do something big. . . ."[23] Where do we draw the line and why do we draw it, between the untrained woman or man who erects strange backyard objects, a Simon Rodia, and a Kurt Schwitters?

Still better known is Louise Nevelson, whose striking all-white or all-black wooden constructions, collages, and environments created over the past thirty years have come to be very well received indeed. Besides showing these room-sized structures which not only fill, but totally dominate the interior spaces of the rooms in which they are placed, she also has placed them within her own living quarters. Thus she lives surrounded by floor-to-ceiling boxes painted all white or black containing assorted objects and bits and pieces all arranged to shape the space around them. The result possesses the surreal quality of a dream. What she has created goes far beyond placing paintings on walls or sculptures on pedestals: she has created a home that is all environment, using the word in its artistic sense. But Nevelson's, Rodia's, and Schwitters' art merely externalizes and makes explicit what can occur within any home at the tacit level, albeit, for the most part, less aesthetically.

Every homemaker (if not every housewife), after all, creates an ambience that marks her family's home as peculiarly theirs. The colors they or she repeatedly choose, the kinds of material, the period of furnishings, the presence or absence of clutter, even the odors all contribute to the total effect. Typically, the average homemaker does not consciously think out every component of the ambience she creates to the same extent an artist would. If she did it would no longer be tacit, but explicit. Nonetheless, she is aware of certain effects she wishes to achieve, just as she knows quite clearly when a result violates her inner sense of what is appropriate to her.

Furthermore, it is common for a homemaker to physically construct, as well as buy and discover, the objects in her home. Often she engages in one or more of the so-called domestic arts—sewing, embroidery, spinning, weaving, quilting, knitting, pottery making, and other assorted crafts. But the fact that these arts are typically labeled "domestic" and "crafts" automatically trivializes them in the eyes of many people who may, nonetheless, applaud these same arts when they are performed by men (and sometimes women) outside the homemaker's role. The following commentary on embroidery is representative:

> Embroidery may rightly be considered as one of the oldest of arts, but it has unfortunately not received the study it deserves; mainly because it is regarded as an applied art and also because it is often despised as feminine.[24]

Yet often the difference between what a housewife and an "officially recognized" artist like Nevelson does is merely a matter of degree. An artist, even one whose work is highly intuitive, is usually highly attuned to the inner feelings and images which go into his or her art. By contrast, a homemaker may correspondingly grope for inner feelings and images, sometimes recognizing their embodiment in what she produces, but just as often failing to actualize them in finished form. Whether or not a housewife "succeeds" from an external perspective by producing recognizable, artistic products, the *process* involved in her acts is creative. Like an officially recognized artist, she engages in the age-old endeavor attributed in all cultures to deity or demiurge, whereby

> [deity] create [s] the heavens and the earth. The earth [is] without form and void, and darkness [is] upon the face of the deep . . . (Genesis I:1–2).

6
CARETAKING

According to an old jingle, "though she works from sun to sun, a housewife's work is never done." Just as her tasks are many, the underlying ritual significance of what a housewife does includes more than community with ancestors and the various facets of cosmization. Caretaking is another primary religious pattern inherent in housekeeping. Aside from caring for the objects, plants, and pets which constitute elements of her physical world, a traditional housewife is expected to care for others—children, aging parents, spouse, and sometimes other relatives or in-laws. In her role of caretaker what she does is largely invisible and seemingly product-free, as in the case of cleaning. Mary Gordon captures this quality well in the voice of Isabel Moore, her protagonist in *Final Payments:*

> Care of an invalid has this great virtue: one never has to wonder what there is to do. Life is simple and inevitable and straightforward. . . . My life had the balletic attraction of routine. Eleven years of it: bringing him breakfast, shaving him, hating to look at his face, twisted from the stroke in a way that made me forget the possibility of beauty. And the bath. Moving his body around, the incredible weight of that body even though it appeared so thin, his left side paralyzed because something had gone wrong with the right side of his brain. Sliding bedpans under

him, looking at the misery of his buttocks. And the smell of his urine and his feces that, loving him as I did, I ought never to have known. And then I would pull him in the chair and wheel him into the kitchen because after all that, the morning was gone and it was time to make lunch.[1]

Just to keep an invalid or infant alive requires enormous expenditures of energy. But a day spent maintaining a life seldom has anything to show for it. The individual survives but that is what was expected. Or, if it is an infant, on an ordinary day she won't have grown visibly, won't have spoken her first intelligible word, and won't have learned to totter precariously for the very first time in an upright position.

"Growing" a human being is so very slow that nothing seems to happen. One of the most illuminating accounts of the process is, ironically, the creation of a purely imaginary child. In Edward Albee's play *Who's Afraid of Virginia Woolf?*, the leads, George and Martha, engage in a game of "Bringing up Baby," as part of a long evening of not very funny games with their young guests Nick and Honey. But "Bringing up Baby" merely culminates years of previously private pretense that they are, in fact, the parents of a son now about to turn twenty-one. In their version of child-rearing he had

> teddy bears and transparent floating goldfish, and a pale blue bed with cane at the headboard when he was older, cane which he wore through . . . finally . . . with his little hands . . . in his sleep. . . . And a croup tent . . . a pale green croup tent, and the shining kettle hissing in the one light of the room that time he was sick . . . those four days . . . and animal crackers, and the bow and arrow he kept under his bed. . . .[2]

And in their imagined reminiscences the pretend child takes shape: a composite of their two imaginations, sometimes grotesque, sometimes sentimental, the result a caricature of what any parent is apt to recollect. As in this purely imaginary case, it is only after the fact that the tangible results of growth and progress can actually be seen. At the time almost nothing seems to happen.

Yet, conversely, the time of growing a human can feel so perversely short that nothing seems to get done at all. When that happens chaos disrupts the anticipated order of the way everything *should* be. John Updike captures this demonic face of caretaking in *Rabbit, Run*, when the young parents, Rabbit and Janice, try to adjust to the crying of their second baby, newly brought home from the hospital. Her crying, for which they can find no particular reason, disturbs their day:

> Outside the sky holds a wide queenly state, blue through the hours, and Rabbit is further panicked by the thought that on such a day his parents used to take them on long pleasant walks, that they are wasting

a beautiful Sunday. But they can't get organized enough to get out. . . . They sip soup by the flickering light of Rebecca's urgent cries, her fragile voice is a thin filament burning with erratic injections of power. But . . . amid the stacked dishes on the sink, under the worn and humid furniture, and in the coffin-like hollow of the plaited crib . . . suddenly she is quiet, leaving behind a solemn guilty peace. They had failed her.[3]

But a failure still more profound awaits them. In one of the most frightening child-rearing scenes in literature, Updike details horror of the kind which makes caretaking of any sort so onerous. Janice, who has been drinking, fills the bathtub, preparing to give Rebecca her bath.

> The wavery gray line of the water is almost up to the lip of the tub. On the skin quick wrinkles wander and under it a deep mass waits colorless. . . . [Janice] tips too much trying to dig the tiny rubber thing out of the chair so drops to her knees and scoops Rebecca into her arms and carries her into the bathroom. . . . She drops gently to her knees by the big calm tub and does not expect her sleeves to be soaked. The water wraps around her forearms like two large hands; under her amazed eyes the pink baby sinks down like a gray stone. . . . And she knows, knows, while knocks sound at the door, that the worst thing that has ever happened to any woman in the world has happened to her.[4]

The horror of that drowning scene, with Janice trying to retrieve the slippery, elusive baby is "only a moment, but a moment dragged out in a thicker time."[5] "Thicker times" are what consistently fill the caretaker's life with dread. A back turned for just an instant may occasion irreversible damage, even death. The back door of a fourth-floor apartment momentarily left unlatched and a toddling two-year-old wanders out onto the unscreened fire escape; the spaghetti pot of boiling water left unwatched for just the moment it takes to walk across the floor to the phone; the Drano accidently set under the bathroom sink instead of in the locked cellar cabinet: any one such moment can change a child's life forever. It is to avoid such catastrophes that women have consistently set aside their own lives and lived for others. Such is the nature of caretaking.

Occasionally, however, caretaking, despite its ordinarily goal-less nature, partakes of questing. To actually preserve a life can lift a caretaker far out of her normal pattern, taking her, in effect, into what is traditionally considered a more exciting, masculine mode: questing. Eudora Welty vividly presents such a shift in her short story "The Worn Path," in which a black woman, so aged that a passerby thinks she must be a hundred years old, functions as caretaker to her ailing, lye-scarred grandson. Regularly, when his medicine runs out, she walks the long

miles to town, often forgetting, through senility, either where she is or
the nature of her errand. Yet she manages this quest for healing, even
to the point of scrounging a few pennies for a small gift for him. As
recollection of why she has come all this long way slowly comes back
to her, she expresses the essence of caretaking in its most positive form:

> "My little grandson, he sit up there in the house all wrapped up,
> waiting by himself. . . . We is the only two left in the world. He suffer
> and it don' seem to put him back at all. He got a sweet look. He going
> to last. He wear a little patch quilt and peep out, holding his mouth
> open like a little bird. I remembers so plain now. I not going to forget
> him again, no, the whole enduring time. I could tell him from all the
> others in creation."[6]

Equally positive for a woman may be the caretaking involved in her
role as a giver of physical nourishment which may also include the
planting of crops and the husbandry of animals. As in other tasks she
undertakes, in preparing food for herself and her family a housewife
may or may not be performing ritual enactment. Surely if she loathes
cooking and seizes any excuse to serve frozen T.V. dinners or hot dogs
and canned beans to a family she has raised to accept and even prefer
such fare, she is unlikely to engage in her task in such a way as to break
through the profane level of performance. But if she lovingly pours over
cookbooks and selects with care the choicest produce and meats she can
afford, chances are she enters, at least occasionally, the sacred realm of
the great goddesses.

In this realm, abundance is the primary attribute. The essence of this
particular kind of traditional feminine abundance is well described in
Willa Cather's *My Antonia* when, towards the end of the book, the
narrator, Jim Burden, stops off to see his old friend Antonia, now a
middle-aged mother of nearly a dozen children. At the urging of several
of Antonia's younger children, Jim tours the fruit cellar where he sees,
among other things "three small barrels . . . one full of dill pickles, one
full of chopped pickles, and one full of pickled watermelon rinds."[7] That
the abundance of this cellar, which matches that of the dinner table, is
a reflection of Antonia is made explicitly clear in this passage:

> She had only to stand in the orchard, to put her hand on a little crab
> tree and look up at the apples, to make you feel the goodness of planting
> and tending and harvesting at last. All the strong things of her heart
> came out in her body, that had been so tireless in serving generous
> emotions.
>   It was no wonder that her sons stood tall and straight. She was a
> rich mine of life, like the founders of early races.[7a]

In myth there are several variations on this theme of the all-providing mother. Often it is a vessel or magic object, as in the case of the well-known "endless-pitcher" from Ovid's tale of "Baucis and Philemon." In this tale Jupiter and Mercury, weary of Olympus, wander on earth in disguise, searching for someone to invite them in for a meal. After receiving countless refusals, they are finally welcomed into the lowly hut of Baucis and Philemon who immediately prepare the best their poverty allows. As the two guests drink, their hosts' wine flagon miraculously remains full. Slowly it occurs to the old couple that their wine vessel has become endless. A similar motif occurs in the Grimms' fairy tale "The Table, the Ass, and the Stick." Here the owner of a magic table has only to utter the words "table be covered," for it to be immediately set with a full meal. Such endless vessels and magical providing objects reflect a child's early relationship to its mother when her milk appears endless and food seems magically to issue from her. Though such abundance may seem to be primarily for her family, its presence may carry an entirely different meaning for the woman herself. To her it may well symbolize her own strength and self-sufficiency, particularly if, like Antonia, she plants and tends as well as prepares the provisions she feeds her family.

As with various facets of cosmization such as ordering, purification, and ritual buying, the acts concerned with gathering and preparing food need not exclude the woman herself. Though providing for her family's nutritional and gustatory needs may appear, and often is, primary, a housewife may also engage in ritual eating on her own behalf to include taking care of herself as well as others. For example, she may treat herself sporadically, or on a daily basis, to coffee brewed only for herself, a ritual which may function as her own private communion, not unlike one Randall Jarrell details through his child persona in his poem "The Lost World":

> . . . some coffee—
> One spoonful—is poured out into my milk
> And the milk, transubstantiated, is coffee.[8]

For a housewife, as for Jarrell's child-persona, the ritual transubstantiation verifies the actuality of the "adult world," and legitimates the existence of the communicant in it. In her case, however, it may not be the "same" adult world shared by fathers; instead, she typically reestablishes her membership in the world shared by mothers. As with any of the tasks she performs, this self-serving coffee break can link her back to her own mother and the company of foremothers. Furthermore, by preparing the coffee *especially* for herself, she functions as priestess—or mother—to herself, an important sacramental benefit of the ritual transubstantiation.

Yet the food-giving side of housework also has its demonic as well as its divine and profane manifestations. Ordinarily whatever a housewife cooks—even if she has worked for hours or even days—is destroyed almost the minute it is completed. Occasionally a guest or family member may remark of a particularly spectacular creation, "It's too pretty to eat." Yet, pretty or not, the handiwork is always eaten. To work so hard and yet end up with no tangible evidence of her labor is a familiar pattern of a housewife's life. But although the interconnection between creation and decreation, order and chaos is everywhere apparent within the rituals of housekeeping, it is truly startling in those related to food. When a housewife cleans and orders for the purpose of returning un- wanted chaos to the expected order of the household, her children and family members will quickly destroy its order of cleanliness. But whereas dirt and mess are tangible, cleanliness is a negative state, generally understood as an absence of disarray and filth rather than as a positive presence of order. Therefore, when cleanliness is destroyed, something is added. By contrast, prepared food is visibly and positively present; when it is consumed something is lost.

The rapid decreation which eating effects parallels that of dance and music in contrast to the plastic arts. As choreographer Yvonne Rainer says, "I remember thinking that dance was at a disadvantage in relation to sculpture in that the spectator could spend as much time as he re- quired examining a sculpture, walk around it, and so forth—but a dance movement—because it happened in time—vanished as soon as it was executed."[9]

For a housewife who is oriented towards end products and tangibility, such deconstructive patterns are difficult to cope with. Yet contemporary artists who normally work in more tangible mediums than the space of dancers sometimes intentionally create objects, works, or enactments intended for immediate destruction. Widely known in this regard is the Swiss-born artist Jean Tinguely, who in 1960 created a gigantic assem- blage called *Homage to New York* out of bicycle wheels, automobile tires, string, rubber balloons, piano parts, and broken planks. This assemblage was supposed to consume itself in flames in the garden of the Museum of Modern Art in New York City. Ironically, destruction did not take place without some help from the New York City fire department.

As anthropologist Victor Turner says, behind such impulses towards ritual destruction there may lie the "human impulse to assert the con- trary value to structure that distances and distinguishes man from man and man [sic] from absolute reality, describing the continuous in dis- continuous terms."[10] To illustrate his point Turner details a ritual of decreation among the Bomba of northeastern Zambia which precedes a young woman's marriage. For a number of days pottery figurines are made, each representing a different obligation of the bride. Within two hours of the figurines' creation they are suddenly pulled apart and destroyed.

For a housewife, cooking undeniably functions to some extent this way. Of course she also eats. But she may disengage her creating self from her consuming self. That way she can simultaneously experience meals as decreation rituals, for only when consumed can her food, no matter how beautiful, be said to have fulfilled its end. Furthermore, because the food a woman prepares for her family seems also to be an extension of her all-nourishing breasts, family meals may function at one level as analogues of the Eucharistic feast. As Sartre says, "To eat is to appropriate by destruction; it is at the same time to be filled up with a certain being." Every meal can thus be seen at one level as a sacrifice in which the bountiful mother is symbolically consumed through the food she proffers.

Such a matrifocal view, which suggests that humans perpetually feast on their mothers, runs strongly counter to Freud's persuasive argument in *Totem and Taboo* for just the opposite position. According to him, in prehistoric times humans killed what he calls the primal father. Over the course of time this original sin was commemorated by ritual re-enactment. Sacrificial feasting on the forbidden totem animal which stood in the father's place allowed the guilty descendants periodically to reexperience the ancestral deed.

Freud considers the consumption of Christ's body and blood in Holy Communion as continued expiation for that early crime, thus ignoring the naturally observable phenomenon that we are all born of the water and blood of *women!* By Freud's reasoning, Christ functions as a kind of primordial mother goddess, disguised as a man. Freud says: ". . . in the Christian doctrine mankind most unreservedly acknowledges the guilty deed of primordial times because it now has found the most complete expiration for this deed in the sacrificial death of the son. The reconciliation with the father is the more thorough because simultaneously with this sacrifice there follows the complete renunciation of women, for whose sake mankind [sic] rebelled against the father."[12] Without arguing either for or against Freud's view you can nonetheless affirm that a continued daily feasting on the sacrificial mother exists tacitly alongside the periodic ritual of Holy Communion.

The reverse side of the sacrificial mother is just as terrifying. You need only think of such figures as the witch in "Hansel and Gretel" or the wicked queen in "Snow White" to recall the potential exchange of roles in this death-dealing pattern. Then decreation extends beyond the food and its cook to those who consume it as well. Literal poisoning by housewives is relatively rare, but metaphorically and stereotypically mothers are frequently thought to poison their children's minds or to "devour" them with their love. Less open to question, perhaps, is the tendency of some mothers to overfeed or even force-feed their children and mislead them into poor lifetime food habits by bribing them with sweets to behave or perform according to maternal requirements. Little wonder that the food-giving aspects of housewifery remain so highly charged for most individuals for life, sometimes resulting in such extremes as obesity, anorexia nervosa, and the compulsive eating of bulimia. In such demonic reversals of what *caretaking* ordinarily suggests, the words *I'll take care of you* assume a deeply menacing quality.

Homecoming

To be taken care of in the fullest, most positive sense is to come home. Homecoming, a ritual which closely relates to the rites surrounding food, requires a family dwelling that is truly a home, not merely a house. As a home, this dwelling effectively protects its occupants from profane intrusion and successfully externalizes selfhood. Furthermore, it represents both physical and psychic safety. It makes its occupants feel "at home," freeing them to be who and what they most deeply conceive themselves to be. Profane masks and roles have no place here. As when Jews and Christians confront the Old Testament God, occupants must dare to enter metaphorically naked. Ideally, they are freed from shame, no matter what their secret transgressions.

When a housewife is truly functioning as a priestess presiding over the sacred space of her home, she embodies welcome. For small children, she may rush out the door, arms extended for a body-encompassing hug; for teenagers she may sit quietly, an after-school snack awaiting their entry while she remains at the kitchen table prepared to share their day. And for her spouse, a loving smile, gentle hug, and freely-given kiss suggesting later consummation may combine with odors of roasting meat and perking coffee to manifest welcome. And for guests to whom she opens her home, she may smile, offering an outstretched hand, a warm hug, or perhaps a kiss. In these ways the priestess and her temple imperceptibly merge to equally welcome homecomers. Thus the woman of the house functions as its *numen* or genius, making visible its otherwise hidden essence.

Mystery—which connects naturally to "home" and "origins"—is central to homecoming. To the extent that a homemaker is willing to embody this mystery by enacting the role of welcoming mother to her spouse as well as her children, she may feel satisfied.

But family expectations of maternally warm welcomes place a heavy burden on a homebound woman. Particularly is this so if she feels uncomfortable enacting the role of earth mother. If that role never matches her self-image, being forced into it may make her so ill at ease that she wonders how and why she ended up in her particular life context. If she sees herself as a princess, or worse, a prince, she can't help but abhor her lot as earth mother. Furthermore, if welcoming is a chore for her instead of a means for giving pleasure, homecoming will result in a failed communion. At times neither wine nor wafer uplifts; comparable failure threatens every homecoming. Just as certain aspects of housekeeping are frequently perceived as chores—dusting, ironing, washing—but may be experienced as sacred rituals, ones more often experienced as joyful rituals may lose their meaning. When that happens, as in the situation of communion wafer clinging gummily and indigestibly to the roof of a dry mouth, homecoming goes flat and gray, losing its original promises of fullness and goldenness. What was so joyfully anticipated, at whatever level of awareness, now eludes both husband and wife in the suddenly stifling air. In contrast to a positive return in which familiar odors, colors, sounds, shapes, and textures all seem to leap forward as the housewife greets the returnee, now everything remains a bleak and dreary undifferentiated mass as she stands there with eyes glazed feeling the moment slip away. Against its falling, and her inner feelings of helpless rage at this imposed burden of priestly greeter, she stands inert; she might as well be officiating in the stale-smelling, blandly appointed interior of a Holiday Inn.

With such a start, the celebration subsequent to homecoming, whether the traditional shared daily evening meal or a sit-down dinner for twelve, is unlikely to succeed. But even if the initial stage of homecoming, the act of greeting, is successful, the following event may nonetheless go flat. One of the funniest, yet saddest, literary depictions of such failure occurs in Ann Beattie's book *Chilly Scenes of Winter*, in which two contemporary young men attempt to conduct a civilized sit-down dinner for themselves:

> "Well," Sam says. "This is a fine celebration."
>
> "I'm glad you like it."
>
> "Beats Christmas dinner all to hell. She [his mother] really *had* parsnips, to shut Eleanor up. Have you ever tasted a parsnip?"
>
> "Not to my knowledge."
>
> "They're foul. They smell like Vanish."
>
> "What's that?"
>
> "Stuff you put down your toilet."
>
> "Shut up about the toilet when I'm eating."
>
> "Sorry. I was just thinking about those rotten parsnips."

"Drop it. I don't want to think about the toilet when I'm eating."

"More lima beans?" Sam says.

"Thanks," Charles says.

"More than that?" Sam says.

"That's fine."

Sam dumps the rest on his plate trying, unsuccessfully, to hold back the water with his fork.

"Some frozen vegetables taste very good," Sam says.

"These were canned," Charles says.

"Oh yeah? Well, they're very good. There's plenty of vegetables I don't mind. Hell. I never eat vegetables any more."

"We're probably going to get scurvy or something. Did you know that when old people have varicose veins it's the start of scurvy? Malnutrition?"

"Shut up about disgusting diseases while I'm eating. You don't hear me talking about the toilet, do you?"

"Stop mentioning the goddamn toilet."

"This is really very good wine," Sam says.

"It ought to be."

"It was awfully nice of you to fix us this big dinner."[13]

In this amusing parody of unsuccessful dinner hours, the scene inevitably keeps returning to the disagreeable talk of toilets, the way so many spouses' conversations trigger dinner table arguments.

Aside from the ever-present danger of such demonic inversions of homecoming, another associated liability threatens a traditional housewife. While she can perform the ritual of homecoming for her spouse and children, she herself can seldom participate except as priestess. In a traditionally structured family her husband and children leave home on a daily basis for work and school, but as a full-time homemaker she does not. Thus the sharp distinction between home and not-home experienced by those fortunate enough to travel freely and regularly between both worlds blurs, sometimes even becoming nonexistent for her. Like a psychiatrist or priest who ministers constantly to others, she may find ritual release difficult or impossible for herself.

This difficulty is compounded by the fact that homecoming, for many husbands, is most fully realized through sex. In the act of love a man most truly goes home in the sense that Norman O. Brown means when he says, "all coitus is a return to the womb." In coitus the return to origins is symbolically complete—but only for him, not for her. That discrepancy raises very serious issues. To what extent, if at all, can she go home? By what means can she return: Where is the symbolic womb for her to reenter? Though she can both inhabit and symbolically be home for him, for others, and even for herself, by what means can she be enabled to return to a home outside herself as a man can? Most importantly, is this difference actually the disadvantage it appears to be given the phallocentric assumptions our culture perpetuates in the think-ing of women as well as men?

Some women do experience this inability to enact the return home in the manner of men as if it were a deprivation. When women react this way they are placing their major emphases on the past, idealizing the uterine state at the expense of what initially enabled it to exist: the uterus or the mother herself. The negative side of this orientation, which con-stitutes a major theme of our Western culture, is not only regressive and infantile, it also lies at the heart of phallocentric consciousness. While both its regressiveness and infantilism are self-evident, its phallocentric nature needs careful examination. Relevant here are some of Sartre's comments on holes, alluded to earlier in connection with a housewife's relation to the interior spaces of her home. In this particualr passage, now well known to most feminists, Sartre views the hole in its most negative aspect:

> The obscenity of the feminine sex is that of everything which "gapes open." It is an *appeal to being* as all holes are. In herself woman appeals to a strange flesh which is to transform her into a fullness of being by penetration and dissolution. Conversely woman senses her condition as an appeal precisely because she is "in the form of a hole." . . . Beyond any doubt her sex is a mouth and a voracious mouth which devours the penis—a fact which can easily lead to the idea of castration. The amorphous act is the castration of the man; but this is above *all* because sex is a hole.[14]

Sartre's negative words depict the counterpart of a woman's experi-ence of deprivation: Sartre, too, emphasizes loss, but from a masculine perspective. Yet a man's experience is an anticipated or feared loss of what he has; a woman's, an absence or loss of something she has never had. Implicit in Sartre's words are Freud's theories of feminine penis-envy and masculine fear of castration.

In what ways, if at all, is it legitimate to speak of penis envy? Most feminists have bitterly denounced that theory, seeing in it additional glorification of masculinity and its most prominent accoutrement. Yet if two underlying meanings of Home are womb and mother, the question remains: How can a woman imaginally project herself back into that original of all sacred spaces? Unless you totally discount body and body parts in considering the relationship between ritual and myth, then differences in female and male body parts do make a significant differ-ence. This difference matters not just at the level of body surfaces, but deep within an individual's psyche as Freud claims. To feel yourself as an interior space is simply not the same as to experience yourself as a solidly enlarging projectile. By what ritual act, if any, can a woman possibly duplicate that archetypally masculine experience of enlargement which *fills* space instead of *becoming* space? Perhaps more importantly, why does she feel she must do so? Is it because she has so internalized a masculine value system that she assumes it is an essentially *human* experience?

But if such a ritualized imaginative return to origins does exist for women, the principle involved should be the same as that described earlier for women's relationships to interior space and the objects within it. The imagined stretching she enacts to fill an interior is very much a vaginal image in which she feels herself expand to approximate a circle or a hole. By contrast, the image described earlier of a woman ironing (or sweeping or vacuuming as the case may be) focuses on the woman as arm: all the essence of her being pours into that one limb, which in turn attaches to the iron before uniting her to the shirt beneath. In that situation she is her arm and her arm is she. Similarly, from what numerous male writers say, in the act of sex a man "becomes" his penis: all his being focuses and concentrates in that one organ. And while a woman may similarly "become" her vagina, that is a very different experience.

Unless you consider a woman's clitoris, a woman has no organ comparable to a penis by which she can *propel* herself. And unlike amputees who experience phantom pain in the region of their severed limbs, women have no body image of an organ by or with which to imaginally experience penile propulsion. To "imagine," in the sense that I can imagine a purple rhinoceros wearing a flower-bedecked straw hat, is not what is involved here. Rather, a full body experience of the kinesthetic sort is required. In such an experience my muscles, skin, and bones must feel, without necessarily physically moving at all, an imitation of what they would feel if they actually were in motion. For instance, if I am riding in the front seat of a car driven by my heedless aunt who insists on driving at forty miles per hour right up to within five feet of the car stopped at the red light in front of her before she begins to brake, I am apt involuntarily to "brake" for her. Yet politeness forbids my actually moving my leg; the "braking" takes place entirely within the memory of my bracing leg muscles. For that kind of body imagination to occur, as opposed to the purely mental imagination we ordinarily mean when we use that word, necessitates an appropriate body part. Thus, for a woman to propel herself back into a womb by means of a sex organ she does not possess, seems unlikely, despite Norman O. Brown's contention that women imagine penises for themselves. For a woman the sex act is not homecoming, but its inversion: she is the welcomer who provides the homecoming. Like it or not, on one level in the sex act she is the mother, just as her partner is the son. While their relationship is undeniably complementary, it is not the reciprocal relationship that Norman O. Brown's words "all coitus is return to the womb,"[15] imply. Being the womb is not the same as entering it.

For a woman to circumvent the emptiness at the center of her home-bound experience and keep it from engulfing her demonically instead of enlarging her divinely, demands a different ritual model. As with a man, homecoming for her necessitates prior leave-taking, for how can there be home*coming* for someone who has been at home the whole time? For her, the ritual must therefore vary immensely: she must, par-adoxically, go somewhere else, away from home.

In contrast to the ubiquitous mother/son patterns of ancient myth which sexual intercourse ritually reenacts at one level, the myth of Demeter and Persephone reflects a countering mother/daughter pattern. In this tale Demeter is the mother goddess whose beloved daughter, Persephone, disappears one day while plucking flowers in a field. Un-beknownst to Demeter, Hades, god of the underworld, has abducted her to be his bride. Demeter's subsequent sorrow with its attendant withering of the earth so devastates the world that Zeus intervenes. Persephone may return to her mother on the condition that she has not partaken of any food in the underworld. But sly Hades offers her three pomegranate seeds which she unwittingly consumes. The agreement is necessarily changed: Persephone will spend two-thirds of the year with her mother and the remaining third with her husband. Every year there-after she rises up from Hades at the appointed time to live with her mother; conversely, she must also return at the end of eight months to her husband. Persephone therefore has two homes: her home of origins with her mother and her present adult home with her husband. Because the story is told from the perspective of her mother, Persephone's home-coming is her ascent to Demeter, not her descent to Hades.

Although the emphases of this myth generally stress the death and resurrection or seasonal themes, there is another way to look at it. The sources which merge both mother and daughter into one image (fre-quently given the general name Kore), are many. The descent into Hades can be seen as departure from the natural mother, the process which occurs in traditional society when a woman marries. In the myth, of course, the marriage and the descent are overtly equivalent. The return to the mother (which is particularly blurred) very much suggests, in addition to its accustomed meanings, the maturation rather than the regression of the daughter, a condition, which renders her virtually indistinguishable from her mother. When, or if, a woman achieves this stage, she has achieved the capability of being mother to or caretaker of herself, a very significant step for any human.

Thus, is it possible that, for women, homecoming necessarily involves a return to a mother or her surrogate rather than the presence of her husband? The patterns of some women do, indeed, suggest that this may be a possibility. It is not at all uncommon, for instance, that homemakers, particularly young ones, seek each other out and unconsciously function for each other as surrogate mothers. You frequently see two young mothers pushing their strollers side by side. Often such homebound women form loose networks whereby they informally extend their otherwise nuclear families to include a number of similarly confined young women and preschoolers. Husbands may or may not be included for evening socializing.

Besides a shared daily walk, various women friends may also share such chores as grocery shopping, baby-sitting, and even ironing. Furthermore, morning coffee, even lunch, are frequently shared as well. In this way a woman who goes to her friend's home can experience to some degree the ritual homecoming traditionally habitual to her spouse. Though it is not her own home which greets her, she may well discover in her visit the joy of being cared for and fussed over maternally. For example, she may be intimate enough with one or more women to freely pop in and out at any time just as she typically does with her own home. Consequently, she may sometimes reexperience her lost childhood role as she sits at her friend's kitchen table drinking coffee and watching her iron. How often she sat just so (minus the coffee) in her mother's house, talking of the school day's events. Conversely, when her friend comes to her house she may reciprocate by plying her with some homemade tidbit or other. Simultaneously, she enacts the gracious hostess and the all-providing mother.

These intimate friendships between women frequently involve the same taken-for-granted quality usually reserved for family alone. Close women friends typically will assume without question the care of one or more children when a crisis occurs. Of course, almost anyone will perform such service briefly in an emergency, but these are gifts of time and care far more lavish—full care of a one-year-old for three days, a full week of daily morning help during a convalescent period, daily dinners for a temporarily wifeless husband. Yet this closeness of homebound women is frequently maligned by men and professional women. Typically, males dis-value it by humor, selecting for particular mockery the coffee klatch.

Though the coffee klatch phenomenom does, perhaps, seem like a luxurious "waste" of time to individuals forced into masculine, linear time, to construe it that way is to miss its significance. In one sense, it is both life saving and life giving, helping to alleviate the truly terrible loneliness so characteristic of the traditional homebound feminine existence. To wake up day after day with no externally imposed routine and nowhere in particular to go is terrifying for anyone accustomed to the fixity and precision of school or job. A reason to "dress up," if only in presentable jeans, rather than to "schlep" around in a grease-stained robe, makes a critical difference to your inner state of being.

But not all traditionally housebound women are in a position to enjoy this kind of surrogate homecoming. Those who are isolated from close female companionship must either find some inner means to perform the priestly function for themselves, or be excluded from ritual benefits all other members of their families can experience.

Consequently, for some of these women fulfilling the need for homecoming must assume a very different form. In contrast to the bodily return sex permits their husbands, or the bodily presence a coffee klatch allows many of their sisters to enjoy, their attempted return is not enacted. Instead, it is further removed from the original condition it seeks to recapitulate, and substitutes for it a partial quality.

Though the specific means may vary, these attempts to achieve homecoming all involve what Freud calls sublimation. This term, borrowed from the alchemical tradition, refers in its original context to the process whereby a solid is purified by heating it directly to gaseous state with no intervening liquid phase. By analogy, Freud, in a latter day gnosticism, uses the term to indicate the process by which highly socialized humans "purify" their bodily, sexual impulses by transforming them into "higher," less bodily form. The work of an artist is held, in this view, to embody the artist's sublimated instinctual drives. To the extent that the human impulse to come home implies and includes a bodily component which seeks some form of physical, ritual enactment, any substituted means which omits the body as body thus sublimates the original drive. This is the case for those women who seek conpensatory satisfaction through habitual television watching. For them a figure like Phil Donahue may come to assume the character of a beloved family member. To tune in to the shows on which he and other surrogate friends and family members appear is to feel welcomed into a sphere not directly a woman's own. To sit sipping a cup of coffee in the phantom presence of Phil Donahue is to be welcomed momentarily into another world. It is to leave the confines of your own cosmos and seem to enter, by proxy, one in which problems belonging to someone else are shared and essentially solved.

As numerous scholars have indicated, a number of issues arise from the phenomenon of television addiction, whether the addicts are housewives, their spouses, or their children. Of greatest relevance in the context of housewives' lives is the relationship between television viewing as substitute for homecoming and its enacted variant. Is there a significant difference between frequent coffee klatching and habitual TV watching?

The issue hinges on two difficult words: transcendence and escapism. Both indicate a process by which humans can metaphorically leave their given physical situation for some other, less tangible realm. In its positive form—as transcendence—the experience allows you to rise above the factual realm. By most accounts the transcendent realm is "better" than its earthly counterpart. Instances abound in religious and folkloristic tales of heroes who manage to transcend their ordinary milieus.

A familiar example is the story of "Jack and the Bean Stalk," in which a lazy boy acquires some seemingly worthless beans in exchange for the family cow. Tossed out as worthless by Jack's angry mother, the beans sprout overnight into a gigantic vine leading up to heaven. Jack climbs this vine only to discover that it leads to a giant's castle. Inside the castle he meets the giant's wife who warns him to hide lest the giant eat him. Subsequently, Jack makes off with the giant's treasures, one item at a time, until he acquires them all. This story with its vine connecting earth to heaven typifies all such tales of transcendence in which vines, ladders, boats, or bridges exist to transport the hero from this realm to another, whether sky, inner earth, or a land on the "far side" of the world. In all cases a sharp distinction separates "this" world from "that." Always in such journeys the issue is whether the hero is merely escaping his present world or actually transcending it.

In the process of transcendence something of value is brought back from the other world. By contrast, in escapism, not only is nothing brought back, frequently something of the hero is lost. Frequently, too, the escape itself merely compounds the problems it was initially designed to avoid. But to say categorically, as some critics do, that all television watching is escapist is to miss the point that the Jack tale makes so well: even the most frivolous-appearing medium may lead to transcendence. It is not safe to generalize about it; only the specific individual can say for sure whether she or he "returns" spiritually refreshed or not. If she feels dull, heavy, and lethargic with little energy for her work, she has merely escaped.

Still other means for attempting to make up for failed homecoming do not involve sublimation but rather what Freud calls displacement. As the word suggests, to displace a desire or act is simply to place it onto something else. A housewife or husband who sits home alone, drinking, is displacing the original impulse to "go home," to return to an earlier, recollected state by dulling her senses and slowing her reflexes. As with television-engendered passivity, this state allows her to be self-aware but not to have the compulsion to act and assume responsibility for herself.

Nowadays, as greater numbers of women exchange traditional house-wifely patterns for contrasting masculine work patterns, the nature of homecoming in both its sacred and its demonic forms is likely to alter. Those who bemoan this shift cry out that the family is eroding. Under-neath their explicit outcry is an unvoiced fear that "Mommy won't take care of *me* any longer." Seemingly, they imply, without the overt pres-ence of the mother goddess figure, the taken-for-granted sacred quality of home could vanish, leaving us all to suffer the profanity of motel-like domains. But for those who probe beneath the layers of meaning in-volved in homecoming, it is apparent that what the ritual ultimately symbolizes is not a return to Mother, but a grounding in self. For what, ultimately, is Home but the space in which you feel secure enough to be most fully yourself? As the familiar phrase "being at home" implies, Home is where you are sufficiently at ease to set aside protective masks. While others may facilitate this task, finally each individual must create *Home* for her or himself. To literalize the ritual, as has generally been done until the recent exodus of women, is to maintain a fiction that can have the devastating consequence of perpetually infantilizing its adherents.

The current emergence of women may therefore turn out to be far different from what those who decry the alleged demise of the "tradi-tional" family believe. In fact, women's emergence may signal an evo-lutionary jump for all humanity. With more and more women able to go out and return on a regular basis, homecoming will necessarily alter its character. Where once only "Mommies" typically performed the welcoming function, now children and men increasingly must learn to do so. Often individuals will also have to enact it entirely for themselves. The emergence of women may consequently be viewed, not as poten-tially harmful to traditional values, but as a very significant step forward in the maturation process of humanity.

If, through our slowly changing rituals, we begin to hear new mes-sages, we may discover that the presumed silence of traditional deity/ ies (of whatever names) has been broken. If we learn to attune ourselves to voices our accustomed ways of being and doing have previously prevented us from hearing, then we may also discover or invent whole new ways of being human. But for that to happen, we must first rec-ognize who we have been in the past and who we are right now. It is for this reason that I consider it essential to probe the theology previously ignored but implicit in housework. Until we can understand the deep significance traditional modes of being still have for many people, it seems unlikely that any of us, women or men, will move beyond the present impasse over issues such as the ERA and abortion.

III

❧ Waiting:
Women's Traditional
Mode of Being

7
WAITING

Nowadays fewer and fewer women in the West still follow the traditional Hestian pattern whereby they spend most of their adult lives primarily as housewives and mothers. Those who do follow this pattern, however, experience life in a very different mode from women who have opted to define themselves—as men traditionally have done—outside the home. An appropriate way to name this increasingly outmoded pattern of being in the home is *waiting*.

The prototype of the waiting woman is Penelope, wife of Odysseus. During her husband's twenty-year absence after the Fall of Troy, Penelope manages to put off one hundred and eight suitors. Homer depicts her as a model of feminine virtue and chastity who spends her time weaving a winding sheet for her aged father-in-law, Laertes. To protect herself from the aggressive insistence of her suitors, she promises to marry one of them once she completes the shroud. But her cunning matches that of her wily husband: by night she undoes the work of each day. What better image could there be of the waiting mode than this Sisyphean undoing of work done?

The medieval English figure called variously Patient Griselda and Patient Grissil possesses equal stamina to endure patiently. Known primarily from "The Clerk's Tale" in Chaucer's *Canterbury Tales*, Griselda

143

is a young peasant girl chosen by the nobleman Walter to be his wife. The story reflects Walter's prolonged and cruel testing of her virtue. First he pretends to send their children off to be slain; then he pretends to renounce her in favor of another wife. Griselda never complains, but waits patiently and submissively until eventually Walter returns to reveal that all along he has been testing her.

Most feminine waiting, however, is more subtle than either of these literary examples. In its contemporary manifestation the waiting mode looks something like this: Gladys, a traditional full-time housewife and mother, finds that, in contrast to her professor husband Harvey, who must know generally where he will be and what he will be doing some-times a full year in advance, she has almost no externally imposed fixity to her schedule. Indeed, one of the things that originally most discon-certs her about housekeeping and motherhood are their relative absence of structure. Following her first baby's arrival, she complains bitterly to Harvey: "I can't accomplish anything. I don't understand it. At school I was always organized, and now nothing gets done. And I once thought housewives did nothing all day!" Gladys is exhausted all the time. Harvey tells her to organize: "Make lists," he says. So she begins reading Heloise's column in the newspaper, and sure enough, other women have the same problem. And, as Harvey suggests, they all seem to make lists. But it isn't a matter of lists. What difference, she keeps asking herself, does it make if I dust the venetian blinds on Tuesday or wait till Wednesday? What she really wonders is: why do them at all?

While this domestic aspect of waiting has diminished considerably in our own culture, waiting, as a mode, still exists. As women develop career aspirations of their own, the issue now centers on who will move or sacrifice an upward move for whom. Traditionally it was the woman who gave up ambitions to follow the man she loved. She might sacrifice college to follow him to graduate school; she might stop a budding career to go where his job called; rarely did she give up a man. Nowadays, by contrast, men are increasingly asked to make the same choices as women, by wives and lovers who have finally dared to risk giving up their men. Yet few men follow their women. Juanita Kreps' husband chose to remain in North Carolina when she went to Washington. Sissy Farenthold's husband and children remained in Texas during her pres-idency of Wells College. One could multiply examples. The point is that few men appear willing to endure the waiting mode that so many women, up until our age, accepted as destiny. Instead, men continue to prefer the contrasting mode of questing.

In a traditional society, it is understood that a man will go out into the world, or quest. The specific way he does so will, of course, vary according to his inclinations, personality, and occupation, but the fact that he goes out gives his life a configuration quite different from that of his spouse. Implicitly, whether he quests for material goods, love, or spiritual boons, his life necessitates self-initiated movement from one place or condition to another. Simply the act of going out of the house each day—even if only to his nearby shop—gives movement, hence a sense of progress or change, to his day. And if he literally journeys, this motion is all the more pronounced. Furthermore, whatever a quester gains or fails to gain typically results from his own efforts, in contrast to the dependency of one who must await someone or something.

Waiting is reaction rather than initiation of action. It is a mode of existence that automatically constrains those forced to endure it to be dependent upon someone or something other than themselves. By definition, waiting implies that someone or something is being awaited. Thus to wait is to place that someone or something as the goal of your existence during the time of waiting. Traditionally, women have been acculturated to believe they *should* wait. Men have told them so; their mothers have taught them how. Implicit in that mode of being is the notion that they would wait chastely. And everyone knows the penalties imposed in traditional societies upon wives or virgins who fail that test.

In extreme form, waiting becomes demonic. When that happens the waiting mode is dominated by a number of qualities generally construed as negative: absence of control, dependency on others, boredom, nothingness, hopelessness, anxiety, anger, nervousness, apprehension, depression, heaviness, lack of self-development, and both patience and impatience. At the far end of the scale is stasis.

Though it is easy to spot these predominantly negative qualities, careful attention suggests that waiting is more than simply an unpleasant mode of existence. Basically it is a time experience radically at odds with the more accepted time patterns of Western culture. Though we know better, we often act as though linear, quantifiable time (associated with masculine questing) were given in nature. Yet linear time is only an externally imposed process of ordering which helps us maintain the illusion of a "first," "second," "third," or "in the beginning," "next," and "then." Though our subjective experiences of time vary, nonetheless we tend to assume that there is some sort of temporal sequence "out there," apart from ourselves.

This kind of time that we assume is "out there" we describe as historic, meaning that it is progressive and nonrepeatable, having a forward motion like the flow of a river. Individuals living in the modern Western world grow up so imbued with this time pattern that it seems given in nature. But there are other ways of conceiving time besides the time of clocks, watches, and calendars. Experiential time, by contrast, is our subjective experience of time.[1] Empty and filled time, subcategories of experiential time, refer respectively to time that seems endless and to time so crammed its passage leaves us feeling breathless. And, whether filled or empty, time can be private or shared. In the latter case, if large numbers of people share it, it becomes public. Thus an entire epoch may be considered filled or empty.

These variations all indicate the multiple nature of time. An even greater difference structures certain experiences of time, however. T.S. Eliot calls the time of such experiences "time out of time"; Henri Bergson calls it "temps durée"; and Mircea Eliade "illo tempore," or mythic time, meaning the time when the gods first enacted all things that have come to be, the time of origins. The paradoxically "timeless" or nonprogressive quality of this kind of time—the time of waiting—often leads us to say that it is not time at all, but eternity.

This sacred or mythic time is, in nearly every religious tradition, the true time of which historical, here-and-now time is a mere shadow or copy. Accordingly, in the view of Mircea Eliade, mythic time is definitionally sacred, and historic time, secular. Yet this distinction blurs when we think of the sacred quality Judeo-Christian thought gives to history, or conversely, of the profane quality some events give to time that is otherwise mythic. Furthermore, both kinds of time are equally capable of demonic manifestation. And, although Eliade sharply distinguishes historic and mythic time, in some instances they intermingle. For example, quests typically exhibit the progressive movement characteristic of historic time, yet within many quests—particularly those with a religious dimension—there are moments of "time out of time." Certainly Lancelot's vision of the Holy Grail occurs within mythic time, and yet his quest, as a whole, is linear. Thus Eliade's clear-cut distinction breaks down if pushed too far.

Nonetheless, bearing this consideration in mind, it is useful to see how a rough distinction between linear and mythic time reflects differences in traditional masculine and feminine time experiences. Women's housebound time is typically characterized by amorphousness or circularity or both, and a content frequently imperceptible within the structures of dominant male culture; above all, it is static.

Typically, within Western patterns of conceptualization, stasis assumes heavily negative connotations. To be static implies lack of progress, absence of motion, and even death. Usually these qualities are not only viewed negatively, but they also reflect a disturbingly different orientation toward time from what is conventionally considered "normal." Thus, much of the fear attached to images of women in folklore and fairy tales may well be less fear of women per se than an associated fear of women's time. Entrapment by a woman—a pervasive theme in numerous variations throughout literature—is life in a time frame so at variance with the quest mode that it feels like living death by contrast. Such women's power of enchantment occurs, for example, in the transformation of Ulysses's men into swine by the witch Circe. In *The Arabian Nights,* the same motif occurs in the tale of "The King of the Black Isles," when the Queen says to her lover, "By virtue of my enchantments, I command thee to become half marble and half man."[2] The stare of Medusa is an extreme instance of a male being so "stuck" or trapped by a woman that he cannot move at all.

Being turned to stone renders a victim totally powerless and reduces him to complete dependency on his enchantress. A modern variant which occurs in Randall Jarrell's poem "Hope" helps explain the underlying meaning of this ancient motif. The speaker of the poem is a wealthy married apartment dweller who longs to break a familial cycle of submission to female dominance. Fearing for his son, the speaker sees himself repeating the role of his own meek father:

> I have followed in my father's light,
>   faint footsteps
> Down to some place under the sun, under
>   the moon,
> Lit by the light of the streetlamp far
>   below.
> Back far enough, down deep enough, one
>   comes to the Mothers.[3]

So little impression did the speaker's father make that his footsteps are barely perceptible to the son who follows them. A downward path leads this speaker to "the Mothers," an allusion to a passage from Goethe's *Faust,* in which Faust is about to journey to the realm of the ancient goddesses known as the Mothers.[4]

Entering this realm can be a perilous enterprise, as Jung says: "There is always a danger that those who set foot in this realm will grow fast to the rocks, like Theseus and Peirithous, who wanted to abduct the goddess of the underworld. It happens all too easily that there is no returning from the realm of the mothers."[5] Like being turned to stone, "growing fast to the rocks" is a visual image of the psychological danger involved when an adult regresses to childlike dependence on its mother. Carried far enough, such dependency, as Mephistopheles' warning to Faust suggests, results in total loss of self. This pattern is present in all tales in which enchantment involves petrification. From a traditional masculine perspective, even if the alluring woman is beautiful, the time experience is purely negative. Not only does the petrified male cease to function in his habitual time sphere, he accomplishes nothing at all, being metaphorically dead to the world.

Such deadness is apparent in the following case, in which Charlotte, a woman in her thirties, increasingly cannot get up in the morning. Instead of rising with her family, she stays in bed until she wakes up. Even then she frequently lingers, preferring the warmth of the bedcovers to getting up and facing the day. Sometimes after she finally does arise she does not even feel like showering or exercising. She may go down to breakfast, there to dally over the morning paper for an hour. Halfway through the paper she may suddenly feel like getting up out of her chair to scrub an annoying spot on the kitchen carpet. But thinking of eliminating that single spot may remind her of all the other long-unscrubbed spots in her house. Meanwhile, she sees that her kitchen table remains littered with empty dishes, crumbs, and the morning paper. Rather than scrub or clear the table she would prefer to call Martha, whom she hasn't seen for three days. She reaches for the phone, dials the first three digits, then stops. Feeling the tug of all that work undone, she slowly puts the phone back on its hook. As she continues to sit at her littered table, she stares into space. Maybe if she got up and took her shower now she would be able to start doing something.

So far, Charlotte's morning has revealed its demonic side. Chaos has swallowed her up, leaving her totally rudderless, incapable of any movement whatsoever. Although her inner voices can scarcely be considered Svengali like, at this moment none stands out as a true voice for Charlotte. In this kind of time pattern the victim is essentially turned to stone: he or she fails to exist in a pattern most of us recognize as living, for nothing at all seems to change or be accomplished.

Certainly not all creatures who lure humans out of their accustomed time frame or paralyze them are females; nonetheless, witchlike power is more commonly attributed to women than to men. In either case, it is logical to question whether or not it is a *power* that such supposed enchanters possess, or whether such a time frame is one that society automatically imposes on those outside the mainstream. For example, if a traditional woman generally experiences time amorphously without much to demarcate and differentiate one moment from the next, then a man who succumbs to her fully may choose to enter into that time frame with her.

And it is partly this choice which contributes to the immense shift in relationship that frequently occurs after a couple marries. Once he feels she "belongs" to him, a man characteristically leaves his beloved's time to return to his own. But she, remaining there, feels neglected and moans, "but *before* we were married it wasn't like this. Then you didn't want to go out with the guys; then you didn't go off golfing in your free time." For as long as romantic love or infatuation fills this amorphous kind of time it feels positive, but as soon as this emotion diminishes or vanishes, it may become a heavy, depressing, anomic experience to cope with. In its negative form, such time occasions feelings of hopelessness typical of anyone whose life is without recognizable structure. For instance, sociologist Helena Z. Lopata compares a housebound woman to retirees: "Having left her job, she experiences most of the difficulties of absence of work rhythm and relation maintenance that upset newly retired men."[6] Common to both groups is the feeling that the future is completely closed off.

When this happens life seems to be passing by, in the way the words, "ceaseless round" suggest. Most household chores are so obviously circular that their completion scarcely can be experienced. The cliché that "a woman's work is never done" accurately reflects the lack of closure characteristic of this time experience. Furthermore, for women who are mothers as well as housewives, the period of child-rearing necessarily so focuses attention on the needs of children that these women can seldom call their time their own. Long-range experiences of time are therefore apt to feel as demonic as shorter ones in contrast to those of their husbands or older, less encumbered, women. Even the most traditional woman is unlikely to view herself exactly as she did before giving birth. Now she lives for someone else in a way she might never have conceived possible before. Deep within herself she feels that without her this baby would die. Even so routine an act as crossing a street may assume new coloration for her. Where once she might have crossed unthinkingly, she must now pause, fully conscious, whether she likes it or not, that she must take care of herself: someone else now depends on her almost totally.

To what extent then can she possibly call this time her own? During this period of her life, which may extend over twenty or thirty years if she makes a "profession" of mothering, she lives at a remove from her own individual life. If it is a question between sleeping or feeding the baby, there is no choice. Although the responsibility can be shared and often is nowadays, in a traditional pattern in which there is only one primary caretaker, virtually no other choice exists: either the mother gets up, or the baby cries. Few can tolerate the latter option, if for no other reason than that it disturbs sleep.

So nongoal-oriented does this pattern often feel to an individual whose education has prepared her for the goal-orientation typical of life in a masculine mode, that she may become deeply frustrated. To assume closure and completion as norms, and then to seldom or never experience them, may lead a victim of the circular time pattern into severe depression. Such depression occasioned by loss of future is characterized by blankness or feelings of not knowing who you are, even to the extent of not being able to recognize your own feelings. You seem to stagger through blackness and thick, heavy fog. You experience frequent blanking—a blotting out, a feeling of not knowing what to do or where to turn, a total slowing down of time, a not being there, a dissipation of yourself into droplets.

An appropriate image for this condition is a large, dark, gaping hole in which each action slows so that you can actually examine its different components bit by bit. Ordinarily you dress without paying particular attention to the single steps involved in the process. If you put on a pair of jeans you just step into them quickly without thinking about it. But in a depressed state you may slowly put one leg in and, as you do so, watch what you are doing, and then very, very slowly roll up the bottom cuff of that leg and then equally slowly put your other leg into the jeans pant and repeat the entire process. Each step, therefore, rather than forming a quick and nearly indistinguishable whole, becomes a discrete moment in and of itself, thus altering the normally accepted time scale.

Even later on, when family demands intrude less insistently, a variant of this same, frequently depressive, circular time pattern may dominate a woman's life. As in the early years of motherhood, her personal goals may be submerged by family objectives. Who, for example, is going to leave work early so that Timmy won't come home from kindergarten to an empty house? Who is going to give up an evening relaxing to watch Gerry in the first-grade play? Though such questions now begin to seem commonplace, within a traditional pattern they weren't even asked. Then, typically, a woman's time was *not* hers to fill as she pleased. Though she was not ordinarily a slave in the technical sense of the word, her culture so conditioned her to assume responsibility for the needs of her children and spouse that her own desires for filling time her way often did not even reach her conscious awareness.

This level of space-time experience, so typical of women confined to the home, depends heavily on the amorphousness and circularity of mythic time. By contrast, that of traditional men is dominated by characteristics associated with space. Assuming he is neither slave nor servant, a traditional man is free to experiment with space-time in ways quite different from his wife. Whereas a traditional woman is likely to be projected into space-time by means of a baby, a man will be extended by some archetypal masculine implement such as a sword, pen, plow, or axe. If he knows how, he can construct an edifice, monument, art work, or poem sufficiently strong that it will far outlast him. But whereas a sword or shovel (masculine implements) extend the holder's arm spatially, a baby metaphorically extends its progenitors in time, for the instantaneous quality of the spatial extension is lacking with a baby. Furthermore, because the sword is an inanimate object it can readily receive its owner's projections without it either protesting or being harmed. Such is far from true, however, with a baby, who has a mind of its own. In fact, the baby who is forced to bear a heavy weight of parental projections and expectations may actually be emotionally harmed. Yet the baby who is allowed appropriate autonomy may correspondingly drain off its mother's emotional strength. Thus, rather than adding something to its mother's life as prevailing wisdom teaches, a baby may destroy its mother's individuality. Furthermore, as the baby increasingly becomes its own person, it may quickly cease to function at all as an extension of its mother, thus depriving her of even that vicarious existence. Even more frightening, a child can always destroy its mother's life work by rejecting all the values she has tried to inculcate. Worse, it can also do so by physically abusing, even killing, itself.

By contrast, the physical monuments traditionally created only by men can theoretically last indefinitely. Thus a man can experience himself in space-time far differently from a traditional woman. Where she must respond to the demands of others, and remain within nature, he may learn to command and stand against the natural world. It is this stance, not hers, which we have learned to call culture. And it is culture—not nurture and nature—which forms the "important" stuff of history from which women have so consistently found themselves excluded.

Yet the static waiting pattern which so long denied women entrée to history does not always manifest itself as depression; nor is it necessarily always "bad"; it is simply another mode of being, one that stands at the opposite end of the spectrum from action. It may imply rootedness of a positive as well as a negative sort. As such it is a condition essential for growth.

The ambivalent nature of traditional woman's static time experience is readily apparent in many fairy tales containing the motif of the "supernatural lapse of time," in which a human of either sex discovers him or herself in a new realm where he or she feasts and enjoys for what appears to be a short time. Once returned home, however, such an individual discovers those five minutes were one hundred years in "ordinary" time. In cases like this, clock time, as the dominant masculine culture ordinarily defines it, is replaced by what we call eternity or mythic time by contrast.

One of the best-known tales of this type concerns the Welshman Herla, king of the ancient Britons, who is trapped into a bargain with a dwarf to attend the dwarf's wedding.[7] When the wedding day comes, Herla is led through a dark cave into the realm of the dwarves where the marriage is celebrated. After fulfilling his obligations as a guest, Herla and his retinue return home, only to discover that the seemingly short feast time has been a period of two hundred years by mortal reckoning. Any man who dismounts instantly crumbles into dust. Herla's Rade, as the group is known, is said to ride yet along the Welsh border, unable either to dismount or return to Dwarfland.

Though we often speak of eternity as positive, the message typical of most such stories involving the supernatural lapse of time is that the individual who enters this kind of time does so at peril of missing his "real" life. But why isn't this so-called "supernatural" time just as real or valid in terms of itself? It is only by contrast with "official" time that it seems negative; it all depends which vantage point you accept as a norm. One of the very few tales which reflects the relativity of the situation is an Italian swan-maiden tale whose hero marries Fortune.[8] When he loses her, he follows her to the Isle of Happiness where he believes he stays two months. By mortal time, however, it is two hundred years. When he wishes to return to visit his mother, Fortune accompanies him back to his greatly changed homeland. When an aged hag approaches, Fortune warns him that she is Death. When next they meet a monster, she warns him it is the Devil. When the hero finally realizes that his mother has died long ago, he willingly returns with Fortune to the Isle of Happiness. But he is one of relatively few mortals to do so.

Two elements of this supernatural time are its unhurried quality and its ability to stretch out "normal" time. Both traits are also crucial components of feminine time. Being unhurried often allows for possibilities prohibited by linear time. In contrast to Charlotte, whose time experience was so negatively chaotic that she experienced aimlessness, there is Clara, who has just returned from a weekend out of town. Needing to unpack and return to this world, two choices lie before her: she can hurry, or she can unpack leisurely. Somewhat to her surprise, she finds herself actually wanting to take her time, to be able to unpack and reenter her habitual time frame in an orderly fashion. If she rushes these chores she will lose a certain dimension of living which simply evanesces, poof! It will never even have been. She can easily dash out first thing in the morning to campus and try and work on her research. Or she can choose not to get up with her husband, simply sleeping until she awakens. Now what determines the latter choice? When her husband arises she still has half an hour before breakfast time, so she sleeps. But when he again awakens her to see if she wants to get up or sleep, she feels such extreme tiredness that she knows she will be exhausted all day. She knows that if she forces herself when she feels so tired, she will subsequently regret her self-induced pressure. So she stays in bed, not awakening until close to nine o'clock. Then, rather than hurry or coerce herself, she slowly exercises and showers, allowing herself time to ruminate between movements, time to listen to the phoebes calling to each other outside the window, time to slip in and out of conscious awareness of her surroundings. For her, letting go is neither frightening nor purposeless as it was for Charlotte.

This is the positive face of chaos, a letting go into the possibilities that freedom from externally fixed routine allows. This face of chaos allows you to be one with the moment. Responding in this way to the whim of the moment is markedly different from imposing your own will on time. This way is both passive and totally free. It involves responding to the combination of your innermost self and the particular moment. This mode of being allows you to disregard all the shoulds and all the fixed structures. The passivity so induced is that of a light object thrown into the water; it is not the object that determines its direction, but the movement of the water.

How very different this passive acceptance is either from Charlotte's frenzied flight or from the assertive striving more typical of the masculine temporal mode, questing. Though unacknowledged, this disparity between the accepted Western time pattern of most men's lives and the largely unrecognized, but experienced, time of traditional women's lives suggests that both history and story, traditionally so full of quests as to be virtually synonymous with them, may not be formally appropriate to express traditional feminine experience. In fact, both forms may so consistently have obscured women's experiences in the waiting mode as to have rendered women largely invisible not just to men, but even to themselves.

8

STORY
AND HISTORY

The story of the Prodigal Son vividly contrasts the major difference between the two time patterns of waiting and questing: remaining home as opposed to regularly leaving it. In that tale, although there are two stories, only one is explicit. The story of the son who never ventured forth, but remained faithfully at home performing his expected duties, is never told. This unvoiced tale, which so clearly falls within the waiting pattern, is an archetypally feminine story, which, like that of Hestia, traditionally is *not* told.[1]

But if stories of the Prodigal Son's brother, Hestia, or housewives were to be told, what might they be like? That question, which sounds so fanciful, actually raises the kinds of significant questions which, until the advent of the women's movement, were not even asked: Why are there few such stories? What does their relative scarcity mean? Would the telling of those stories now, automatically right ancient wrongs? Or would creating such stories paradoxically exacerbate harm already done?

To even begin answering such questions we must understand how stories function. Although by *story* we typically intend a fictional account, the word is very closely related to *history*, a factual record. Both mean a learning by inquiry, a narrative. Even now the two are used interchangeably, as when I ask an eyewitness to an accident to give me the story of what happened; conversely, novelists often give histories of entirely fictitious characters.

History has two distinct senses: it means both events that occur in time and a record of those events. The marked lack of records about women's lives makes women appear to be absent from history in both senses. Although content may sometimes distinguish history from story, structurally they are alike, so the following discussion of story is intended in the broad sense to include both history and story.

Story is one of the modalities that many thinkers—particularly many contemporary male religionists, such as Sam Keen, James Wiggins, Michael Novak, and Stephen Crites—consider central to the experience of being meaningfully human. Crites says that experience itself is "an incipient story."[2] Sam Keen goes so far as to assert that "to be a person is to have a story to tell."[3] And feminist thinker Carol Christ, picking up this thread, claims that "without stories there is no articulation of experience. Without stories a woman is lost when she comes to make the important decisions of her life. . . . She does not learn to value her struggles, to celebrate her strength, to comprehend her pain. Without stories she cannot understand herself."[4] Other feminists, in addition to religionists, assume a similar stance, as does Beverly Tanenhaus in these words: "without a literature, one does not know that one exists. For the great service of literature is to show us who we are."[5]

At first glance what these thinkers say about story seems inarguable. Do not all of us constantly engage in storytelling and history-making? Consider, for example, a situation in which an individual driving along a superhighway suddenly sees a fleshy-looking carcass in the left hand lane. What is she likely to do? Further imagine that before the horror of that first shocking carcass dissipates, she sees another, and then another, until she counts close to twenty? What process is her mind apt to engage in?

Likely her first thought will be, "There must have been a terrible accident. Driving conditions aren't hazardous so these bodies must be the result of the first accident. Probably a second car slowed down . . . but there aren't any wrecked cars. Surely the police would never tow away the cars and leave the bodies . . . that doesn't make sense." Seeing carcasses beyond numbers likely to be occasioned by even the worst highway fatalities intensifies her horror so that she no longer wants to look: "This has to be some horrible cult murder! A group was traveling together in a van and the leader made them all take cyanide pills and jump. And they're all naked because. . . . No, they aren't full

bodies. He must have gone berserk and sliced them up. . . ." The accompanying impulse to that thought leads her to speed up. All the while
her mind is frantically trying to make sense of this ghoulish, unprece-
dented sight. How could so many bodies possibly be strewn about In-
terstate 90? When she finally comes to an overturned tractor-trailer with
the words "Fennel's Meat Packing" on the side, once again she must
tell herself an explanatory tale, this time one that turns horror to laughter
as she realizes her initial mistakes.

It is the unusual person whose mind does not engage in such expla-
nation-seeking, whether it is a bizarre situation, such as this one, or a
more prosaic one in which an older man escorts a young girl into an
expensive restaurant: "It's his daughter," one story goes; "It's his mistress," goes another. Ordering, or attempting to make sense of our
environment through telling stories is essential to human nature: we do
it all the time. Whatever we encounter we automatically place into a
context in order to understand it.

But accepting the naturalness of this human need and ability to make
up stories differs greatly from granting it primacy among human activities. Why, after all, is story emphasized by some Western religionists
almost to the exclusion of any other mode of artistic expression? Why
do we hear comparatively little within Western theology about painting,
sculpture, music, weaving, and the like? As religionist Ted L. Estess
asserts, "story is *one* form of the possible, and we can speak of life *as
if* it were a story. . . . We talk about life in a multiplicity of ways, not
through story alone."[6] Certainly, as Estess suggests, other, equally valid,
modes of being and becoming human exist that are not necessarily narrative at all: ritual enactment, spectacle, image, dance, vision, trance,
and music.

One reason for the heavy contemporary academic emphasis on story
is a long historical bias in favor of the word. Partly through the Greek
word *Logos,* the word *story* has often mistakenly come to be considered
prior to material reality. This confusion is due to the fact that *Logos*
translates as *word,* giving the impression that it means the same thing
as *word* does in English. However, in the original Greek context *Logos*
means *primary reality, rational principle, reason,* and *cosmic order.* Thus the
opening words of the Gospel According to John: "In the beginning was
the word, and the word was with God, and the word was God," actually
mean, "In the beginning was the primary reality. . . ." But misunderstanding of the meaning of the original Greek has led to a common belief
that this gospel account denigrates the actual world we perceive through
our senses and elevates an ideal, unperceived world deemed to exist
prior to and beyond this one, a world composed not of materiality but
of imagination. This is also the Platonic view as opposed to the Aris-

totelian, in which the idea precedes and surpasses actuality; it is subsequently the gnostic view which vehemently denounces the sensory
world in favor of its ideal, nonmaterial prototype. While few would
deny that ideas, words, and language are great human gifts, surely such
linguistic traits are not, of themselves, the only distinguishing qualities
of humanness.

But some would argue that without words we cannot think. Recent
research, however, conducted on human beings with surgically severed
brain hemispheres suggests that this is not the case. Experiments with
a rather complicated eye device known as a half-field occluder enable
researchers to block off vision in such a way that data enter only one
sphere of the brain. When the left sphere, the verbal side, is denied
access to the stimulus, the right hemisphere takes over. Apparently the
right brain can recognize, but not name, what it sees. For example, an
experimenter will place a series of cards before her subject. On each is
a simple picture showing, perhaps, a cat, a dog, or a house. The re-
searcher will point to one object and ask the subject, Do you recognize
this? The subject will nod, but when asked to name it, remain mute.
Only when asked specifically, Is this a dog? can the subject agree or
disagree. Repeated experiments indicate that the subjects always know
what they see, but simply cannot find the words to match their
knowledge.[7]

While you can reasonably argue that without language, it would be
difficult to communicate, that does not mean that without words people
are not thinking. Similarly, it is reasonable to assume that just because
some people don't tell stories that does not necessarily mean that nothing
is happening to, or inside, them.

Another major argument against the primacy of stories for human
understanding is the question, Where are all the women's stories? Usually that question is asked from the masculine perspective which assumes that stories are not only good, but also necessary. That means
that the question is typically asked like this: Why haven't women been
as frequent storytellers (writers) as men? Or, Why haven't women generally been part of the story of history? Or, Why can't women tell stories?
Jokes? Such questions imply a lack in women.

Recently, some feminist thinkers have countered this supposed lack
by finding increasing numbers of little-known women such as Anne
Buras[7a] or Susan Keating Glaspell[8] who either actively engaged in history
or who wrote important, but unacclaimed literary works. Besides seeing
formerly ignored individuals—whether women or minority figures—included in the official canons of history and story, we are also witnessing
an expansion of what is defined as history.Whereas history once primarily centered on military and political battles, it now includes social

and psychohistory as well. Furthermore, it increasingly concerns inner history, the often hidden, and scarcely articulated, source for visible actions. Obviously, these are all important steps towards placing women in the stream of history.

But even though more women are now telling stories and entering history, the imbalance is still marked. Considering that women constitute slightly more than half the human species, it seems odd, indeed, that the output of a fraction of the numerical minority should be considered essential to the genesis of all being and becoming human. Furthermore, such placement of women in history takes for granted that being in that stream is good, and that categories like history and story are asexual. But what if, in fact, history and story are actually masculine constructs? Then they may not accurately reflect the experiences of women who have lived out traditional, stay-at-home lives. Furthermore, telling stories and placing women in history automatically translates the waiting mode into another form and, hence, as in all translations, at least partially obscures it. While some individuals of both sexes may welcome such translation, others may question whether the shift does not inevitably entail some loss.

Yet how can these seemingly gender-free categories of history and story possibly obscure women's experiences? To understand that possibility we need to take a close look at how both function in our lives. Consider, for example, a statement like this one made by an aged Chinese wood-carver:

> The right pace, neither slow nor fast, cannot get into the hand unless it comes from the heart. It is a thing that cannot be put into words; there is an art to it that I cannot explain to my own son. That is why it is impossible for me to let him take over my work, and here I am at the age of seventy, still making wheels. In my opinion it must have been the same with the men of old. All that was worth handing on, died with them; the rest, they put into their books. . . . What you [read, therefore is but] the lees and scum of bygone men.[9]

Women's traditional enactment has scarcely been hampered by "the lees and scum of bygone men" (or women). Indeed, searching out the art of housework has been as freely available to women as discovering the art of making wheels has been to the wood-cutter.

As the wood-cutter's words indicate, story may not be an appropriate vessel for capturing the actual experience of either women or men. After all, expanding on the implication of the Chinese wood-carver's words, there are false stories as well as true. As George Steiner writes in *After Babel*, "Hypotheticals, 'imaginaries,' conditionals, the syntax of counter-factuality and contingency may well be the generative centres of human speech. . . . [They] do more than occasion philosophical and grammatical perplexity. No less than future tenses to which they are, one feels, related, and with which they ought probably to be classed in the larger set of 'suppositionals' or 'alternates,' these 'if' propositions are fundamental to the dynamics of human feeling . . . ours is the ability, the need, to gainsay or 'unsay' the world, to image and speak it other wise. . . . We need a word which will designate the power, the compulsion of language to posit 'otherness.' . . . Perhaps 'alternity' will do: to define the 'other than the case,' the counter-factual propositions, images, shapes of will and evasion with which we charge our mental being and by means of which we build the changing, largely fictive milieu of our social existence. . . ."[10] If we accept Steiner's view, what we create by words and what we create by other methods may not necessarily bear any true relationship, either to each other or to external "reality." For instance, within most stories women appear as victims or dependent creatures. By contrast, many males appear as heroic savior figures. Are those roles necessarily based on any factual truth? The words we originally use do not necessarily relate to something called "external reality." But as those words assume power and validity of their own, our actions subsequently come to resemble the words. Consequently, in many instances words do create our realities, but falsely. This situation is what Douglas R. Hofstadter in *Godel, Escher, Bach* terms counter-factual-almost situations. As an example he describes a picture by artist René Magritte entitled *The Two Mysteries*, which depicts a pipe against a neutral background above a floor. Underneath the pipe are written the words "Ceci n'est pas une pipe," This is not a pipe.[11] Obviously, this picture defies common sense. We look at a picture of something recognizably a pipe—yet the words beneath that object deny what we see.

This concept of the counter-factual is useful in discussing what commonly happens to women when they are defined by masculine thinking. For example, if I go out and play a tough game of tennis and beat four or five different men in the course of an afternoon, my behavior may be labeled unladylike, bitchy, or overly aggressive. Those labels are counter-factual. If I have won fairly, then why should I be called such names? To give a more important example, how about the woman whose consistent depression leads her eventually to be hospitalized because she has been labeled "crazy" or "mad"? Suppose that her own experience seems so totally divorced from what the external world calls it that the discrepancy between the two duplicates that between the conception of the pipe and the words denying it is a pipe. Such is the message of Marge Piercy's book, *Woman at the Edge of Time*. Here the female protagonist, Connie Ramos, experiences within herself space in which she is a hero. Yet, in contrast to her inner experiences of strength and compassion, others see her as a child-abusing troublemaker — a crazy Latino.

On the other hand, words and stories frequently do suggest the capacity for human liberation and transcendence. What might be referred to as a "transcending" story in contrast to a false one is one whose final purpose or result is the transformation of an actual situation. Even if the intended liberation fails to occur, the intention will be clear from the context of the story. Such is the case with the parables of Jesus. But it is by no means appropriate to so enshrine words and stories as to make them the primary avenue of human transcendence. Often stories are merely escapist. (I think in that connection, of Flaubert's poor Emma Bovary or any of her contemporary sit-com or soap opera counterparts.) And at their worst, stories become positively demonic, as with the outright counter-factual stories told as propagandistic distortions of what their tellers know to be true.

Consequently, rather than automatically assuming that story and history are positive, gender-free categories, it makes more sense to question them closely. It may even be the case that women's traditional absence from storied activity allows them to start from the very beginning, as if they were just coming into being for the first time. At first glance, that beginning seems to be the obvious one of entering fully into history and story as well as into what was formerly called "a man's world." But it could also be the far more radical beginning involved in refusing to make those entries at all, choosing instead to look into the essentially nonstoried, a-historic past of women for modes *other* than those perpetuated by masculine culture. In that case, the fact that nowadays we seem to be living in an increasingly nonverbal age probably bears a much greater relationship to women's traditional mode of being, the waiting mode, than has yet been realized. Contemporary emphases on musical and visual media at the expense of literature and fully developed conversation are frequently deplored by intellectuals. Yet oral cultures were once displaced by literate ones. The current shift into an electronic culture is not necessarily bad—it is simply different. The passivity typically associated with this shift away from the participation involved in reading strongly resembles the negative face of women's traditional waiting pattern. The positive parallel has generally received less critical commentary so far. But surely it exists. Similarly, the relative absence of women in story and history, which seems to be a negative situation when articulated from a masculine perspective, may actually be cause for celebration from a feminist one. Humanity may now be witnessing something genuinely new: as more and more women depart from the illusive Land of Happily Ever After, they may reveal in the process the theological significance of waiting as a viable, not just an untenable, mode of human being. But to understand why this may be so, we must examine some of the components of story.

Though it would appear simple, defining *story* is difficult. *Story* is a word whose meaning is so commonly assumed that few literary critics actually define it, generally preferring instead to speak of fiction, the novel, or the short story. Yet discussion of what is loosely called story has occupied philosophers and critics ever since the time of Plato and Aristotle. In fact, the *locus classicus* for modern conceptions of the term remains Aristotle's *Poetics* despite numerous contemporary deviations from Aristotle's thought. As Aristotle conceived it, the *sine qua non* of story was wholeness, by which he meant a unity with a clear-cut beginning, middle, and ending. What we rather imprecisely call story more closely resembles what Aristotle called epic, one of three basic literary forms, the other two being drama and lyric. As elaborated in our own century by James Joyce, certain distinguishing features characterize each of these modes.[12]

Epic is distinguished from both the lyric and the dramatic modes by the presence of a narrator through whom the information we receive is mediated. The Grimms' tale, "The White Snake," for example, opens like this:

> A long time ago there lived a king whose wisdom was celebrated far and wide. Nothing was unknown to him, and the news of the most secret transactions seemed to reach him through the air.[13]

Here we experience a flow of events in time through the mediation of an unseen storyteller. Whatever else story may be, it is narrative in form; thus the two words *story* and *narrative* are often used interchangeably. *Narrative* automatically implies telling or narration, hence a narrator.

By contrast, in the dramatic form the artist presents material directly to the audience through the words and actions of his characters; and although drama enacts what we also call a story, the presentational aspect replaces narration. However, some twentieth-century stories— such as those of Hemingway—approach the dramatic mode. Consider, for example, his famous story, "The Killers," in which almost nothing is told in the narrator's voice. Instead, most of the story unfolds through the dialogue between the various characters just as typically occurs on stage. With their words they reveal most of what the reader needs to know. Only information awkward or impossible for the characters to state is mediated as when the unseen narrator opens the story by saying, "The door of Henry's lunch-room opened and two men came in. They sat down at the counter."[14] Aside from bits of equally spare commentary, everything else unfolds without mediation, as dialogue.

The lyric mode is just as immediate as the dramatic, but here the artist does not envision an audience apart from himself. Instead he presents material immediately to himself as it happens. Ordinarily we associate certain kinds of poetry with the lyric mode, but some prose falls in this category as well. Lyric typically concentrates on a single image considered in its timeless aspect, as in this example from Samuel Beckett's short story "The Calmative":

> I see a kind of den littered with empty tins. And yet we are not in the country. Perhaps it's just ruins, a ruined folly, on the skirts of the town, on a field, for the fields come right up to our walls, their walls, and the cows lie down at night in the lee of the ramparts. I have changed refuge so often, in the course of my rout, that now I can't tell between dens and ruins."[15]

By contrast with the static, timeless quality of these words, epic typically simulates a far more temporal effect, in which there is progress from point A to B to . . . Z. The formulaic opening "once upon a time," signals that kind of movement. In a sense, all literature, whether oral or written, is temporal in contrast to the visual arts which are inherently spatial, although serial effects may allow temporal elements into them as well. This is so because of the sequential nature of words which can only be heard or read in succession, whereas images can be absorbed at a glance. But of all the written and spoken forms—argument, exposition, description, and narration—narration is the most specifically and intensely temporal. And it is this temporal dimension of stories that makes them so suspect as vehicles for traditional women's experience just as absence of temporality as it is typically construed may also largely account for women's conspicuous lack of history and their comparative absence as writers of stories.

Plot

Of all the traditional Aristotelian elements of story—plot, character, setting, thought, and diction—it is plot that most strongly militates against story as an appropriate vehicle for traditional women's experience. This is so because plot is so inextricably linked to time, being the element that formally shapes time in both story and history; its most basic elements are incidents or episodes. Although these facts are elementary, it is precisely their familiarity that makes them suspect. If we stop to think about the concept of plot as the arrangement of incidents, then we begin to understand the problem of storying women's experience. First, what traditional women do with their time is so minimally perceived by most males that it simply has not registered with much impact upon our culture. Dusting, washing dishes, making beds, sweeping, watching children: such chores require women to maintain a status quo. Therefore, what women do largely involves "sameness" without apparent differentiation. For example, who ever notices the shiny-floored, dust-free house if it is always in that condition? Only if that same house becomes fingerprinted and glopped with clay does it become noticeable as a negative deviation from the norm.

A closely related variant of this phenomenon is the fact that certain things and processes are not only unnoticed (except in their absence), but also typically disvalued. Such is the case with women's work. This is partly because such work is primarily maintenance work as opposed to creative effort, although you might reasonably argue that maintaining an existing creation is not to be denigrated if that creation was worth the initial effort to make it. Nonetheless, traditional women's work is typically conceived as trivial compared to men's work, when it is even noticed at all. Consequently, it is considered unsuitable to plotting for two reasons. First, plotting demands that there be clearly definable incidents with which to build plot, hardly the case with much amorphous women's work. Second, those incidents must have sufficient stature to rise above the level a culture defines as trivial.

Much as plots in traditional stories run a gamut from highly epic to lightly plotted, in the feminine waiting mode a similar situation occurs. Certainly not all women's lives—even the most sheltered, housebound sort—are entirely devoid of traditional plots in recognizable story form. However, the plot forms most characteristic of women's housework are typically not progressive. If we think of typical chores such as cooking, caretaking, and cleaning it quickly becomes apparent why this is so.

For a caretaker life often approaches stasis, particularly if her charge is an invalid. In that case there are likely to be days of hope when promise of renewed life appears possible. Yet overall, progress typically does not occur. The underlying pattern of such an existence is appropriately reflected in the French fairy tale known as "The Three Wasted Wishes" in which a poor man is unexpectedly granted three wishes by Jupiter. He rushes home to tell his wife and they sit down to decide what to wish for. In so doing the man forgetfully wishes for a sausage. So enraged does his wife become at his stupid waste of a precious wish, that she tongue-lashes him severely. To retaliate, the humiliated husband wishes the sausage onto the end of her nose. After prolonged debate, the husband relinquishes his final wish, and instead of lifelong riches, orders the sausage away. As the tale begins, so it ends, a brief remission of the status quo having marked its body.

A more extreme form of this reversion to "nothingness" occurs in the story of "The Fisherman and His Wife." Because of its greater length and complexity, this tale is more heavily plotted than "The Three Wasted Wishes." The only difference is that this time the wishes of the simple man are not wasted. Instead, following the advice of his ever-more-greedy wife, he first wishes for a cottage to replace his miserable hut. Next he is goaded by her to wish for a stone castle; then she must be King, Emperor, Pope, and finally God. With the last wish thunder resounds, the sky darkens, and the man and his wife return to their original hovel. Once again, the underlying pattern is from "nothingness" to "nothingness," this time interrupted with a series of apparently progressive incidents.

A somewhat different negative plot form exists in Sean O'Casey's play "The End of the Beginning," in which a man so taunts his wife about her easy role as housekeeper, that she eventually agrees to change places with him.[16] Once she leaves, her husband's nearly blind, bumbling friend Barry comes over. The husband, Darry, now begins to understand how wrong he was. As the day starts slipping away from him, first one thing then another goes wrong. Starting with a broken jug, the damage progresses through shelves of broken crockery, a broken window, a burned electric fixture, spilled oil, and a roped cow dangling midway between chimney and ground. By the time Darry's wife returns the original order of the house is totally destroyed. In this play drawn from an Irish fairy tale, the movement is from something to nothing, from order to chaos, without the subsequent return to order typical of an Aristotelian story. This pattern appropriately reflects the decreation so evident in the rituals of cooking, cleaning, and ordering, immediately followed by a destructive return to chaos.

Waiting as a structure is present in even more extreme form in an entire category of tales known as formula tales, which all exhibit the waiting pattern. Included in this group are cumulative tales such as "The House That Jack Built," in which it is not what happens, as in plotted stories, that dominates, but how it happens. And the element of repetition, through very slow enumeration, is the dominant principle:

> This is the house that Jack built.
>
> This is the malt
> That lay in the house that Jack built.
>
> This is the rat,
> That ate the malt
> That lay in the house that Jack built.
>
> This is the cat,
> That killed the rat,
> That ate the malt
> That . . .[17]

And so on.

Catch tales, unlike cumulative tales, seemingly tell a story. They begin clearly enough, progress to a middle, but then, as something unexpected happens, abort in *medias res*. Instead of reaching a climax, some irrelevant lines intervene, on purpose, to trick the reader rather than to fulfill her or his expectations. Shaggy dog stories fall in this category.

Another variation, unfinished or endless tales, fold in upon themselves like this:

> It was a dark and stormy night, and the men sat round the campfire. "Captain," said the lieutenant, tell us a story." Said the Captain, "It was a dark and stormy night, and the men sat round the campfire. " 'Captain,' " said the Lieutenant, " 'tell us a story.' "

Similarly, rounds repeat themselves *ad infinitum*.

Though these three tale types are all classed as tales, they are certainly not stories in the Aristotelian sense of the word, having no plot as such, nor any clear-cut beginning, middle, and ending. Their purpose is not to express content, but form qua form. In that respect, they far more closely approximate waiting, women's traditional pattern of being, than do stories like those of Penelope and Griselda which can *tell* about waiting, but have difficulty encapsulating it. These traditional types have existed for generations, yet their presence has not made nearly the impact that "regular" stories have. Unlike poetry, which they somewhat more closely resemble than stories, they do not exploit language so much as they do formal patterns alone. Until recently, such tales seemed little more than childish curiosities.

But starting along about the time of Chekhov, Flaubert, and Henry James, the Aristotelian legacy with its heavy emphasis on plot, began to change. Yet the term "story" persisted as the name for seemingly plotless stories which sometimes plunged in *medias res* and had no end. Since that time, we have seen Dorothy Richardson invent stream-of-consciousness, closely followed by the experiments of other writers like James Joyce, Virginia Woolf, William Faulkner, and Anaïs Nin. And finally, we have watched as absurdists like Ionesco, Pinter, and Beckett virtually destroyed whatever vestiges of traditional story remained. Furthermore, what they didn't demolish, metafictionists like John Barth and William Gass did. Rather than following the traditional progressive notion of time and history that I have labeled masculine, such writers so flout the convention of time as we customarily construe it, that what remains is surely as motionless or amorphous at times as the most vituperative Medusa could wish. In these writings clock time virtually ceases. Consider, for example, this typical sample from Beckett's *Endgame*, when Hamm asks, "What time is it?" and Clov responds, "The same as usual."[18] Such an odd response to an everyday question immediately suggests to the reader that no temporal progression has occurred at all.

When recognizable temporal progression ceases in story, narration, as we typically use the term, ceases as well. Without plot, the lyric mode dominates and we end up with the paradox of storyless stories—stories in which nothing happens, just as "nothing happens" in traditional women's mode of being, the waiting mode.

It is possibly for this reason that instead of writing stories women as a class have been more prone to engage in a different form entirely—the journal. As reviewer Holly Prado says of this form which so clearly reflects the waiting mode:

> The journal, I believe, is a feminine form. The feminine principle, as has been said often enough, is inclusive and cyclical rather than single-minded. If there's any form of writing which reflects this principle, it's the journal. Everything fits, just as everything fits into women's daily lives. The feminine is also multiple. . . . [19]

Yet in the United States, it is only since the 1960s, with the rise of the new social history derived from the Annales School of French historical study that this affinity of women for journal and diary writing has become generally known. The names of those who kept them are likely to remain largely unknown, for most of them were ordinary women engaged in traditional domestic endeavors; literary exemplars like Anaïs Nin being relatively rare exceptions. As Maryjane Moffat says in *Revelations: Diaries of Women*:

> The form has been an important outlet for women partly because it is an analogue to their lives; emotional, fragmentary, interrupted, modest, not to be taken seriously, private, restricted, daily, trivial, formless, concerned with self, as endless as their tasks.[20]

Point of View

But it is not just plot, with its temporal essence, that makes story a less appropriate structuring device for women's traditional experiences than the journal. The point of view of most story tellers is equally suspect. This is a component of stories not included in the original Aristotelian analysis. But ever since writers like Henry James and Joseph Conrad began making point of view an integral part of their stories, the stance of the teller has been recognized as a crucial component of literature. Who tells the story and how is just as important as what is told. Now that even minimally trained readers are aware of this dimension of story it seems startling to realize that it was ignored for centuries.

Applied to the situation of women, point of view has generally been equally ignored. Although the literary use of the term typically focuses on differences in point of view from one individual to the next, in a broader sense the term becomes indistinguishable from group perspective or *weltanschauung*. Thus histories typically refer to the *weltanschauung*, or world view, of a specific culture in a particular age. But this sort of group point of view can be extended still more, becoming in its broadest sense the structures of Western culture as a whole. These structures, which are the shared assumptions upon which everything we label "knowledge" has been erected, have been largely the ideas of males. The comparatively few women who have been writers have typically been those who were educated, and phallocentric thinking has been at the center of education. Until this century, education was typically the province of the few—the elite white males sufficiently moneyed to be able to afford the time it takes. The stories they read, like the histories they studied, all passed along a man-centered conception of the world. Few of the women granted the masculine privilege of education deeply questioned its underlying structures in their thinking or in the stories they wrote.

This preeminence of a phallocentric perspective in Western culture, more than any other factor, is what makes the current emergence of women so problematic. On the surface, women's emergence appears straightforward—women have been oppressed victims, confined by masculine injustice to the prison of home. Now, however, like other previously oppressed groups, they are finally assuming seats in corporate boardrooms. But their nascent "success" in so doing, often reflects an assumption that corporate boardrooms are not only good, but necessarily better than isolated houses. Point of view has taught women and men alike that certain places and modes of being are "better" than others. So far most women have not sufficiently recognized equivalent structures of their own through which they can adequately view their lives from a genuinely gynocentric perspective. That lack places all but a few culturally uncontaminated women in an extremely awkward position: how can they be sure they are experiencing life in ways authentic to their innermost natures and not simply aping the supposedly superior ways of men?

The perspective historically promulgated throughout Western culture teaches girls as well as boys to value masculine culture more highly than its feminine counterpart. This is one of the reasons why questing is storied and waiting is not. Women like men, have consequently learned to judge the two modes accordingly.

The thinking responsible for fostering in women such woman-rejecting thinking has its roots in the ancient classical world. According to

Aristotle who, in contrast to Plato, gave voice to the accepted beliefs of his fellow Greeks, "the woman is as it were an impotent male, for it is through a certain incapacity that the female is female, being incapable of concocting the nutriment in its last stage into semen."[21] In the Judeo-Christian tradition this notion of woman as a misbegotten or lacking male takes a slightly different turn, as the Genesis account indicates. Here woman is seen as lacking because she is not created directly from God like man is, but is instead a being derived from man. Paul reasserts this view in statements like, "For a man indeed ought not to cover his head, for as much as he is the image and glory of God: but woman is the glory of the man." (I Cor. 11:7).

Taken out of context, as he frequently is, Augustine also appears to reinforce the patriarchal emphases of the Genesis and Pauline positions by statements like, ". . . the mother herself no more creates the nature of her child than she creates herself."[22] But he also makes equivalent statements for men: "Neither the wife nor the husband's part is anything, but it is God who fashions the form of the offspring; nor is the mother who bears and brings the child to birth anything, but it is God who gives the growth."[23] While it is still the so-called masculine principle which is credited with the woman's role, it is not human males who receive her due as is so strongly implied when the passages are not cited in full.

These notions of women as derivative creatures and misbegotten males come together in the thirteenth-century writings of Thomas Aquinas. In his *Summa Theologica,* Thomas grounds the traditional Christian subordination of women in the Aristotelian notion that woman is a defective male lacking vital force. In his first point he says:

> It seems that woman ought not to have been produced in the original production of things. For the Philosopher [Aristotle] says that the female is a male *manqué.* But nothing *manqué* or defective should have been produced in the first establishment of things; so woman ought not to have been produced then.[24]

He then goes on to argue in his second point that subjection and inferiority are a result of sin and that woman is by nature of lower capacity than man. In his third argument he says that woman ought not to have been produced, because all occasions of sin should be eliminated. Even in his reply, Thomas says nothing to mitigate the harshness of his view. Instead, he justifies God's creation of woman on the grounds that "it is not good for man to be alone; let us make him a help that is like himself"; that subjection of women to men is for *women's* benefit; and that "if God had removed everything from the world in which man has found an occasion of sin, the universe would have remained incomplete."[25]

In the nineteenth century Darwin gives such traditional misogynist thought a new twist in *The Descent of Man* when he claims that sexual selection accounts for the differences between men and women:

> With respect to differences of this nature [the mental powers of the two sexes] between men and women, it is probable that sexual selection has played a highly important part. . . . The chief distinction in the intel lectual powers of the two sexes is shown by man's attaining to a higher eminence, in whatever he takes up, than can woman—whether requiring deep thought, reason, or imagination, or merely the uses of senses and hands.[26]

In the twentieth century, Freud's unwillingness to give up these inherited phallocentric assumptions that women are deficient unnecessarily encumber his thinking. When he works out his otherwise elegant Oedipus theory, he realizes, somewhat belatedly, that his system is a bit awkward when it comes to explaining the same problem (*mutatis mutandis*) for girl children. The sleight of hand necessary to "save the appearances" of his system, is his theory of penis envy, leading him to assert that girls develop a castration fear like that of their brothers:

> The castration complex of girls is also started by the sight of the genitals of the other sex. . . . They feel seriously wronged, often declare that they want to "have something like it, too" and fall a victim to "envy for the penis." . . .[27]

Even so enlightened a thinker as Norman O. Brown clings to a phallocentric perspective, saving the appearance of its system rather than admitting that a new one might better fit the facts: ". . . the penis is the 'narcissistic representative,' or 'double,' of the total personality; the phallus 'a miniature of the total ego.' "[28] When he speaks of the ego as the image of the penis, Brown raises an interesting point for women, for unless women are deemed totally without ego, he seems to be saying that the prevailing psychological image for women as for men in our society is phallic! The impact of this thought is staggering. It would mean that *there is no image of the feminine!* In other words, in psychiatric thinking there is no view from the "known," but only from the knower. But because literal knowers may be either male or female, this anomalous situation unbalances the commonly accepted masculine/feminine dichotomized superstructure upon which Brown builds. Hypothetical constructs have to be added to save the appearances. Thus Brown resorts to the strange concept of a "female penis" to "save" the system, even though the comments he makes otherwise generally attack that system.

This type of thinking tends to place flesh-and-blood women in a very awkward position. If they keep silent, following the model of "the feminine," then the negative stereotypes of feminine submissiveness, non-existence, stupidity, animality, and the like appear to be substantiated. On the other hand, if they speak they necessarily must use the very superstructure which is based upon a masculine mode of thinking. The situation is indeed a vicious circle.

Many women, too, wish to "save the appearances" generated by masculine perspectives. Undeniably, there is a great deal in what we generally call Western culture that is worth saving. There is much, too, that women understandably wish to try for themselves. But again, the problems arise when they try to determine what they authentically value as opposed to what a phallocentric perspective masquerading as "Western culture" has taught them they should value. This is a variant of the problem that emerges for any out group as it tries to achieve equality within a dominant caste.

A major contributing factor to this issue of perspective, which adds to the common problem of women's false consciousness, complicates it exceedingly. The masculine/feminine dichotomy that seems to necessitate sexually distinct points of view is a misleading structure. On the surface it appears to be a symmetrical relationship in which women are opposite to men and feminine is opposite to masculine. In fact, however, the system is inconsistent. Sometimes the terms reflect an asymmetrical opposition, sometimes, a symmetrical one. Reformulating the opposition of masculine and feminine in terms of something concrete like salt and pepper clarifies the problem.

Asked to name the opposite of salt, many people will respond "pepper." But some will say, "non-salt." How *very* different these two answers are. One specifies and delimits, making the answer approximately equal to salt; the other incorporates everything that is not itself salt. Consequently, the "non-salt" answer is infinite, whereas "pepper" is finite.

A comparable split governs thinking about the polarity of masculine/feminine. Sometimes the two are spoken of as if they were salt and pepper; sometimes as if they were salt and non-salt. By analogy, while I could presumably find words appropriate to pepper, how could I ever find them all for non-salt? To do so, obviously, salt has to be the point of reference. Comparably, this is what has happened to women and the feminine. In one model "the feminine" exists; in the other, it does not. The latter model dominates: our language is mainly relational, just as women's lives traditionally have been.

Three quite different paradigms suggest the complexity of this issue of perspective relative to women's role. First, I can adopt the familiar view that there is a single human nature, traditionally modeled on a *masculine* perspective, from which women have historically been deemed to diverge sufficiently to make them somewhat less than human. Given this view, a useful model is the familiar fairy tale, "The Frog Prince." After all, the frog is not *really* a frog, but a human being. Consider the pain it must feel to be hurled against the wall and to be called ugly. Yet inwardly it knows only its false self is being so abused. If its tormentor only knew that the frog really was human, there would be no problem. In the end, of course, the frog triumphs and enters its rightful place as a handsome prince. Here the inner sense of self is both human and masculine, the outer experience less than human. For many women, this is a fairly accurate model. It occurs when a girl patterns herself after men rather than women. Usually the process is so unconscious that she has no idea that she is incorporating into her thinking masculine values which denigrate women to a status less than fully human. Because her observations of the world tell her that it is men, not women, who wield power and experience relative freedom, and her reading confirms what her senses and intellect convey, it is not surprising that it is the Prince, not the Princess, with whom she identifies. To her way of thinking, she must eventually triumph. How shocking to discover, usually at, or shortly after, puberty, that unexpected obstacles block her way. For her, conflict typically emerges when she struggles to be her boyish self and yet simultaneously attract the attention of males. The question is whether she experiences true consciousness or not. Is that inner male-identified self a reflection of true or false consciousness? What is her own genuine perspective?

A second, very different, paradigm reflects the previously mentioned ancient belief that there are not one, but two, distinct human natures: whereas man derives from God, woman derives from man, making her clearly inferior from the start. This belief in two different human natures is typically voiced from a masculine perspective, to show why women are so very different from men. Whereas the single human nature view, imagined in terms of the Frog Prince, at least allows the possibility for a woman metaphorically to achieve selfhood, albeit as a man, this model does not. It derives from the well-known folkloristic motif of the Loathly Lady. Best known from Chaucer's "Wife of Bath's Tale," the Loathly Lady typically first appears to a troubled young man as just what her name indicates—an ugly hag. She promises to aid him on condition that he subsequently grant her a boon. The boon turns out to be marriage to her. When the young man finally kisses her, lo and behold, she turns into a beautiful young woman. Though Chaucer tells it as an exemplary tale about youth and age, the metamorphic aspect, as with any trans-formative tale, raises the issue of whether one of these is the true woman? Does one form represent her authentic self, the other merely a falsely assumed one? In fairy tales that same motif often appears with the addition of fairy glamour which makes the aged hag merely appear young and beautiful to an enchanted mortal male. This paradigm suggests that false consciousness is simply a survival technique, the counterpart of shuffling among blacks.

But what happens if a woman is so taken in by her own glamour that she believes the role she assumes? Obviously there are degrees of self-awareness and degrees of masculinity and femininity within women. But in general, women have been conceived of either as what they "should" be: feminine, or as deviant: masculine. Yet those two ways of seeing women merely reflect the division of the sexes legitimated by patriarchal religions. Is it possible that there is some other way of proceeding?

A third paradigm is suggested by Wallace Stevens's poem "A Rabbit as King of the Ghosts," in which the reader enters into the reality of a rabbit, "to feel that the light is a rabbit-light,/In which everything is meant for you/And nothing need be explained. . . . The trees around are for you,/The whole of the wideness of night is for you,/A self that touches all edges,/You become a self that fills the four corners of night."[29] It seems reasonable to suppose that, like the rabbit of this poem, women, too, can enter a "woman-light" in which everything is meant for them and nothing need be explained. But to fully enter this woman light women have to realize that they may be lucky not to have told many stories themselves. As critic Robert Scholes says: "Knowing one thing is a way of not knowing something else."[30] By and large, most women have known a nonstoried existence, a situation far preferable to that engendered by false stories.

Character

The shared assumptions of Western culture, which constitute point of view in the broad sense, are seemingly common to both women's and men's experiences while actually being phallocentric. As a result, character is correspondingly distorted. Typically it is only men who are cast as heroes in literature. While the Greek word *hero* has numerous meanings ranging from gentleman (as Homer used the term) to superhuman male (as in the case of a figure like King Arthur) its significance in this context rests on the fact that a hero is a fully autonomous individual who is not defined solely in relation to other characters. Whatever else he may be, he is clearly a self.

Some women, such as the biblical Deborah, Judith, and Esther, have also functioned as heroes. But more commonly women who achieve autonomy are portrayed as negative exceptions who are in some way "fallen" or "bad." Frequently the name "witch" is hurled at them, a term of opprobrium most women prefer to avoid. By contrast, to be what women are typically expected to be—heroines or princesses—is the counterpart of being "good niggers." Such ways of naming represent powerful tools of masculine control over most women's behavior.

Unlike men, whose quests may or may not be for love, those women who do attempt quests are usually assumed to do so for either love or revenge. And when a woman quests for love she is ordinarily removed from the category of acceptable womanhood unless she is still chaste, a condition almost definitionally opposed to active female questing. Consequently, if a woman does "make it" into story or history, her success is usually counted as a social failure for which she will pay heavily.

But if she still functions as a woman but tries to act on her own initiative, what happens? Then she may well fail to be either a hero or the unequal, but more common, equivalent of a heroine. Instead she becomes an antihero. In contrast to a hero, who is typically better than the average man, an antihero is worse or lower. The case of Leopold Bloom in James Joyce's *Ulysses* is particularly illustrative. In contrast to the heroic Ulysses of Homer's *Odyssey*, Bloom is a common man. Where Ulysses is king, leader, and warrior, Bloom is both cuckold and buffoon. Instead of battling monsters and circumventing enchantments like his prototype does, Bloom peddles advertising space along the dirty streets of Dublin.

For a woman, being an antihero is apt to equal whoredom. Typical of such female antiheroes are the numerous women who figure prominently in the novels of Jean Rhys. Typically in Rhys' works the central character is a sensitive, intelligent woman who is kept by various men. Although her role as mistress or lover would seem to place her more in the heroine category, she is seldom rescued and never permanently. Furthermore, she often ends up in this role because she originally chose adventure. As Julia, in *After Leaving Mr. Mackenzie,* says to one of her male friends,

> "I wanted to go away with just the same feeling a boy has when he wants to run away to sea—at least that I imagine a boy has. Only, in my adventure, men were mixed up, because of course they had to be. You understand, don't you? Do you understand that a girl might have that feeling?"[31]

Such a woman epitomizes the horror of the failed feminine quest, exemplifying the largely unspoken nightmare of middle-class women: What would happen to me if no one were around to take care of me? To avoid this nightmare, many young women have preferred the "safe" role of heroine.

Unlike a hero, a heroine does not save herself from whatever predicament befalls her: a male savior inevitably comes along to rescue her. If it is Sleeping Beauty, the passive heroine par excellence, the prince need only part the concealing thorns and plant his euphemistic kiss to "save" her; if it is little Red Riding Hood, who tried so hard to do things her way, the rescuing axman must kill the wolf in grandma's clothing. And if it is Andromeda, Perseus must kill the menacing dragon.

In daily life as in myth, the role of heroine has hampered women's development into fully mature, autonomous human selves. This is so largely because cosmos and eros thoroughly intertwine for most women. Often we smile to hear a young lover say, "I couldn't live without my beloved." Though such a statement is made by men as well as women, for many traditionally reared women it has been almost literally true, although not for precisely the reason they thought. Until recently many middle-class women were groomed so exclusively for marriage that they were scarcely fit to survive any other way. Some, blessed with prudent parents, were trained for a womanly pursuit like teaching, just in case. But in contrast to their brothers, such young women were seldom encouraged to think of their pursuits as anything but back-up strategies. Nowadays, emphasis on careers for women makes notions of lifelong commitment to career less foreign to ambitious females.

But as Colette Dowling points out in a *New York Times Magazine* article, a traditional woman typically grows up associating future loved ones with security—the familiar savior prince syndrome.[32] Like Mommy and Daddy, Prince Charming will provide for all physical needs when he comes along. If he actually does so, however, a woman may well remain, as many critics of both sexes have noted, an infantilized adult who fails to achieve autonomous selfhood. Unlike most Western men, who grow up expecting to support themselves and their families, such a woman typically has little or no life apart from her home sphere. Her entire cosmos is permeated with her spouse's presence. By contrast, his work sphere is totally separate unless he works at home. Chances are that most of the home's furnishings were bought and paid for by him, though she may have selected most of them. Everywhere she looks she sees evidence that without him she could not physically survive. As many feminists put it, she is one man away from welfare.

If she comes from an extreme of wealth or poverty her situation will differ, of course. In one case her family of origin will presumably support her in the style to which she is accustomed. In the other, she might actually be better off without her Prince Charming. But for the vast majority of women in the middle, to think of subsisting alone was, and still is, almost overwhelming. Consequently, any change in her relationship with her husband automatically disrupts her entire cosmos, threatening to revert it to chaos. If he leaves on a journey at all perilous, his absence signals potential loss of support. She therefore finds herself forced constantly to reenact her need of "rescue" by him: every time he returns he once again "saves" her from independent existence on her own. Although her psychological and physical needs to play heroine instead of hero are frequently intense, a traditional woman finds her life so circumscribed by this enforced role that she may be incapable of finding words to speak about her experience. As Simone de Beauvoir points out in her crucial book *The Second Sex*, women have been defined historically as Other.[33] And to internalize otherness is almost definitionally to be unable to speak in the language of self. Much as animals do not name themselves but receive their names from men, so with women. Not only have they been named by men, women have been defined, told exactly what they were to be, with an implicit "or else" menacing them through the words men use to shape them. To experience being Other is often to feel so schizophrenically torn, that not even a clandestinely authentic "I" dares to speak.

To be Other is to make statements like, "But of course a wife should be willing to give up her work for her husband and move where he goes." Or "I don't understand what all the fuss is about. I've been working at a man's job for thirty years and I've never experienced any discrimination. If I could do it, why can't they?" To be Other is also to see and judge yourself through the imagined eyes of someone else, momentarily borrowing that person's subjectivity through imagination and seeing yourself through *his* eyes. For instance, a young girl walking down a small-town street thronged with adolescent males may feel such dread that she crosses the street. She may also suddenly see herself as she fancies the boys see her: a nubile body in slightly too-tight jeans and faded blue T-shirt.

Through these borrowed boy-eyes she experiences herself as a clumsy, but sexually provocative "piece," and wishes now for the comforting concealment of a sloppy sweatshirt and jeans a size too large, for sneakers instead of three-inch slides. In her mind she already hears their insults and obscenities as she passes by. Never once does it occur to her to think of *them* through her own eyes . . . not now, not while she is within calling distance. This young girl's experience is totally Other for the agonizing moment in which awareness of the boys' subjectivity destroys her own. With such repeated experiences of Otherness, to expect women to be able to speak in authentic voices is a little like looking at rocks, trees, or catfish to demand that they speak in the language of humans. This is what it means to exist in women's traditional pattern of being: the waiting mode.

Setting

Although it seems unlikely at first glance, setting and character are often so closely intertwined for women as to blur the normally accepted distinctions between them. For instance, to make a statement like, "A woman is the belly of the whale," sounds very odd indeed. By contrast, we assume that, "When reading a novel we can obviously tell the characters apart from the inanimate world around them; we have little difficulty knowing that Catherine Earnshaw is a character and that Wuthering Heights is a house."[34] It seems absurd to even make a statement which is so obvious on one level that it should not even require saying. Or so it seems. Actually, however, both statements, from opposite points of view, raise a very serious issue.

In traditional tales, for instance, the locale of a woman is frequently an island, a castle, or a garden. Typically, her attributes are mirrored in her surroundings, making person and place analogous. As Renaissance poets from Ariosto to Spencer attest, the setting, particularly in its garden form, is characteristically an earthly paradise perceived as a place of danger to men. In such gardens, according to Renaissance scholar A. Bartlett Giamatti, "a man is tempted to let down his guard, to succumb to the desire for security and female domination which the garden promises."[35]

Certainly the interrelationship Giamatti notes between persona and place is not limited either to the time period of the Renaissance or to the female sex. The setting of Edgar Allan Poe's "The Fall of the House of Usher" is but one of hundreds of examples focused on the interrelationship of place and man. In it, the decaying state of the house clearly mimics the emotional instability of its owner:

> Minute fungi overspread the whole exterior, hanging in a fine tangled web-work from the eaves. Yet all this was apart from any extraordinary dilapidation. No portion of the masonry had fallen and there appeared to be a wild inconsistency between its still perfect adaptation of parts, and the crumbling condition of the individual stones.[36]

But unlike men as a class, all women are treated like settings instead of persons in certain, crucial circumstances. Consider these words by Dr. J. C. Willke, president of the National Right to Life Committee:

> Enactment of the human life amendment is the central focus of the entire movement. It would restore legal personhood and return civil rights to an entire class of living Americans. The discrimination they suffer is based on the place of residence: the womb. If a kid could move to a new location, his life would be protected. Now a private citizen, the mother, has the right to destroy a life.[37]

In what he says Willke totally ignores the personhood of women. To make his point, he has to see women, as countless men before him have done, as mere settings or homes of unborn children. It is a view which ignores the fact that such "settings" have rights and feelings, too.

This view of women as settings, or objects, led historically to the English legal phenomenon known as coverture. When a woman married she became *covert*, "in Latine *nupta*, that is, 'veiled'; as it were, clouded and overshadowed; she hath lost her streame. . . . Her new self is her superior; her companion, her master. . . ."[38] The law of Coverture gave sole administration of a woman's property, including her personal possessions, to her husband.[39] Even to retain her own jewels if he predeceased her necessitated a specific bequest in his will. Coverture also prohibited her from any legal rights regarding her own children; her husband could dispose of them as he so desired. Nor could she make contracts or be tried in court. Similarly, an unmarried woman was legally as much governed by her father's authority as her married counterpart was by her husband's.

Structuralist Juri M. Lotman provides some useful guidelines for analyzing this phenomen whereby one human so objectifies another as to nullify her existence and render her an immobile setting. Looking at literary texts, Lotman sets up an opposition between immobile and mobile elements. Immobile elements represent all the structures of the hero's environment, mobile ones the hero.[40] He further distinguishes between mobile characters, heroes, and immobile ones, personified circumstances which name their surroundings. Lotman's technique very well illustrates the way humans are able to transform fellow humans into "Others"—objects or settings at the immobile end of the scale. Only the hero, the one from whose point of view we follow the story, is mobile. Hence, only the hero appears to be alive. Whatever is not alive surely need not be treated as though it were human. Such is the pattern of logic by which some men—but women as an entire class—have been placed in an immobile time frame distinct from the mobility implicit in history.

Thought and Diction

Like perspective and character, which are fairly obvious in their phallocentricity, thought and diction are equally biased sexually. Although the two are not identical, Aristotle deals with both together in the nineteenth chapter of the *Poetics*; it therefore seems appropriate to maintain the connection between them. As he uses the terms, diction means "the art of delivery," as it is nowadays taught in drama schools. Thought, (*dianoia*) on the other hand, is an inclusive word covering reasoning, experience of emotion, and "every effect which has to be produced by speech . . . proof and refutation; the excitation of the feelings, such as pity, fear, anger, and the like; the suggestion of importance or its opposite."[41] Aristotle then deals with language separately in the next chapter, in a discussion limited entirely to grammar.

For our purposes, the important element is language as Aristotle deals with it under thought. What is the language of the feminine? Since men have been the predominant spokesmen in our culture, do we have only their phallic language? When women have spoken, have they, therefore, used this same phallic language?

Does that mean that no such thing as a language of the feminine exists? No language that can be called language? Is language, by fiat, a product of the phallic, so that once you use language, you are automatically in the phallic mode, no matter what? Such a view simply repeats, in Norman O. Brown's language, what Freud and Jung said somewhat differently: the unknown, whether it is called the unconscious, the feminine, the vaginal, can only speak through the conscious, the masculine, the phallic.

There is a terrible danger in this kind of thinking, however, for literalism inevitably will take it to mean that the female only speaks through the male, a view already too long accepted as worldwide suffragist struggles well attest. Furthermore, this view, promulgated by Brown, makes us all masculine in our conscious mode, all feminine in our unconscious. This is clearly one mode of conceptualizing, the one that both Freud and Jung followed.

Some language theorists, however, argue that there is, indeed, something called women's speech. To take just one example, Robin Lakoff argues that men and women develop two different languages whose characteristics she carefully analyzes.[42] Women's language is typified by nine distinct traits. First of all, women, like men, use more specific words in areas of interest to them; hence words like *magenta, shirr,* and *dart,* all of which relate to clothes and sewing, are less likely to be used by men than women. A second characteristic of women's language Lakoff isolates is prevalence of empty adjectives—words like *divine, charming, cute.* (This point seems highly debatable when you think of typical contemporary student usage from both sexes: *great, decent, really,* and *really excellent.*)

While tag questions such as "Isn't it," added on to any factual statement—"It's a nice day, isn't it?"—seem legitimate, hedges such as *well, you know,* and *kind of,* seem just as problematic as empty words, to anyone familiar with student language. Use of the intensive *so* as in "It's *so* warm out today," or "He's *so* cute," seems more appropriately woman-connected. But whereas hypercorrect grammar may once have been gender-specific it no longer seems prevalent in either sex. The last three characteristics Lakoff singles out are superpolite forms of expression (Has she ignored the influx of four-letter words from both sexes since the 60s?), the lack of joke-telling among women, and speaking in italics, by which she means frequent heightened emphasis on key words: "He s very cute."

Whether a language theorist like Lakoff is correct or not, her analysis of presumed differences between women's and men's speaking does not sufficiently probe the seriousness of the problem. More important than these observable, surface distinctions is the tacit dimension at which unspoken assumptions are taken for granted. At this deep level the words a culture has never thought necessary—thus never conceived— are extremely significant. Thus it seems legitimate to ponder absences such as any positive, joyous words for menstruation, which is, instead, given such derogatory names as "the curse." Similarly, why are there no positive words for older women? And why are self-directed women so often labeled witches, or considered masculine, instead of being given exultant, positive names equivalent to the masculine "hero?"

This marked absence of certain kinds of woman-centered words reflects a problem that runs deeply throughout the assumptions of Western culture: woman in myth equals the totality of what can be known, and the hero equals the knower. By extension, "knowing" is equated with masculinity. Such an equation, whether it involves the knowing of a hero on his quest or of a scientist with his matter is bound to confuse a woman.

It means that if women want "to know," to be active and not passive, they are trapped by a structure of received human thought processes that says women are known and men are knowers. If the function of myths and stories is to tell us who we are as human beings, only the male form of human being is thus given satisfactory definition. Definitions of women have been couched in terms that can only satisfy a "knower," but not what is known. That places a paradoxical burden upon those women who wish "to know" rather than to be known, for there are virtually no satisfactory images of women as knowers. Women who wish to "know" must deny within themselves their inherited senses of what it means to be in the form of woman: they must repress certain aspects, not only of themselves, but of their worlds. Even more destructive, since the entire edifice of Western thought has been built from masculine perspectives, a woman must also continuously distort her world view, herself, or sometimes both. Otherwise what she seeks to know will not make sense. In addition, it means she will fail to develop a language authentically reflecting *her* joys, *her* fears in contrast to those expected of her by the dominant cultural point of view. Fortunately, a few feminist thinkers like Mary Daly, Adrienne Rich, and Susan Griffin typify women (though still a small minority) who are truly struggling against the weight of inherited patriarchal language to create new linguistic possibilities to express women's actual experiences.

If they are ultimately successful, the experiments of such innovators may refocus attention on some of the still largely ignored, positive aspects of women's traditional experiences. Such a refocusing could help change the denigration, so typical of spokeswomen of the left and spokesmen of nearly all positions, of women's traditional housewife role.

To ignore such innovative possibilities and continue acting on the assumption that the more traditional modes of ordering time and space— history, story, and image—are normative, seems foolish indeed. Similarly, to keep expanding the definitions of story and history to include "storyless" stories and "inner history" raises some disturbing questions. If constructs like story and history in their more traditional forms are both masculine constructs, then widening the definitions to include formerly excluded elements may, at the same time, obliterate bits that don't quite fit the structures even in their expanded forms. In the process of transforming previously omitted material into history or reinterpreting heroines as heroes, are we simply translating the "language" or the experience of a subject group into that of the dominant one, and in the process losing whatever subtle nuances don't readily shift?

While I am in no sense arguing for a reactionary return to the old traditions, I worry that something of value from women's traditional mode of being may be irretrievably lost as we hurry to assume places in what is still predominantly a man's world. Ultimately, waiting appears to name a *via negativa* that so far has been construed as the inenarrable counterpart to questing. As such, it is neither inferior nor superior, but merely different. Now it is time to find appropriate means to explore the nature of that difference.

9

THE BORING
AND THE
MYSTICAL

At the same time that some feminists are struggling overtly with the inherited structures and contents of Western thought, a parallel, nongender-related phenomenon crucial to understanding the theological significance of women's traditional mode of being, the waiting mode, has been occurring in the arts. The evolution of Aristotelian story into "storyless stories," noted under plot has its parallel in the visual arts. If plot still seems central to what the average individual defines as story, image is its counterpart in painting. But it has been years since one could take for granted that canvases would contain recognizable images.

When images do appear, frequently they are distorted, as in the work of an artist like Yves Tanguy. Or, themselves undistorted, they may nonetheless distort perspectives, as occurs, for example, in Picasso's *Girl Before a Mirror*. Still more disturbing to many viewers, however, is the trend in minimal art towards dispensing with what some people would call images at all, if by image they intend a relationship between what appears on the canvas and something external to it. Typically an image exists at a remove from its source, even if that source exists solely in the artist's mind, much as a word exists at a distance from its referent. Conceivably instead of using words, we could manipulate the actual things to which they refer, as Swift depicts for the Lagadano who "speak" with objects in *Gulliver's Travels*. Then we would not be removed from our speech the way we now are by words. Similarly, minimal artists who paint monochrome or single subject canvases are attempting to delve beneath interpretation and focus on immediate perception of objects at the level of pure sensation. Thus they concentrate on pure form, color, line, plane, and texture, as such, without attempting to "mean" anything beyond the forms themselves. Instead of trying to create a semblance of something, what they create is itself the "something." The painting is exactly what our senses tell us it is: color, line, texture, form and plane—no more and no less.

Underlying such minimal endeavors is an existential philosophic stance which follows Sartre's dictum that "existence precedes essence," rather than vice versa. According to art critic Allen Leepa, "rather than deal with meanings that are abstracted from their referents, the minimal artist deals with a more immediate objective, an 'impersonal' world of phenomenological meanings."[1]

This emphasis on things themselves rather than transcendent meanings relates directly to what waiting has meant in women's lives. Ordinarily when we use the word *waiting* we add a *for* after it as in *Waiting for Godot*. But what if we drop the *for* and simply look at waiting as waiting, the way minimal artists look at forms as forms rather than asking, What do the forms mean? Then waiting can be seen as having a meaning in and of itself quite apart from any end.

Two qualities are common to these twin developments away from story and image in literature and painting: boringness and mysticism. Each is also a way of naming a dominant quality of women's waiting mode. But *boringness* is an awkward term. Changing it to *the Boring*, makes it slightly easier to work with, for that at least places it in an aesthetic category comparable to the more traditional categories of the Beautiful, the Ugly, and the Sublime. But it is still problematic. As in the case of the Ugly, there is inherent in the word *boring* the notion of turning away. Thus the artist or the critic working with this category risks making his material too boring to sustain his audience's attention.

There is also an inherent semantic difficulty that makes the term awkward to work with. Although you may turn away from the Ugly, you do not do so in fear of becoming ugly or uglified, unless you still believe in imitative magic. By contrast, you turn away from the Boring to avoid becoming bored. Thus, although the terms *boredom* or *ennui* in the arts would sound less awkward, neither is accurate. Both refer to an effect of *the Boring* on a percipient, not a cause. Yet to further confuse the situation, sometimes boredom does occur within a work itself, for a *character* may experience it. Consequently, there is danger that the term *the Boring* may slip, sometimes meaning an aesthetic component of a work, sometimes meaning an emotional state more properly character- ized as boredom.

Despite these difficulties, *the Boring* is one way to accurately describe what lies beyond story and image, as mystical or *the Mystical* is another. A number of qualities, also applicable to traditional women's experience, characterize both: monotony, abstraction, plotlessness, minimalness, repetitiveness, incompleteness, to name a few. Many of these phenom- ena occur, too, in certain traditional religions through chanting, drum beats, ingestion of various drugs, twirling, fasting, engaging in lengthy vigils. All are used to induce a trance-like, mystical state in which con- sciousness is altered and rationality put in abeyance. Similarly, when you are bored without being turned away from the source of the bore- dom-producing stimulus, you are thrown into such a state.

In art, literature, and traditional women's lives a mystical state may be produced by manipulating these "boring" qualities in varying ways. Monotony, for example, occurs in its most literal sense, as a single tone or color, in numerous contemporary paintings. You need only recall an Ad Reinhardt all-black or all-navy blue canvas in this respect. Closely related is lack of variation. Too close a focus on a single theme frequently occurs in many of Andy Warhol's works. How different can one Camp- bell's soup can be from another? Similarly, think of the monotony and lack of variation involved in such household tasks as drying dishes or ironing one white shirt after another after another. . . . Is monotony of this sort any different from that produced by countless repetitions of the word *om?* In all these instances an individual's sensitivity to stimuli is being abnormally manipulated.

Two characteristics of the Boring and the Mystical slightly more dif- ficult to evaluate are: elements devoid of interest and elements conducive to tedium. Both are inherently subjective. Thus, while you can objec- tively call an Ad Reinhardt black canvas monotonous, one viewer might nonetheless consider it interesting while another sees it as devoid of interest and hence conducive to tedium. Similarly, one woman may consider ironing interesting while another does not. In this respect the Boring and the Mystical, like the Ugly and the Beautiful, are only partially amenable to objective analysis.

Besides analyzing the objective and subjective elements of the Boring and the Mystical you can examine different types of each as well. One type is caused by surfeit. Too much of anything overwhelms a percipient. Such excess can result from too many stimuli on the one hand, or too great an expanse on the other. For this reason, a picture crammed full of various elements can be as boring as one too little filled. In contrast to surfeit, the latter kind of boringness results from deprivation. Here you might compare the overstuffed house full of antimacassars and objets d'art to its blank-walled, nearly furnitureless counterpart.

Both surfeit and deprivation occur in what might be called the Boring of the large, such as you experience when confronted with vast stretches of space or time. Either temporally or spatially, such vastness seems infinite, tending to overwhelm you. Opposed to this overwhelming type of the Boring there is the Boring of the small in which there is too little to occupy your mind. Hence, you are bored for exactly the opposite reason. Whereas story tends to create illusions, either of reality or of make-believe, elements of the Boring or the Mystical reverse the process, breaking apart illusions instead. Generally we tend to see disillusionment as undesirable and negative. Actually, however, if we think of it as dis-illusionment, separating the prefix from the root, its opposing, positive meaning is more apparent.

Almost any fairy tale involving metamorphosis deals with disillusionment in this sense. The familiar stories of swan men or maidens are all illustrative. In the Grimms' story of "The Six Swans," for example, an archetypally evil queen-stepmother enchants her six stepsons by witchcraft, giving the illusion to the world at large that they are swans. To dis-enchant them their sister must neither speak nor laugh for six years. The task nearly costs her her life, and deludes her husband into thinking that she is evil. When she is falsely accused of killing their own children, unable to speak in her own defense, her silence does create the illusion that she is the evil woman he mistakes her for. Nonetheless, she completes the task, dis-enchanting her brothers at the appropriate time:

> The swans came close up to her with rushing wings and swooped round her, so that she could throw the shirts over them. And when that had been done the swan skins fell off them, and her brothers stood before her quite safe and sound.[2]

And with her brothers' dis-enchantment comes the dis-illusionment of her husband. Now, as she talks for the first time in six years, the illusion that she is an evil woman shatters for good.

As a means of helping us see through images that hold us in thrall, dis-illusionment, though painful, is a vital source of growth. What is revealed through such shattering of images is mystical knowledge, which is characteristically difficult to put into words because it has broken through to a realm *beyond* words or named images.

As agents of dis-illusion, elements of the Boring and the Mystical similarly help counter enthralling images. Take any Andy Warhol sequence of Marilyn Monroes. Monroe is an obviously enthralling image, at least for most males. Yet Warhol's endless repetitions with minimal variation change their original fascination. By multiplication he creates surfeit. One Marilyn Monroe is a fascinating image: twenty Marilyn Monroes first appear tedious, then somewhat frightening. As we look at them we begin to stare uneasily, questioning what we see. Why should there be so many look-alikes? What does that mean? What has become of individuality? With only one we are far less likely to think consciously that it *is* an image. With twenty we can hardly do otherwise. And yet these images do not seem to exist as images ordinarily do. If we are looking at an image, what is it an image of? *Is* there anything behind it? The ontological questions are insistent; hence our fear.

Such dis-illusionment or breaking of images is typical of any initiation rite that seeks to reach the sacred. To reach the sacred an initiate must die. That way he may return to the absolute beginning, to chaos. Only then can his or her rebirth on a new, spiritual plane take place. An artist purposely working with the Boring strives to disengage attention, scatter it, and force the viewer back upon herself. This effect closely resembles what happens to a novice enduring his initiation ordeals. Typically he will be left in a special hut or even by himself in the forest. Given no food, he will be instructed not to sleep. In such a setting he will inevitably enter a trance after periods of restlessness and sleepiness.

Mircea Eliade describes this initiatory, mystical process of dis-illusionment in the rites of Tantrism known as *tchoed* in which

> the novice submits himself to an initiatory ordeal by stimulating his imagination to conjure up a terrifying vision, which, however, he masters by the power of his thought. He knows that what is before him is a creation of his own mind; that the Goddess and the demons are as unreal as is his own body and with it, the entire cosmos. . . . This initiatory meditation is at the same time a post-mortem experience, hence a descent to Hell—but through it the novice realizes the emptiness of all posthumous experience, so that he will feel no more fear at the moment of death and will thus escape being reborn on earth. The traditional experience of bodily dismemberment . . . serves as an instrument of knowledge; by virtue of it the novice understands what is meant by the universal void, and thereby draws closer to final deliverance.[3]

As with the novice, so frequently with the housewife. Particularly during the years when she is also mother to young children, she must endure prolonged periods of sleep deprivation in response to her children's often nightly demands. Such deprivation, combined with the repetitiveness of her daily chores, is apt to make her as restless, sleepy, and bored as an initiate. Once she passes beyond these surface responses, however, she, too, is likely to enter into a trancelike state in which seemingly negative conditions alter into their positive counterparts. Whether responding to art, initiation, or housework, the body of viewer or participant inevitably reacts to this situation which is so radically unlike more traditional artistic attempts to focus attention on an intense situation and force viewer/reader identification with an appealing character.

Bertolt Brecht's alienation effect—which purposely introduces illusion-shattering devices at appropriate intervals—obviously works this way to prevent viewers from over-identifying with characters. Yet if alienation from the situation at hand is too great, the reader, viewer, initiate, or housewife will become so thoroughly disengaged that the potentially mystical stimulus loses its effectiveness. When that happens he or she will turn away completely, severing the potential connection between viewer and performance, initiate and rite, or housework and task. Conversely, when no alienation separates a viewer from a story or an initiate from an ordeal dis-illusionment is unlikely to occur. Then an individual remains so caught up in the image or story that she remains hooked at the stage of idolatry, rather than gaining sufficient distance to move into the nothingness beyond.

Those who tout story as the *sine qua non* of human existence frequently view this nothingness as bad, as the words of Michael Novak suggest: "Not to have any story to live out is to experience nothingness: the primal formlessness of human life below the threshold of narrative structuring. Why become anything at all? Does anything make any difference? Why not simply die?" Or instead of demonizing nothingness, story advocates may simply try to encapsulate it within another, more encompassing story. In that case the nothingness is framed on either side by content as is promised, for example, in the play *Harvey* when Elwood P. Dowd explains that Harvey has the ability to stop time for as long as he wants. That time-stoppage, in which normal life abates, is another way of naming what we otherwise variously call "death," "eternity," "a mystical state," or "nothingness." But in that context, or any of many fairy-tale versions of it, story frames and controls it. But if that "nothingness" is valued for its own sake, the need for such framing disappears, the situation which is frequently exploited by practitioners of minimal art.

In addition to the minimal aspects of art that lead into the Boring and the Mystical, there is often associated with both an altered attitude towards humanness that has great bearing on the way women might possibly come to be perceived. Usually when we think of stories, we think of humanity. In fact, one of the traditional characteristics of stories is character. Even in stories about machines or animals, the "protagonists" assume human characteristics. It is difficult to think of many stories without characters. Ray Bradbury's "There Will Come Soft Rains" comes to mind, but even there, the house has humanoid qualities. By contrast, many contemporary works of fiction deemphasize human roles. Absurdists like Ionesco and Beckett create characters who approach some outer limit of humanity (particularly Beckett's Unnamable). Surely this shifting of humanity out of center stage means something. And surely it is no accident that we tend to equate the Boring with things we cannot identify with, thus suggesting that the Boring in part alienates percipients because it is in some way "beyond" them. Frequently we even use that metaphor to describe how we feel when a work bores us: "It's beyond me" or "that's nothing," we may say with a shrug of dismissal.

It is precisely this nothingness or beyondness that is important. Contrasted with story, which stands for and/or creates a finite something, the Boring is an artistic mode that mirrors infinite nothingness. Consider this small segment from Beckett's *Waiting for Godot*, which helps clarify this point. In Act II Vladimir sings this song:

> A dog came in the kitchen
> And stole a crust of bread.
> Then cook up with a ladle
> And beat him till he was dead.
>
> Then all the dogs came running
> and dug the dog a tomb—
> Then all the dogs came running
> And dug the dog a tomb
> And wrote upon the tombstone
> For the eyes of dogs to come:
>
> A dog came in the kitchen
> And stole a crust of bread.
> Then cook up with a ladle
> And beat him till he was dead.
>
> Then all the dogs came running
> And dug the dog a tomb—
> Then all the dogs came running
> And dug the dog a tomb.[5]

Is this story? Or is this something else? Clearly it has some of the characteristics of story: a rudimentary plot; a character of sorts in the form of the dog; action; and a climax. Yet despite all these qualities, it lacks the *sine qua non* of story: a clearly articulated beginning, middle, and end.

What then, has Beckett created instead? In this song which Vladimir sings Beckett has abridged an endless series, abstracting from it its actual length while giving up in part the feeling of the whole. By its form, he indicates eternal progress, making this an "endless story," hence no story at all in the Aristotelian sense. In other words, he has used a *pars pro toto* technique to present an image of the infinite in finite form. By having only the single repetition he has minimized the physical time span for the percipient at the same time that he expresses the *essence* of the greatest possible time span.

To borrow from Suzanne Langer's terminology, what Beckett has created is "virtual" rather than actual Boredom.[6] Thus while we may feel the boredom presented in his compressed presentation of the boring nature of infinity, because this is such a carefully abridged, and therefore delimited, version of the whole, there exists a strong enough counteractant to the boredom to carry us on through without making us turn away.

A similar phenomenon occurs visually when an artist like Nassos Daphnis chooses to cover an entire canvas in black with only two white stripes to relieve its sameness. And Brecht deliberately destroys the continuity of his plays every time he obtrudes one of his editorial comments upon the scene, reminding his audience that this is indeed a play, not an illusion of life.

What I. A. Richards says of poetic metre in his *Principles of Literary Criticism* suggests a possible analogy. He says: "metre adds to all the variously fated expectancies which make up rhythm, a definite temporal pattern, and its effect is not due to our perceiving a pattern in something outside us, but to our becoming patterned ourselves."[7] A poet who uses a too highly regular metre will inadvertantly create a monotonous effect, thus lulling his reader into an almost hypnotic state. Likewise, an artist may deliberately choose to use elements of the Boring to so pattern his audience.

It is here that we see just how strongly the Boring, whether in art or housework mimics mystical states. As opposed to story and image, the Boring does not offer the reader a vicarious experience of some virtual space-time. Instead, the Boring *alters* space-time. It is this same characteristic which transforms some enactments of housework and sacred rituals.

To understand the significance of this distinction between virtual and altered space-time, consider what Aristotle says of the aesthetic aspects of tragedy:

> . . . a beautiful object, whether it be a living organism or any whole composed of parts, must not only have an orderly arrangement of parts, but must also be of a certain magnitude and order. Hence a very small animal organism cannot be beautiful; for the view of it is confused, the object being seen in an almost imperceptible moment of time. Nor, again, can one of vast size be beautiful; for as the eye cannot take it all in at once, the unity and sense of the whole is lost for the spectator.[8]

Obviously the unspoken measure here is human. Now while such an anthropocentric view appears to be the only logical one, you could argue that its implied fixity makes it a somewhat static measure—that humanity could indeed learn to expand and contract its powers of attention in accordance with altered space/time intervals. It is just such stretching and manipulating of human response that appears to be part of the rationale for minimal art. Thus Andy Warhol presents the public with a movie showing a single face and nothing else for a period of two hours. Here is the Boring in art indeed, art that would bore most people. But, if you contrast the amount of time given to a single entity in the movie with the amount given to a face in "normal" time, it is obvious that something once unconsidered is occurring here. The dislocation of the normal time sense has been exploited in such a way that the viewer's whole space/time perception is put into question. What we ordinarily accept tacitly has here been made glaringly explicit. While writers from Swift on have exploited such qualities as variations in size vis à vis our human scale, it is not until this century that such experience has been presented directly, minus the framing device of a story about it. And it is just such unframed experience that traditional women have enacted through their lives, for centuries.

Much as the old Euclidean notion of space/time has been altered scientifically in favor of complex non-Euclidean models, our human sensibility to that continuum appears to be undergoing a similar artistic recreation. On the one hand, there is a surfeit of stimuli in certain multimedia works of art. On the other, there is minimal artistic input. It would seem that humanity is being stretched aesthetically beyond its old mean, in two directions at once.

Once story and image were central to art. Increasingly now, art pushes both aside. Usurping their place are elements of the Mystical and the Boring. Whereas story, as Aristotle defined it, was made to human measure, the Mystical and the Boring extend beyond us.

And, whereas story and image are artistic modes which reveal some-*thing*, the Boring is a mode which reveals *Nothing*. Story and image both *fill* space, but the Boring and the Mystical, conversely, lead into the emptiness of space itself. As vehicles of revelation, these two modes are therefore radically different from both story and image. To say of anything boring, as we commonly do, "that's nothing," is therefore highly appropriate. But to also turn away from it, as if *nothing* were equivalent to *meaningless*, is to ignore the significance of that nothingness.

If we take the view that all art and literature, not just so-called sacred texts, are revelations of the *divine* then the repeated emergence of *the Boring* in so much contemporary work has to be revealing something in us with great insistence. Surely anything that insistent demands our serious attention.

Rather than deplore these tendencies, which are already abating to some extent, as other modes of painting and writing in turn develop, it makes more sense to ask what they mean. From a feminist perspective, such seeming absence of images and stories, instead of signifying a horrifying emptiness, suggests that women's traditional mode of experiencing life has finally been given shape artistically. Whether women or artists choose to remain in this mode or not is another issue.

Furthermore, the emergence of this waiting mode from obscurity into art indicates that at this stage in what is still called human history, we may be engaged in a second Copernican Revolution. But our Copernican crisis is not between our expectations of where the earth should be relative to the sun and the planets. Ours is the discontinuity we feel between the spot human males have traditionally occupied in human thought relative to women, children, animals, plants, and inanimate objects, and the place women are beginning to assume for themselves.

The so-called Death of God theologies of the 1960s foreshadowed this crisis. To the extent that the ultimate term humans can conceive—*God* in the Judeo-Christian tradition—has been envisioned as masculine, the term has revealed more about human minds than about anything truly ultimate. This situation has been equally true, of course, in cultures whose symbols of ultimacy have been feminine or theriomorphic (in the shape of animals), and multiple, as well as monotheistic. When a number of theologians such as Gabriel Vahanian, Thomas Altizer, William Hamilton, and Richard Rubenstein took up Nietzsche's statement that God is dead, they spoke of this death in various ways. In Vahanian's view this death of God reflects the demise of a certain way of thinking. For Vahanian, if that particular mode of envisioning and speaking about ultimacy dies, that in no way means that the ultimate itself dies. Rather it means that a certain, conventionally accepted human way of constructing ultimacy no longer works for an entire community of believers, although it may linger indefinitely for many. Following Vahanian's thought, when that long-accepted symbol begins to lose its potency for enough people that it "dies," that indicates that something significant is occurring within a number of human minds. Much emphasis has been laid on numerous negative affiliates of this death: the loss of a sense of human purpose, coupled with scientific theories of indeterminacy, pluralism, leveling of transcendence into immanentism, and estrangement from ancestral Christendom. But few thinkers have pointed out that concurrent with this Death of God theorizing is another important cultural phenomenon: towards the beginning of the period often referred to now as the *post mortem dei* era feminist theology began.

Consequently, simply to replace the old masculine God with a feminine variant called the Goddess is to ignore the implications of the Death of God theologies. Similarly, to retain the biblical God and His Son but to repristinate the meanings of both terms as others would do is also to ignore those theologies. But to see in feminist theologizing a correlation to Death of God theologizing is to move closer to understanding what is happening to *homo* [sic] *religiosus* at the present time.

For woman, the silent partner in the term *homo*, what is happening is discontinuous with a whole previous history. A traditional woman's life was once so fully bound up with waiting that she was merely an egg's way of ensuring another egg.[9] Nowadays, that view, which implicitly values the life process above all else, with no concern for quality of life, is being questioned and disavowed by thousands of women. Many flee it in horror. At this point, relatively few have yet discovered how to be whoever they think they are without polarizing their lives into either/or choices. Many find themselves caught: either they can exist primarily in the familiar mode of waiting with its day-to-day emphasis on housework, or they can adopt an alternative masculine quest pattern. Relatively few have learned to cope with the ambiguities inherent in both patterns. Until they do, it is unlikely that many will be able to create genuinely new modes of being forged from the best of both traditions.

This predicament shared by so many women is cogently expressed in Martin Buber's parable, "The Query of Queries":

> Before his death, Rabbi Zusya said, "In the coming world, they will not ask me: 'Why were you not Moses?' They will ask me: 'Why were you not Zusya?' "[10]

For most women the first task now is to stop being "Moses," whether a Moses locked into the home or one aspiring to be a man in a "man's world." The second is to discover, acknowledge, and then create a Zusya born, not from Adam's rib, but from Eve's womb. Only when women can accomplish both tasks will they legitimate themselves as full human beings in female form. Such self-legitimation will free them from accepting internalized masculine conceptions of who and what they should be. That legitimation depends on carefully examining the ambiguities of their past, a past neither worthless nor glorious. Instead, it is a past spent for the most part living out an ambiguous Hestian pattern of enactment characterized by waiting. From one perspective this pattern is profane, experienced primarily with despair as meaningless. From another, however, it is felt as sacred, opening out alternatively into the demonic realm of the Boring or the divine space of the Mystical. To ensure the birth of a Zusya, it makes sense for women to ponder both poles of that sacred dimension, lest they find themselves quoting Yeats:

> . . . what rough beast, its hour come round at last, Slouches towards Bethlehem to be Born?''[11]

Notes

Introduction

1. I derive my concept of tacitness from Michael Polanyi's *The Tacit Dimension* (Garden City, New York: Doubleday Anchor, 1967).

2. *The Cloud of Unknowing* (Baltimore: Penguin Books, 1961), pp. 134–35.

3. See Gustave Flaubert's *Madame Bovary*. Emma Bovary was a bored married woman who so longed for a romantic, exciting life that she allowed her fantasies rather than common sense to lead her into a disastrous love affair. The word "bovarist" is derived from her character.

4. "Republic," in *Dialogues of Plato*, ed, J. D. Kaplan, trans. Jowett (New York: Pocket Books, Cardinal edition, 1953), p. 269.

5. Harold Pinter, "The Room," in *The Birthday Party and the Room* (New York: Grove Press, 1960), p. 103.

6. Marabel Morgan, *The Total Woman* (New York: Pocket Books, 1973), p. 116.

7. For a full discussion of women's failure see Matina Horner's "Sex Differences in Achievement Motivation and Performance in Competitive and Noncompetitive Situations" (unpublished doctoral dissertation for the University of Minnesota, 1968).

8. For the parallel between the civil rights movement and the views of certain Roman Catholic feminists I am indebted to Professor William Barnett of Le Moyne College, Syracuse, New York.

9. Eugene Ionesco, "Jack or the Submission," in *Four Plays* (New York: Grove Press, 1958), p. 109.

10. At the 1981 Senate hearings on sexual harassment, Phyllis Schlafly declared that "sexual harassment on the job is not a problem for the virtuous

woman. . . . Sexual harassment can also occur when a non-virtuous woman gives off body language which invites sexual advances." She also asserted that women "have abandoned the Commandments against adultery and fornication." These remarks are quoted in Toni Carabillo, "Through the Looking Glass Upside Down," *National NOW Times,* June 1981, p. 9.

11. "Bad Trips. Women Travelers Find Safety and Harassment Can Be Major Problems," *The Wall Street Journal,* 5 March 1980.

12. Elizabeth Dodson Gray, *Why the Green Nigger: Re-mything Genesis* (Wellesley, Mass.: Roundtable Press, 1979), p. 7.

13. James Ogilvy, *Many Dimensional Man: Decentralizing Self, Society, and the Sacred* (New York: Oxford University Press, 1977), p. 113.

14. William King, An Essay on the Origin of Evil, tr. from the Latin with Notes and a Dissertation concerning the Principle and Criterion of Virtue and the Origin of the Passions, by Edmund Law. M.A., Fellow of Christ College in Cambridge, 2nd ed., (London: 1732), quoted in Arthur O. Lovejoy, *The Great Chain of Being: A Study in the History of an Idea* (Cambridge, Mass.: Harvard University Press, 1973), p. 213.

15. Aristotle, "De Generatione Animalium," trans. Arthur Platt in *The Oxford Translation of Aristotle,* ed. W. D. Ross (Oxford: Clarendon Press, 1912).

16. Dorothy Soelle, *Political Theology,* tr. John Shelley (Philadelphia: Fortress Press, 1971), p. 40.

17. Soelle, pp. 78 and 80.

18. Soelle, p. 80.

19. Leonard Swidler, *Biblical Affirmations of Woman* (Philadelphia: Westminster Press, 1979), p. 13.

20. Swidler, p. 15.

21. Catherina Halkes, "Feminist Theology: An Interior Assessment," in Concilium 134 (4/1980): *Women in a Men's Church,* ed. Virgil Elizondo and Norbert Greinacher (New York: The Seabury Press, 1980), p. 110. The following points in this paragraph all come from this same essay.

22. Elizabeth Schüssler Fiorenza, "Women in the Early Christian Movement," reprinted in *Womanspirit Rising: A Feminist Reader in Religion,* ed. Carol R. Christ and Judith Plaskow (New York: Harper & Row, 1979), p. 86.

23. Phyllis Trible, *God and the Rhetoric of Sexuality,* (Philadelphia: Fortress Press. 1978). p. xvi.

24. Trible, p. 4.

25. Trible, p. 201.

26. Barbara Burris, "The Fourth World Manifesto," in Anne Koedt and Shulamith Firestone, eds., *Notes From the Third Year: Women's Liberation* (P.O. Box AA, Old Chelsea Station, New York, NY 10011, 1972), p. 118.

27. Quoted in Letty M. Russell, *Human Liberation in a Feminist Perspective— A Theology* (Philadelphia: The Westminster Press,1974), p. 111.

28. Russell, p. 27.

29. Russell, p. 21.

30. Rosemary Radford Ruether, "Mother Earth and the Megamachine," in *Liberation Theology: Human Hope Confronts Christian History and American Powers* (New York: Paulist Press, 1972), pp. 115–16.

31. Ruether, p. 125.

32. These ideas appear in Joseph G. Ramisch, "Towards a Male Critique of Christianity," an unpublished paper presented at the Eastern International Regional Meeting of the American Academy of Religion, Syracuse, New York, April 1980.

33. Sheila Collins, *A Different Heaven and Earth* (Valley Forge, Penn.; Judson Press, 1974), and Carol P. Christ, "The New Feminist Theology: A Review of the Literature," *Religious Studies Review* 1977, 3(4), pp. 203–212.

34. David Tracy, *Blessed Rage for Order: The New Pluralism in Theology* (New York: The Seabury Press, 1975).

35. Naomi Goldenberg, *Changing of the Gods: Feminism and the End of Traditional Religions* (Boston: Beacon Press, 1979), p. 96.

36. Tom F. Driver, *Patterns of Grace: Human Experience as Word of God* (New York: Harper & Row, Publishers, 1977), p. 28.

37. Driver, p. 12.

38. Judith Plaskow, "The Coming of Lilith: Toward a Feminist Theology," in *Womanspirit Rising: A Feminist Reader in Religion,* ed. Carol P. Christ and Judith Plaskow (New York: Harper & Row, Publishers, 1979), pp. 198–209.

39. Mary Daly, *Gyn/Ecology: The Metaethics of Radical Feminism* (Boston: Beacon Press, 1978), p. 355.

40. Daly, p. 378.

41. Penelope Washbourne, *Becoming Woman* (New York: Harper & Row, Publishers, 1977).

42. Carol Christ, *Diving Deep and Surfacing: Women Writers on Spiritual Quest* (Boston: Beacon Press, 1980), p. 117.

43. Naomi Goldenberg, *Changing of the Gods: Feminism and the End of Traditional Religions* (Boston: Beacon Press, 1979), pp. 126–27.

44. Goldenberg, p. 25.

45. Jean-Paul Sartre, *Being and Nothingness: An Essay on Phenomenological Ontology,* trans. Hazel E. Barnes (New York: Philosophical Library, 1956), p. 383.

46. Daly, p. xi.

47. John Updike, *The Centaur* (New York: Alfred A. Knopf, Publisher, 1963).

47. Plato, "Symposium," in *Dialogues of Plato,* pp. 188–192.

49. Carlos Castaneda, *The Teachings of Don Juan: A Yacqui Way of Knowledge* (New York: Ballantine Books, 1968), p. 127.

50. Castaneda, p. 173.

51. Sartre, p. 383.

52. Aeschylus, "The Eumenides," in *The Oresteian Trilogy,* trans. Philip Vellacott (Baltimore: Penguin Books, 1969), p. 172.

Chapter 1

1. Rudolph Arnheim, *Visual Thinking* (Berkeley: University of California Press, 1969), p. 251.

2. Gaston Bachelard, *The Poetics of Space,* trans. Maria Jolas (Boston: Beacon Press, 1969), p. 3.

3. Robert Frost, "The Death of the Hired Man," in *The Poetry of Robert Frost* (New York: Holt, Rinehart and Winston, 1969), p. 38.

4. I am indebted to Professor Daniel W. O'Connor of St. Lawrence University for information in this paragraph and the one immediately following it.

5. Xenophon, *Oeconomicus*, 3.12.

6. Ann Douglas, *The Feminization of American Culture* (New York. Avon Books, 1978).

7. For a full discussion of this process see Amanda Porterfield, "The Domestication of Theology," in *Feminine Spirituality in America: From Sarah Edwards to Martha Graham*, (Philadelphia: Temple University Press, 1980).

8. For an excellent account of Beecher's life and work see Kathryn Kish Sklar, *Catharine Beecher: A Study in American Domesticity* (New York: W. W. Norton & Co., 1973).

9. Valerie Saiving, "The Human Situation: A Feminine View," in *Womanspirit Rising: A Feminist Reader in Religion*, ed. Carol P. Christ and Judith Plaskow (New York: Harper & Row, Publishers, 1979), p. 37.

10. Christ and Plaskow, p. 37.

11. Betty Friedan, *The Feminine Mystique* (New York: Dell Publishing Co., 1963).

12. For a fuller discussion of the historical development of houses see Lord Raglan, *The Temple and the House*, (London: Routledge and Kegan Paul, 1864), p. 2 ff.

13. For an interesting interpretation of this Egyptian reversal of the otherwise universal association of the masculine with the sky and the feminine with the earth, see Marie-Louise von Franz, *Interpretation of Fairy Tales* (New York: Spring Publications, 1970).

14. Lord Raglan, p. 88.

15. Quoted in Naomi Goldenberg, *Changing of the Gods: Feminism and the End of Traditional Religions* (Boston: Beacon Press, 1979), p. 104. Zsuzsanna E. Budapest, founder of the Sisterhood of the Wicca and The Susan B. Anthony Coven #1, inherited her powers from her Hungarian mother, who came from a long line of witches.

16. Marianne Alireza, *At the Drop of a Veil* (Boston: Houghton Mifflin Co., 1971), p. 108.

17. John Steinbeck, *The Grapes of Wrath* (New York: Penguin Books, 1977), p. 452.

18. Information in this paragraph comes from Lord Raglan, pp. 16–17.

19. Walker Percy, *The Moviegoer* (New York: Alfred A. Knopf, 1973), p. 139.

20. Nathanael West, "The Day of the Locust," in *Miss Lonelyhearts and the Day of the Locust* (New York: New Directions, 1969), p. 81.

21. Shirley Jackson, *The Haunting of Hill House*, (New York: Viking Press, 1959), pp. 34–35.

22. Suzanne K. Langer, "The Modes of Virtual Space," *Feeling and Form: A Theory of Art* (New York: Charles Scribner's Sons, 1953), pp. 86–103.

23. Marianne Alireza, p. 33.

24. Wallace Stevens, "Anecdote of the Jar," in *Collected Poems* (New York: Alfred A. Knopf, 1969), p. 76.

25. See John G. Neihardt, *Black Elk Speaks* (New York: Pocket Books, 1959), p. 36.

26. Randall Jarrell, "Well Water," in *Collected Poems* (New York: Farrar, Straus and Giroux, 1969), p. 300.

27. Robert Frost, "Directive," in *The Poetry of Robert Frost*, ed. by Edward Connery Latham (New York: Holt, Rinehart and Winston, 1969), p. 377.

28. For a useful schema of the qualities of the Ouranian versus the chthonic dimensions of religion, see Philip Wheelwright, *The Burning Fountain: A Study in the Language of Symbolism* (Bloomington: Indiana University Press, 1968), p. 175.

29. Marcel Proust, *Swann's Way*, trans. C. K. Scott Moncrieff (New York: Modern Library, 1956), pp. 65–66.

30. Ray Bradbury, "There Will Come Soft Rains," in *The Martian Chronicles* (New York: Bantam Books-Doubleday & Co., 1970), pp. 166–172.

31. Vladimir Nabokov, *Speak, Memory, An Autobiography Revisited* (New York: Pyramid Books, 1966), p. 13.

32. Joseph Campbell, *The Hero With a Thousand Faces* (Cleveland: The World Publishing Co./Meridian Books, 1968), pp. 40–41.

33. Samuel Beckett, *Endgame* (New York: Grove Press, 1958), p. 27.

34. Carl Gustav Jung, "Individual Dream Symbolism in Relation to Alchemy," in *The Portable Jung*, ed. Joseph Campbell, trans. R. F. C. Hall (New York: Viking Press, 1971), p. 324.

35. For discussion of Jung's concept of the mandala see C. G. Jung, "The Secret of the Golden Flower," in *Alchemical Studies*, Bollingen Series XY, Collected Works, vol. 13, Cary Baynes, tr.

36. William Butler Yeats, "The Second Coming," line 3, from *the Variorum Edition of the Poems of W. B. Yeats*, eds. Peter Allt and Russel K. Alspach (New York: The Macmillan Company, 1968), p. 402.

37. For more information on this subject see *Existence: A New Dimension in Psychiatry and Psychology*, ed. Rollo May, Ernest Angel, and Henri F. Ellenberg (New York: Simon and Schuster/Clarion Books, 1958).

Chapter 2

1. For great numbers of people Christianity remains the other-worldly vision it has traditionally been thought to be. However, it should be noted that from a critical-*praxis* point of view Christianity is a profoundly this-worldly religion; that is what allows for liberation theology.

2. Michael Robinson, *The Long Sonata of the Dead: A Study of Samuel Beckett* (New York: Grove Press, 1969), p. 259.

3. Ernest Hemingway, "A Clean, Well-Lighted Place," in *Rhetoric and Literature* (New York: McGraw-Hill Book Co., 1974), p. 330.

4. Hemingway, p. 330.

5. Hemingway, p. 331.

6. I am indebted to Professor Daniel O'Connor of St. Lawrence University for this information.

7. Anne Tyler, *Searching For Caleb* (New York: Alfred A. Knopf, 1976), p. 108.

8. Charlotte Perkins Gilman, "The Yellow Wall Paper," in *The Oven Birds: American Women on Womanhood, 1820–1920*, ed. Gail Parker (Garden City, New York: Doubleday, Anchor Books, 1972), pp. 334–335.

9. Dick Case, "Happy Harold's World Was Small, But It Misses Him Already," *Syracuse Herald-American*, 23 March 1980.

10. Ramon Oldenburg and Dennis Brissett, "The Essential Hangout," *Psychology Today*, April 1980, p. 82.

11. James Joyce, "Counterparts," *Dubliners* in *The Portable James Joyce* (New York: The Viking Press, 1969), p. 99.

12. James Joyce, "Counterparts," p. 103.

13. James Joyce, "Counterparts," p. 108.

14. From Epictetus, *Discourses*, Bk. II, chap. 23, paragraph 3, quoted in Matthew Arnold, "Wordsworth," *Victorian Poetry and Poetics*, ed. Walter E. Houghton and G. Robert Strange (Boston: Houghton Mifflin Company, 1968), p. 554.

15. *The Book of Common Prayer and Administration of the Sacraments and Other Rites and Ceremonies of the Church* (New York: Edwin S. Gorham, 1929), p. 6.

16. Bruno Bettelheim, *The Empty Fortress: Infantile Autism and the Birth of the Self* (New York: MacMillan/The Free Press, 1972), p. 238.

17. Vladimir Nabokov, *Speak, Memory* (New York: Pyramid Books, 1968), p. 75.

18. William Irwin Thompson, *At the Edge of History: Speculations on the Transformation of Culture* (New York: Harper & Row, Publishers, 1971) p. 9.

19. William Carlos Williams, *Paterson* (New York: New Directions, 1963), II, iiii, p. 78.

20. Dante Alighieri, *Inferno*, Canto V, lines 34–37.

21. This information was taken from Mary Lee Settle's review of *Woody Guthrie: A Life*, by Joe Klein in *The New York Times Book Review*, 7 Dec. 1980.

22. Philip Roth, "A Talk with Milan Kundera," *The New York Times Book Review*, 30 November 1980, p. 7.

23. Jean Rhys, *Quartet* (New York: Harper & Row, Publishers 1929), p. 8.

24. Michel Foucault, *The Order of Things: An Archaeology of the Human Sciences* (New York: Random House/Pantheon, 1970), p. xvii.

25. Foucault, p. xviii.

Chapter 3

1. For a discussion of the historical development of romantic love, see Denis de Rougement, *Passion and Society*, tr. Montgomery Belgion (London: Faber and Faber, Ltd., 1939).

2. Nadine Gordimer, *Occasion for Loving* (New York: The Viking Press, 1963), p. 182.

3. Joan P. Berry, *Faith in the Center Ring: An Elephantine Question* (Philadelphia: Fortress Press, 1978), p. 54.

4. Alda Marjorie Vaughan Curtis, "Homemaker, Volunteer, Rancher," in *The Radcliffe Quarterly*, 64, no. 4, p. 25.

5. Euripides, *The Bacchae*, line 34.

Chapter 4

1. Sean O'Casey, "The End of the Beginning," in *Five One-Act Plays* (London: Macmillan, Ltd./Pocket Papermacs, 1966), p. 10.

2. Michael Polanyi, *The Tacit Dimension* (New York: Doubleday Anchor, 1966).

3. I wish to thank Professor William Barnett of Le Moyne College, Syracuse, New York, for providing this Koan.

4. William Butler Yeats, "Among School Children," in *The Norton Anthology of Modern Poetry* (New York: W. W. Norton and Co., 1973), p. 142.

5. Rainer Maria Rilke, *Lettres à une Musicienne*, quoted in Gaston Bachelard, *The Poetics of Space*, trans. Maria Jolas (Boston: Beacon Press, 1969), pp. 70–71.

6. For a fuller discussion of mythic time see "Waiting", pp. 143.

7. Robert Coles, *Women of Crisis: Lives in Struggle and Hope* (New York: Delacorte Press, 1978), p. 107.

8. See Antonin Artaud, *The Theater and Its Double*, trans. Mary Caroline Richards (New York: Grove Press, 1958), particularly "Metaphysics and the *Mise en Scène*," and "Letters on Language."

9. Artaud, p. 68.

10. Quoted in Barry Laine, "Uniting Words and Motion," Arts and Leisure Section, *The New York Times*, 7 Dec. 1980, p. 18.

11. *National NOW Times*, December/January 1980–81, p. 2.

12. Alexander Solzhenitsyn, *One Day in the Life of Ivan Denisovich* (New York: New American Library/Signet, 1963), pp. 55–56.

13. Syracuse *Herald-Journal*, 2 Dec. 1980.

14. I. A. Richards, *Principles of Literary Criticism* (New York: Harcourt, Brace & World, 1925), p. 139.

15. Mircea Eliade, *The Sacred and the Profane: The Nature of Religion* (New York: Harcourt, Brace World/Harvest, 1959), p. 74.

Chapter 5

1. Geza Roheim, *Australian Totemism: A Psychoanalytic Study in Anthropology* (New York: Humanities Press, 1971).

2. Sir James Frazer, *The New Golden Bough*, ed. Theodor H. Gaster (New York: The New American Library/Mentor, 1959), p. 35.

3. Jean-Paul Sartre, *Being and Nothingness: An Essay on Phenomenological Ontology*, trans. Hazel E. Barnes (New York: Philosophical Library, 1956), p. 613.

4. James Joyce, *Ulysses*, (New York: The Modern Library, 1946), p. 49.

5. Lewis Carroll, *Alice in Wonderland and Through the Looking Glass* (New York: Grosset and Dunlap, 1949), pp. 33–34.

6. H. H. Arnason, *History of Modern Art: Painting, Sculpture, Architecture* (New York: Harry N. Abrams, 1977), p. 662.

7. Rainer Maria Rilke, "Evening," trans. Randall Jarrell, in *Randall Jarrell: The Complete Poems* (New York: Farrar, Straus and Giroux, 1970) p. 241.

8. Wallace Stevens, "A Rabbit as King of the Ghosts," in *Collected Poems* (New York: Alfred A. Knopf, 1969), p. 290.

9. A paraphrase of a line in Stevens, "Notes toward a Supreme Fiction." The original is: ". . . the giant of the weather," p. 385.

10. Gaston Bachelard, *The Poetics of Space*, trans. Maria Jolas (Boston: Beacon Press, 1969), p. 18.

11. Samuel Beckett, *Watt* (New York: Grove Press, 1959), p. 30.

12. E. M. Forster, "My Wood," reprinted in *Here and Now: An Approach to Writing Through Perception*, ed. Fred Morgan (New York: Harcourt, Brace and World, 1968), p. 87.

13. A. L. Kroeber and E. W. Gifford, *World Renewal, a Cult System of Native Northwest California*, quoted in Mircea Eliade, *Myth and Reality*, trans. Willard R. Trask (New York: Harper & Row, Publishers, 1963), p. 44.

14. Wallace Stevens, "Connoisseur of Chaos," *Collected Poems* (New York: Alfred A. Knopf, 1969), p. 215.

15. C. Wright Morris, from "The Ram in the Thicket," reprinted in *Here and Now: An Approach to Writing Through Perception*, ed. Fred Morgan (New York: Harcourt, Brace and World, 1968), p. 73.

16. Wright Morris, p. 73.

17. Wright Morris, p. 77.

18. Wallace Stevens, "Theory," p. 86.

19. Norman Mailer, "The Case Against McCarthy: A Review of *The Group*," in *Contemporary Women Novelists*, ed. Patricia Meyer Spacks (Englewood Cliffs, New Jersey: Prentice-Hall, Inc., 1977), p. 83.

20. Patricia Meyer Spacks, pp. 14–15.

21. Richard Wilbur, "Love Calls Us to the Things of this World," in *The Poems of Richard Wilbur* (New York: Harcourt, Brace & World/Harvest: 1963) p. 65.

22. Wilbur, p. 65.

23. This information was taken from a promotional blurb on the Watts Towers of Simon Rodia.

24. Mary Symonds and Louisa Preece, *Needlework Through the Ages* (London: Hodder and Stoughton Ltd., 1928), p. vii.

Chapter 6

1. Mary Gordon, *Final Payments* (New York, Ballantine Books: 1978), p. 3.

2. Edward Albee, *Who's Afraid of Virginia Woolf* (New York: Pocket Books, 1969), pp. 218–19.

3. John Updike, *Rabbit, Run* (New York: Fawcett Crest, 1960), pp. 203–4.

4. Updike, pp. 219–20.

5. Updike, p. 220.

6. Eudora Welty, "The Worn Path," in *Women and Fiction*, ed. Susan Cahill (New York: New American Library/Mentor, 1975), p. 105.

7. Willa Cather, *My Antonia* (Boston: Houghton Mifflin Co., 1954) pp. 337–353.

7a. Cather, p. 353.

8. Randall Jarrell, "The Lost World," in *Collected Poems* (New York: Farrar, Straus & Giroux, 1969) p. 290.

9. Quoted by Barbara Rose, "ABC Art," *Minimal Art: A Critical Anthology*, ed. Gregory Battcock (New York: E. P. Dutton & Co., Inc., 1968), p. 290.

10. Victor Turner, *Dramas, Fields and Metaphors: Symbolic Action in Human Society* (Ithaca: Cornell University Press, 1974), p. 297.

11. Sartre, *Being and Nothingness; An Essay on Phenomenological Ontology,* trans. Hazel E. Barnes (New York: Philosphical Library, 1956) p. 614.

12. Sigmund Freud, *Totem and Taboo: Resemblances Between the Psychic Lives of Savages and Neurotics,* trans. A. A. Brill (New York: Random House/Vintage, 1946), p. 199.

13. Ann Beattie, *Chilly Scenes of Winter* (Garden City, New York: Doubleday, 1976), p. 154.

14. Sartre, pp. 613–14.

15. Norman O. Brown, *Love's Body* (New York: Random House/Vintage, 1966), p. 133.

Chapter 7

1. The divisions of time mentioned here come from Dominic Crossan, *Raid on the Inarticulate: Comic Eschatology in Jesus and Borges* (New York: Harper & Row, Publishers, 1976).

2. "The King of the Black Isles," in *The Arabian Nights* (New York: Grosset & Dunlap, 1946), p. 55.

3. Randall Jarrel, "Hope," in *The Complete Poems* (New York: Farrar, Straus & Giroux, 1969), p. 310.

4. Johann Wolfgang von Goethe, *Faust,* trans. Bayard Taylor (New York: The Modern Library, 1950), p. 54.

5. Carl Gustav Jung, *Symbols of Transformation* (Princeton, NJ: Princeton University Press, 1970), II, 1082.

6. Helena Z. Lopata, *Occupation Housewife* (London: Oxford University Press, 1971), p. 34.

7. Katherine Briggs, *The Encyclopedia of Fairies, Hobgoblins, Brownies, Bogies and Other Supernatural Creatures* (New York; Pantheon Books, 1976), pp. 247–249.

8. In Briggs, p. 399.

Chapter 8

1. Luke 15:11–32.

2. Steven Crites, "The Narrative Quality of Experience," *Journal of the American Academy of Religion,* 39 (September 1971), p. 297.

3. Sam Keen and Anne Valley Fox, *Telling Your Story: A Guide to Who You Are and Who You Can Be* (New York: Doubleday/Signet, 1973), p. 8.

4. Carol P. Christ, *Diving Deep and Surfacing: Women Writers on Spiritual Quest* (Boston: Beacon Press, 1980), p. 1.

5. From "Lesbians and Literature," paper presented by Bertha Harris at MLA Convention, NY, December 1976. Quoted by Beverly Tanenhaus in her book review of *Burning Questions* by Alix Kates Shulman, quoted in *Chrysalis* #7, p. 105.

6. Ted L. Estess, "The Inenarrable Contraption: Reflections on the Metaphor of Story," *Journal of the American Academy of Religion* 42 (September 1974) pp. 433–34.

7. For fuller details and findings on this procedure see R. W. Sperry, "Forebrain Commissurotomy and Conscious Awareness," *The Journal of Medicine and Philosophy,* vol. 2, June 1977.

7a. Maid to an early Virginia colonist; both reached Virginia in 1608. For a few details see Eleanor Flexner, *Century of Struggle: The Woman's Rights Movement in the United States* (Cambridge, Mass.: The Belknap Press of Harvard University Press, 1976), p. 3.

8. An American writer (1876–1948). For a full-length study and a bibliography see Arther E. Waterman, *Susan Glaspell* (New York: Twayne Publishers, 1966).

9. Arthur Waley, *Three Ways of Thought in Ancient China* (Garden City, NY: Doubleday and Co., n.d.), pp. 15–16.

10. Quoted in Douglas R. Hofstadter, *Godel, Escher, Bach: An Eternal Golden Braid* (New York; Basic Books, 1979), p. 642.

11. Hofstadter, p. 494.

12. James Joyce, "A Portrait of the Artist," in *The Portable James Joyce* (New York: The Viking Press, 1969), p. 481.

13. The Brothers Grimm, "The White Snake," in Grimms *Fairy Tales,* trans. Mrs. E. V. Lucas, Lucy Crane, and Marian Edwards (New York: Grosset & Dunlap, 1945), p. 80.

14. Ernest Hemingway, "The Killers," in *Contemporary Trends: American Literature Since 1900,* ed. John Herbert Nelson and Nelson Cargill (New York: Macmillan, 1949), p. 186.

15. Samuel Beckett, "The Calmative," in *Stories and Texts For Nothing* (New York: Grove Press, 1967), pp. 27–28.

16. Sean O'Casey, "The End of the Beginning," in *Five One-Act Plays* (London: Macmillan Ltd./Pocket Paperbacks, 1960).

17. "The House That Jack Built," *The Oxford Dictionary of Nursery Rhymes,* ed. Iona and Peter Opie (Oxford: Clarendon Press, 1955), p. 229.

18. Samuel Beckett, *Endgame: A Play in One Act* (New York: Grove Press, 1958), p. 4.

19. Holly Prado, a book review of *One to One,* by Christia Baldwin and *The New Diary,* by Tristine Rainer, in *Chrysalis #7,* p. 116.

20. Quoted in Deana Metzger and Barabara Myerhoff, "Dear Diary," *Chrysalis #7,* p. 48.

21. Aristotle, "De Generatione Animalium," trans. Arthur Platt, in *The Oxford Translation of Aristotle,* ed. W. D. Ross (Oxford: Clarendon Press, 1912), vol 5, bk. I, ch. 20.

22. Saint Augustine, *The City of God,* trans. by Gerald G. Walsh, S.J.; Demetrius B. Zema, S.J.; Grace Monahan, O.S.U.; and Vernon J. Dorike (New York: Doubleday & Co., Image Books, 1958), bk. XII, ch. 26, p. 265.

23. Augustine, *The City of God,* bk. XXII, ch. 24, p. 525.

24. St. Thomas Aquinas *Summa Theologica,* Blackfriars (New York: McGraw-Hill Book Company and London: Eyre & Spottiswoode), v. 13, pp. 35–39.

25. Aquinas, pp. 35–39.

26. Charles Darwin, *The Descent of Man,* 2nd ed. rev. (London: John Murray, 1874), pt. 3, ch. 18.

27. Sigmund Freud, *New Introductory Lectures on Psychoanalysis*, trans. James Strachey (New York: W. W. Norton and Co., 1965), Lecture 33.

28. Norman O. Brown, *Love's Body* (New York: Random House/Vintage, 1966), p. 129.

29. Wallace Stevens, "A Rabbit as King of the Ghosts," in *Collected Poems* (New York: Alfred A. Knopf, 1969), p. 290.

30. Robert Scholes, *Structural Fabulation: An Essay on Fiction of the Future* (Notre Dame & London: University of Notre Dame Press, 1975), p. 1.

31. Jean Rhys, *After Leaving Mr. Mackenzie* (New York: Harper & Row Publishers, 1931), p. 51.

32. Colette Dowling, "The Cinderella Syndrome," *The New York Times Magazine*, 22 March 1981.

33. Simone de Beauvoir, *The Second Sex*, trans. and ed. by H. M. Parshley (New York: Bantam Books, 1961).

34. From an unpublished paper by Steven Cohan, "Other People: Character in the Novel."

35. A. Bartlett Giamatti, *The Earthly Paradise and the Renaissance Epic* (Princeton: Princeton University Press, 1969), p. 126.

36. Edgar Allan Poe, "The Fall of the House of Usher," in *The Fall of the House of Usher and Other Tales* (New York: New American Library/Signet, 1960), pp. 115–16.

37. Quoted in *The New York Times*, 15 February 1981, p. 42.

38. J. C. Spruill, *Women's Life and Work in the Southern Colonies* (New York: Russell & Russell, 1969), p.340.

39. This information and what follows on coverture is from Roger Thompson, *Women in Stuart England and America: A Comparative Study* (London: Routledge & Kegan Paul, 1974), pp. 162–3.

40. Juri M. Lotman, "On the Metalanguage of a Typological Description of Culture," *Semiotica* 14:2, pp. 102–03.

41. Aristotle, *Poetics*, trans. S. H. Butcher (New York: Hill & Wang, 1961), p. 93.

42. Robin T. Lakoff, *Language and Woman's Place* (New York: Harper & Row, Publishers, 1975), pp. 8–17.

Chapter 9
1. Allan Leepa, "Minimal Art and Primary Meanings," in *Minimal Art; A Critical Anthology*, ed. Gregory Battcock (New York: E. P. Dutton, 1968), p. 206.

2. The Brothers Grimm, "The Six Swans," *Grimms Fairy Tales*, trans. Mrs. E. V. Lucas, Lucy Crane, and Marian Edwardes (New York: Grosset & Dunlap, 1945), p. 113.

3. Mircea Eliade, *Rites and Symbols of Initiation: The Mysteries of Birth and Rebirth*, trans. Willard R. Trask, (New York: Harper & Row Publishers/Torchbooks, 1958), pp. 105–06.

4. Michael Novak, *Ascent of the Mountain, Flight of the Dove: An Invitation to Religious Studies* (New York: Harper & Row, Publishers, 1971), p. 52.

5. Samuel Beckett, *Waiting for Godot* (New York: Grove Press, 1954), p. 37.

6. For a discussion of the difference between *virtual* and *actual* see Suzanne

K. Langer, *Feeling and Form: A Theory of Art* (New York: Charles Scribner's Sons, 1953), particularly chapters 5, 6, 11, and 15.

7. I. A. Richards, *Principles of Literary Criticism* (New York: Harcourt, Brace & World, 1925), p. 139.

8. Aristotle, "On the Art of Poetry," in *On Poetry and Music*, trans. by S. H. Butcher (New York: The Bobbs-Merrill Co., 1956), p. 11.

9. A paraphrase of a comment in John Langdon-Davies, *A Short History of Women* (New York: The Literary Guild of America, 1927), p. 48. The original reads, ". . . a hen is merely an egg's way of laying another egg."

10. Martin Buber, "The Query of Queries," from *Tales of the Hasidim—The Early Masters*, reprinted in *The Norton Reader: An Anthology of Expository Prose*, 4 ed. (New York: W. W. Norton & Co., 1965), p. 1136.

11. William Butler Yeats, "The Second Coming," lines 21–22, *The Variorum Edition of the Poems* of W. B. Yeats, eds. Peter Ault and Russell K. Alspach (New York: Macmillan, 1968), p. 402.

Index

Also published by The Seabury Press

Robert C. Neville
CREATIVITY AND GOD: A CHALLENGE TO PROCESS THEOLOGY

"Neville possesses a mind capable and willing to face the basic ontological and meta-physical problems that are the heart of any attempt to speak *rationally* of God."
—*Best Sellers*

Jean Leclercq
MONKS ON MARRIAGE: A TWELFTH-CENTURY VIEW

This is a fascinating contribution to marriage studies, surveying twelfth-century classics as well as lesser-known popular works by monks who wrote about marriage with an idealistic eloquence balanced by surprising, down-to-earth psychological insight.

Norman J. Girardot
Mac Linscott Ricketts, Editors
IMAGINATION AND MEANING:
THE SCHOLARLY AND LITERARY WORLDS OF MIRCEA ELIADE

Original fiction and essays by Eliade as well as essays presenting analyses of the her-meneutic of the noted Roumanian scholar's work. Among his writings translated into English and published here for the first time are "The Fact" and "A Great Man."

Janice Nunnally-Cox
FOREMOTHERS: WOMEN OF THE BIBLE

A new look at the key female figures of the Old Testament, at the amazing change in the religious view of women that emerged from the New Testament, and at the difficult and fascinating roles played by women in the early years of the Christian church.